The Future of Democracy

CIVIL SOCIETY
HISTORICAL AND CONTEMPORARY PERSPECTIVES

Series Editors:
VIRGINIA HODGKINSON, *Public Policy Institute, Georgetown University*
KENT E. PORTNEY, *Department of Political Science, Tufts University*
JOHN C. SCHNEIDER, *Department of History, Tufts University*

PETER LEVINE

The Future of Democracy

DEVELOPING THE NEXT GENERATION
OF AMERICAN CITIZENS

TUFTS UNIVERSITY PRESS

Medford, Massachusetts

Published by

UNIVERSITY PRESS OF NEW ENGLAND

Hanover and London

Co-sponsored by the Jonathan M. Tisch College of Citizenship
and Public Service

Tufts University Press

Published by University Press of New England,

One Court Street, Lebanon, NH 03766

www.upne.com

© 2007 by Tufts University Press

Printed in the United States of America

5 4 3 2 1

Library of Congress Cataloging-in-Publication Data

Levine, Peter, 1967–

  The future of democracy : developing the next generation of
American citizens / Peter Levine.

    p.   cm.

Includes bibliographical references and index.

ISBN-13: 978–1–58465–648–7 (cloth : alk. paper)

ISBN-10: 1–58465–648–4 (cloth : alk. paper)

1. Youth—United States—Political activity.   2. Political participation—United States.   3. Social participation—United States.
4. Democracy—United States.   5. Youth development—United
States.   I. Title.

HQ799.2.P6L48 2007

323.6'508350973–dc22   2007011141

University Press of New England is a member of the Green Press
Initiative. The paper used in this book meets their minimum
requirement for recycled paper.

CONTENTS

TABLES AND FIGURES

PREFACE

This book is an argument about why and how we should prepare young people to be active and responsible democratic citizens. I present new data, including statistics from a 2006 survey of American youth and quotations from various recent interviews and focus groups. Most of the empirical base, however, comes from previous quantitative research that I summarize and synthesize.

I also direct attention to *normative* questions: issues of value and principle that are often left implicit in the literature on youth civic engagement. For example, *why* should people participate actively in community affairs? There is evidence that when many citizens participate, public institutions work better. I cite data to support that causal theory. There is, however, an equally important reason for democratic participation that has little to do with its *effects*. To engage in community affairs is dignified and rewarding; to encourage others to participate is a way of demonstrating respect for them. We can explicate and defend the value of civic engagement in such terms, not merely by citing data about its consequences.

Likewise, why should we give serious civic responsibilities to children and adolescents? Advocates of "positive youth development" have shown that by involving young people in important roles, we can increase the odds that they will succeed in school and avoid delinquency. That evidence is worth investigating, but positive youth development reflects a more fundamental ethical commitment. It is a way of treating fellow human beings as responsible agents and enabling them to develop their talents and political autonomy.

It will already be evident that this is an opinionated book, written in the first person singular, and I am solely responsible for the opinions it contains—as well as for any errors of fact or logic. Its empirical basis, however, has been a group effort. To a large extent, the facts come from five years of collaborative effort by CIRCLE (the Center for Information & Research on Civic Learning & Engagement) at the University of Maryland.

Given CIRCLE's enormous impact on this book, the center will receive all proceeds from its sale. I owe especially deep gratitude to

CIRCLE's staff, past and present: our founding and visionary director, William Galston; our scrupulous and dedicated research director, Mark Hugo Lopez; my colleagues Deborah Both, Barbara Cronin, Carrie Donovan, Abby Kiesa, Emily Hoban Kirby, Karlo Barrios Marcelo, Demetria Sapienza, and Dionne Williams; and several cohorts of graduate students, including Gary Homana, who helped me with the book. It is a cohesive, talented, and committed team.

CIRCLE has been primarily funded by The Pew Charitable Trusts and Carnegie Corporation of New York. I must also acknowledge four program officers at these foundations for their vision, guidance, and patience: Michael X. Delli Carpini, Cynthia Gibson, Geraldine Mannion, and Tobi Walker. Cindy Gibson has also been my close collaborator on several projects, notably the Civic Mission of Schools report of 2003, and I have learned an enormous amount from her.

The circle of CIRCLE is large, encompassing twenty-eight members of a distinguished advisory board and at least eighty recipients of CIRCLE's research grants, which were made possible by The Pew Charitable Trusts and Carnegie Corporation of New York. All of these people have influenced this book, and their names fill the notes, but I am especially grateful for the intellectual guidance and personal support of Harry Boyte, Constance Flanagan, Diana Hess, Lewis Friedland, Carmen Sirianni, Judith Torney-Purta, and James Youniss.

INTRODUCTION

"Civic education" sometimes sounds like a rather specialized or optional matter—especially at the beginning of the twenty-first century, when we are desperately trying to make all our students competitive in a global economy that values mathematics, science, and literacy. Under these conditions, it is necessary to explain why civic education is not a luxury that can be considered only after we are satisfied with all of our children's basic academic skills.

Strong, just, robust democracies require the skillful and committed participation of their citizens. It is easiest for people to obtain the necessary skills and commitments when they are young. Therefore, "civic education"—which is not just the name of a course, but is the shared responsibility of schools, families, political institutions, the press, and communities—is a critical component of a struggle to sustaining democracy itself. So this book will argue.

When adults consider the character and behavior of contemporary youth, they often portray decline or decadence. As early as the eighth century B.C., Hesiod complained: "I see no hope for the future of our people if they are dependent on the frivolous youth of today, for certainly all youth are reckless beyond words." In 1906, William James argued that the "gilded youths" of his day ought to be "drafted off" to do some form of civilian national service "to get the childishness knocked out of them, and to come back into society with healthier sympathies and soberer ideas."[1] In 1997, Judge Robert Bork wrote, "Every generation constitutes a wave of savages who must be civilized by their families, schools, and churches." He recalled the "exceptionally large" wave of the 1960s as especially barbarous, devoted to "violence, destruction of property, and the mindless hatred of law, authority, and tradition."[2]

The Enlightenment philosopher Condorcet, writing during the French Revolution, observed that *every* generation accuses itself of being less civic-minded than its predecessors.[3] (And each cohort of adults fears that its children will be even worse.) Such clichés of decline or crisis can be seriously misleading. For example, contrary to popular belief, the adolescent pathologies that most people worry about—teen motherhood, failure to graduate from high school, smoking, violent crimes, and deaths of teenagers by firearms—have moved in favorable directions since the mid-1990s. None of these indicators of moral behavior looks worse than it did twenty-five years ago.[4] Thus it would certainly be a mistake to portray today's youth as especially remiss.

Nevertheless, each generation should worry about the civic and political development of its children. Citizens are made, not born; it takes deliberate efforts to prepare young people to participate effectively and wisely in public life. Good government requires widespread civic participation and virtue; yet the development of the necessary skills and attitudes is not in anyone's narrow self-interest, nor does it occur automatically. Therefore, civic education—again, broadly defined as the job of society, not merely of schools—must be continuously renewed and redesigned to address the specific challenges of each age.

Like the statistics on crime, pregnancy, and health, the data on *citizenship* in America today show some favorable trends. For instance, young people are increasingly likely to do volunteer work and are more socially tolerant than any previous generation for which polling data are available. On the other hand, they score poorly on assessments of civic knowledge; they are relatively mistrustful of other citizens; they are less likely than in the past to join or lead traditional membership organizations; and they usually vote at low rates. Most are skeptical about their own power to make a difference in their communities.

In this book, I will explore two basic models for understanding these challenges. The first is a "psychological deficits" model. It assumes that there are problems with young people's civic skills, knowledge, confidence, and values. These problems are not the fault of young people. Hardly anyone would hold a sixteen-year-old personally accountable for lacking interest in the news or failing to join associations. If we should blame anyone, it would be parents, educators, politicians, reporters, and other adults. Nevertheless, the problems are located (so to speak) inside the heads of young people. We should therefore look for interventions that directly improve young people's civic abilities and attitudes. Such interventions include formal civic education, opportunities for community service, and broader educational reforms that are designed to improve the overall character of schools. The government, the press, and political parties can also enhance young people's civic commitments and skills by directly communicating with them.

As an alternative, I will consider an "institutional reform" model. This paradigm assumes that there are flaws in our institutions that make it unreasonable to expect positive civic attitudes and active engagement. For example, citizens (young and old alike) may rightly shun voting when most elections have already been determined by the way district lines were drawn. They may rightly ignore the news when the quality of journalism, especially on television, is poor. And they may rightly disengage from high schools that are large, anonymous, and alienating. If this model holds, then we do not need interventions that change young people's minds. Civic education that teaches people to admire a flawed system is mere propaganda. Instead, we should reform major institutions.

These two basic models admit variations and combinations. For example, one might hold that there are problems located inside young people's heads—namely, inadequate habits and skills for civic and political participation—but that adolescents would gain these habits and skills if they had more incentives to participate. Then our goal would be to change young people's psychology; but the only way to do so would be to restructure institutions so that they sought and rewarded youth participation more.

This book is not a polemic in favor of one basic model over the other. As I argue in chapters 10 and 11, we need a broad movement that improves civic education while it also reforms the institutions in which citizens engage. We must prepare citizens for politics, but also improve politics for citizens. Neither effort can succeed in isolation from the other. Educational curricula, textbooks, and programs, if disconnected from the goal of strengthening and improving democracy, can easily become means of accommodating young people to a flawed system. But political reform is impossible until we better prepare the next generation of citizens with appropriate knowledge, skills, habits, and values. Students should feel that they are being educated for citizenship, but also that they can help to renew American democracy.

The Future of Democracy

CHAPTER 1

What Is Civic Engagement?

1.1 FROM LISTS TO A DEFINITION

The purpose of civic education (broadly defined) is to enhance the *civic engagement* of young people. "Civic engagement" is a very popular catchphrase in foundations, government agencies, schools, and universities around the English-speaking world. In many contexts, it has supplanted "participation" and "participatory democracy," which were more common phrases in the 1960s and 1970s, when they acquired a politically radical edge. Many specialists in the field prefer the phrase "civic engagement" over "citizenship"—let alone "*good* citizenship"—finding those alternatives old-fashioned, primly moralistic, and limiting. (After all, not everyone holds legal citizenship in the country where she resides, yet everyone can participate in helpful ways.) Despite its popularity, however, "civic engagement" is very rarely defined with any conceptual clarity. Indeed, I suspect that its *lack* of definition, combined with its generally benign connotations, accounts for its popularity. It is a Rorschach blot within which anyone can find her own priorities.

While rarely defined in a coherent sentence or paragraph, "civic engagement" is often operationalized as a list of variables. For example, Scott Keeter and his colleagues designed a major national survey of civic engagement, using questions that emerged from focus group interviews.[1] CIRCLE replicated their study as our 2006 omnibus survey, which I cite frequently below.[2] Both polls measured nineteen core indicators, in three main categories:

- Indicators of *community participation* include measures of membership in various types of nonprofit voluntary associations (including religious groups); regular volunteering and fund-raising; and "community problem-solving," which is defined as a positive answer to the following question: "Have you ever worked together with someone or some group to solve a problem in the community where you live?"

- Indicators of *political engagement* include registering to vote, voting, and various activities that might influence other people's votes, including volunteering for campaigns, displaying political stickers and signs, and giving money to parties and campaigns.
- Indicators of *political voice* include protesting, canvassing, signing petitions, contacting the mass media, contacting elected officials, boycotting products, and "buycotting" products or companies. (To "buycott" is to purchase "something because you like the social or political values of the company that produces it.")

According to Keeter and his colleagues, you are civically engaged if you regularly perform several actions on this list of nineteen.[3]

There are arguments in favor of expanding or changing this list. Some scholars believe that relatively unusual forms of engagement should be included, even though they do not show up in focus groups and national surveys. These atypical civic behaviors include acts of civil disobedience, participation in transnational youth movements (such as the campaign against globalization), and Native Americans' membership in tribal councils.[4] Second, one could argue that some relatively common forms of service were overlooked in the survey designed by Keeter and colleagues: for instance, helping to raise younger siblings, or confronting friends and relatives who use racist or other immoral language. It is controversial whether these forms of behavior constitute "civic engagement." Third, some scholars believe that following and understanding the news and public affairs is a form of engagement.[5] (We could call this "mental" or "cognitive" civic engagement.)

Finally, most of the indicators measured by Keeter et al. are signs that people support and want to improve the regime in which they live. Those who are deeply critical of the status quo may prefer indicators of resistance and revolt, such as participation in violent protests, or the ordinary foot-dragging and noncompliance that is often the resort of poor people in response to coercion.[6] For those who are hostile to the existing regime, a *lack* of engagement in school—as shown by truancy or evident boredom—could be a sign of political resistance, hence an indicator of *civic* engagement.

In short, there are arguments for expanding the list of nineteen indicators to twenty-five or thirty. Such arguments beg the question of what makes any indicator appropriate for the list. What is the underlying philosophy of civic engagement?

Two mechanical objects are said to be "engaged" if they are capable of affecting each other. Likewise, a person who is *civically* engaged somehow connects to the civic domain so that she can affect it. A distinguished committee of the American Political Science Association recently wrote, "For us, *civic engagement includes any activity, individual or collective, devoted to influencing the collective life of the polity.*"[7] But what is the "collective life of the polity" or (as I had put it) the "civic domain"? It can't be everything; otherwise, people would be able to say they were "civically engaged" if they merely participated in their own families or businesses.

Some analysts define the civic domain in sectoral terms, as the set of all institutions that are either part of the government or not-for-profit. On that definition, you are civically engaged if you work without pay (then you are a "volunteer"), if you influence the state (as an "advocate"), or if your paycheck comes from the government or a nonprofit organization (which makes you a "public servant"). This scheme is misleading. Newspapers are civic institutions, even though they are usually profit-making corporations that pay their reporters and editors. A hospital may be organized as a private enterprise, a public agency, or a not-for-profit institution: the difference does not necessarily matter to employees, patients, or members of the surrounding community. Grocery store owners who display fruits and vegetables outside their businesses at night contribute civically by making city streets safer and more attractive.[8] When people boycott and "buycott," they are said to be civically engaged even though they are consumers who attempt to influence firms.

Another way to define the civic domain is to say that it includes any venue in which people work together on public problems. That definition trades one difficult word for another. There is no consensus about what problems are legitimately public. Just because an issue is taken up by a legislature or a court, it does not follow that the matter is public: perhaps the government has reached illegitimately into private affairs. Conversely, the government might fail to address an issue that is genuinely public. Meanwhile, private firms take up public problems, for instance by providing jobs and goods that people need. Firms can also encourage collaboration and problem-solving among groups of their own employees and partners. Nevertheless, most theorists would not define routine business collaborations as "civic engagement." Why not?

1.2 LEGITIMATE PUBLIC CONCERNS

I do not think there is any substitute for a theory that defines public concerns and problems in contrast to those of the private sphere and the market. We can then define "civic engagement" as behavior that addresses legitimate public matters. Unfortunately, no definition of public matters attracts consensus. However, *discussing* the limits of the public's concerns is itself an important and perennial aspect of civic engagement, fundamental to the ongoing debates between left and right.

Liberals, conservatives, libertarians, left-radicals and others hold different views of the public's interests, but they ask some of the same questions. One important question concerns the nature and welfare of the "commons." Although this word has a collectivist ring (reminding some people of "communism"), people of all political stripes—including libertarians and anarchists—care about the commons; it is the definition that varies.

A commons consists of all the goods and resources that are not privately owned. The list of such resources varies depending on how a society is governed: it may include the atmosphere and oceans, the national defense, the overall plan of a city and its physical public spaces, the prevailing norms of cooperation in a society, the rule of law, civil rights and their enforcement, the store of accumulated scientific knowledge and cultural heritage, and even the Internet (understood as a whole structure, not broken down into its privately owned components).[9]

It is difficult or impossible to divide any of these resources among private owners. Things that cannot be divided cannot be traded. No one owns Shakespeare, traditional Southern cooking, national defense, the ozone layer, or freedom of speech. Because markets cannot generate or preserve such public goods, we rely instead on the state, nonprofit associations, or voluntary collaborations among firms, families, and individuals. Part of "civic engagement" is work that protects or enhances the commons. Again, we do not agree on which resources should be treated as common, but debating that question is itself an important part of civic engagement.

We can reach a similar conclusion from a different point of departure. Economists say that an "externality" occurs when some people conduct a voluntary exchange that affects other parties who never consented to their agreement. The externality is the effect on the third parties. It can be positive: for example, a new downtown store can benefit me even if I never shop or work there, by lowering crime, beautifying my city, providing jobs for my neighbors, contributing taxes, attracting visitors, and so on. In fact, many of the best things in life are positive externalities that arise as side effects of market transactions or as the public effects of people's work in private, voluntary associations. An externality can also be negative, and the usual examples are environmental. For instance, smoke can blow from a factory into the lungs of people who never consented to receive it. Coarse or inconsiderate personal acts are also good examples of negative externalities: think of cases when A talks loudly to B on a cell phone, annoying C, D, and E who are sitting nearby.

Much of ethics consists of acting so that one's externalities are as positive as possible. We can define the commons as the sum total of our externalities, the negative ones subtracted from the positive ones. Then civic engagement is work that improves the balance of externalities. People create positive externalities and mitigate negative ones by volunteering and by influencing the state.

This definition of "civic engagement" encompasses some aspects of life that we do not usually tag with that label. For example, fundamental research on cancer promises to provide basic knowledge, which is a public or common good of enormous value. Therefore, a cancer researcher is civically engaged, by my definition. To be sure, science is not identical to volunteering or political participation; it has its own standards, logic, and history. Some features of science can be observed in commercial laboratories that generate patented goods for the consumer market, not only in academic or government-sponsored research labs that tackle public problems. Nevertheless, I believe it is illuminating to recognize that science—along with medicine, art, law, teaching, religious ministry, and other professions—has a strong civic dimension. Licensing bodies limit entry to these professions to people who are trained and pledged to enhance the commons (regardless of how they are paid). Such professionals are supposed to address issues that a broader public has identified as important and to deliberate respectfully with laypeople, including the taxpayers and clients who fund their work. Some sociological theories of science invoke values that we expect of good citizens, such as the open sharing of knowledge, disinterestedness, and a willingness to examine hypotheses critically.[10] Scott Peters finds that scientists in land-grant universities often enter their professions with explicitly civic goals—to work with communities to address common problems—and they are frustrated when they realize that other goals (such as generating commercial patents) have taken over.[11] More generally, Boyte finds "a strong and often painful sense of loss of public purpose" among senior scientists and researchers.[12]

Recognizing the civic potential of *paid* employment prevents us from equating civic engagement with volunteering, which narrows and even trivializes it. Civic engagement is "public work" (in Harry Boyte's phrase): a serious business that ought to occur in families, workplaces, professions, and firms, not only in voluntary associations.

In emphasizing the commons, I have passed over another aspect of politics: efforts to distribute and redistribute private goods. When the state (at any level) taxes some and spends the money on others, it is redistributing. Likewise, when the state provides authors with copyright and inventors with patents, it influences the distribution of goods. When people give contributions of money or time or raise funds through such activities as charity walks (as 84 percent of Americans claim to do annually),[13] they are also redistributing goods—albeit voluntarily and on a comparatively small scale.

Surely the pattern of distribution in a society is a public issue, a legitimate matter for debate. Civic engagement includes participation in that debate, whether from a libertarian, conservative, moderate, progressive, or socialist perspective. I began, however, with civic engagement that enhances the commons—not with struggles over distribution—because there is a tendency to overemphasize the latter. Harold D. Lasswell's famous 1958 book was entitled *Politics: Who Gets What, When, How.*[14] I would say that "who gets what" is a *part* of politics and a legitimate topic for engaged citizens. It is not the whole of politics. Another important aspect of politics is more creative; it involves citizens' work in making public goods that benefit everyone.

There is also the question of who should be *allowed* to do what—the question that arises in debates about abortion, narcotics, pornography, and other controversial social issues. Again, to participate in these debates—from any ideological or philosophical perspective—is to be civically engaged. Around the same time that Lasswell was defining "politics" as a struggle over scarce resources, another classic book defined it as the "authoritative allocation of values."[15] It is important to note, however, that pressuring the state to regulate or deregulate private behavior is not the only way that citizens can change values. They can also build voluntary associations to promote their moral views in civil society, thereby contributing to and helping to shape the common culture.

In defining civic engagement, I have not invoked a contrast between self-interest and altruism. Civic engagement is behavior that influences public matters, which, in turn, include the commons, the distribution of private goods, and decisions about what actions to prohibit or promote. One can influence these matters altruistically, for instance, by trying to distribute more goods to people who are less fortunate than oneself. One can participate in one's enlightened self-interest, trying to strengthen an overall system that protects one's welfare. One can work for the narrow interests of one's own group. Or one can act in one's individual self-interest by, for example, trying to get more personal benefits from the government. We may admire altruistic engagement more than selfish advocacy, but they are both legitimate. Furthermore, self-interest sometimes motivates participation that helps the whole system. For example, justice will be better served if poor people vote in their own interests instead of staying home.

Although we should not exclude self-interested motivations, it is a mistake to assume that participation is always narrowly self-interested. History provides many dramatic examples of altruism and public-spiritedness, including heroic self-sacrifice. And on a daily basis, people frequently define their identities in ways that are not highly individualistic. Often a person participates in civic life not as "I" but as "we"; and the "we" can range from a family to the entire nation. If people always calculated the potential costs and benefits of their behavior to themselves as individuals, then no one would vote. No single vote has any impact on policy unless the election would otherwise be a draw, a highly unusual situation. Nevertheless, about half of the U.S. population does vote; the proportion is even higher in many other countries. This behavior indicates that many people define themselves as members of large identity groups or as citizens of a whole republic on Election Day. They do not vote as "I" but as part of some "we" that collectively has an impact.[16]

1.3 THE ETHICS OF CIVIC ENGAGEMENT

So far, the working definition of "civic engagement" is any effort to enhance the commons or to influence decisions about distribution and regulation, because these are legitimate public concerns. However, an adequate definition should say something about means as well as ends. After all, one can "engage" the government by plotting to overthrow it; one can influence a religious congregation by embezzling its funds, and one can address an alleged community problem by violently expelling an ethnic minority. One might even take some of these actions for decent purposes. For example, the organizers of the coup in Thailand in 2006 claimed that their goal was to end a debilitating political crisis, and perhaps they were sincere. To qualify as "civic engagement," however, the *means* of engagement, as well as the ends, must be legitimate. Civic engagement includes deliberation, persuasion, collaboration, participation in legal politics, civil disobedience, and the giving of time and money. It does not include coercion, violence, or deception.

Again, this is something of a list that needs a conceptual foundation. I now suggest that to be civically engaged is to enhance the commons or to influence state distribution and regulation *in ways that benefit the underlying political structure.* We sometimes define political actors by arraying them on a spectrum from left to right. However, there is another dimension of politics that is orthogonal to this one. At one end of this *civic* spectrum is a highly participatory, constructive, deliberative, and equitable polity. At the other end is a murderous tyranny. Quite apart from where they stand on the issues that divide the Left from the Right, people can either be pro- or anticivic.

To be civically engaged means not only pursuing legitimate concrete goals (including one's own self-interests and matters of moral principle) but also caring about the political system and political culture. Someone who is civically engaged does not merely participate in politics and community affairs. He also pauses to ask: Are most other people allowed and motivated to participate in discussions and decisions (at least within their neighborhoods and schools)? Or are many citizens completely alienated or excluded? Do we seriously consider a broad range of positions? Do good arguments and reasons count, or has politics become just a clash of money and power? Can we achieve progress on the goals that we happen to share, or have our disagreements become so sharp and personal that we cannot ever cooperate?

Defining civic engagement as work that benefits—or at least does not harm—the existing political structure raises two further questions. First, what forms of engagement are most likely to strengthen or harm a regime? That is an empirical question for which the relevant research is surprisingly thin. (For example, no one knows what level of voter turnout is necessary for the stability of a democratic society.) Nevertheless, in the next chapter, I will argue that certain behaviors, including protest but excluding violent insurrection, are valuable to a reasonably just regime.

Second, is our current regime *worthy* of loyal engagement, or should we prefer revolutionary forms of politics? We cannot simply rule out resistance, or even violence, when we consider that the United States began with a violent revolution whose leaders are still seen as paragons of civic virtue. Men like Washington and Jefferson did not enhance the British Empire in which they were born; they broke it apart. I assume that most readers believe, as I do, that American citizens should try to strengthen and ameliorate their society rather than overthrow or partition it. To argue for the basic legitimacy and potential of the American political/economic regime would require a digression inappropriate for this book. But I acknowledge that I have not rebutted arguments for revolution or secession, either of which would entail a very different ethics of engagement.

As a matter of definition, civic engagement need not support or promote democracy. Consider Li Huijuan, a judge in China who stood up for the rule of law when she issued a decision against the interests of her provincial government. Her willingness to resist political pressure was consistent with her lifelong, idealistic commitment to the law as an autonomous institution. She told the authorities, "I will protect my integrity and defend the integrity of the law, even if it means being like a moth that flies into a flame."[17] Judge Li is a member of the Communist Party, and there is no evidence that she favors democracy (which is not the same as the rule of law). Nevertheless, Judge Li's work in favor of judicial independence and consistency in jurisprudence surely qualifies her as "civically engaged." Likewise, there were good citizens in the old monarchies of Europe, many of whom did not favor democracy. Think of Benjamin Franklin, who built much of the civic infrastructure of Philadelphia—inventing great institutions such as the public lending libraries that remain part of our commons—while still a firm supporter of the British Empire.

Notwithstanding the examples of Li and the younger Franklin, there are reasons to believe that democracy is a superior political system. It treats individuals better than other systems do and respects their opinions more; it offers more freedom and equality; it is more sustainable and flexible; and it is especially good at conserving and enhancing public goods, from the natural environment to culture and science (see section 2.4). If all this is true, then civic engagement should support democracy, at least in countries like the United States, where democratic self-government is a realistic option. We should support representative political institutions and norms of equality and participation—public goods that are essential to our democratic commons.

Caring about the quality of our democratic system (its institutions and norms) creates a set of ethical dilemmas. First of all, there is the question of how *much* one should weigh the impact of one's actions on the political system. Imagine that you are trying to "save the earth" by preserving the ozone layer that protects us from disaster. This may appear to be a goal of overriding importance, much more important than your marginal impact on democracy. In that case, even if you feel that American democracy suffers from excessive litigation, you may decide to file a lawsuit on behalf of the environment. Even if you believe that the political debate is generally too nasty, you may demonize an opponent of environmental protection. We can only denounce these choices if we assume that the civic culture is paramount and all other issues are secondary. I am not convinced that that is always true.

To make matters even more complicated, the same political behavior can both help *and* harm democratic institutions. Consider an inflammatory message that is included in a mass-mailing from a political organization. This message may succeed in mobilizing citizens to become active, which is good for democracy; but it may also reduce the chances that citizens will fully understand the nuances of an issue and find common ground with those different from themselves, which is bad for democracy. It is not immediately obvious whether such a message is civically acceptable.

Much of the energy in politics and civic life comes from people who have agendas. They do not support democracy or civil society so much as they want to achieve particular purposes, which may be self-interested or altruistic. It is unrealistic to expect people to put their agendas aside in order to work for the quality of our democratic culture and institutions. The Progressive reforms of the early 1900s provide a cautionary example. In an effort to enhance the quality of public discourse and civic participation, Progressives supported nonpartisan newspapers at the expense of partisan broadsheets. They restricted the influence of political parties, on the theory that citizens should choose individuals, not slates of candidates prescreened by party bosses. They replaced thousands of local elected officials with appointed professionals, believing that elections should be high-stakes contests for a few accountable senior leaders who would employ experts.[18] They reformed college education so that students were no longer exhorted to be active civic leaders, but were instead taught academic and professional disciplines—all in the interests of making them critical judges of public issues.[19] One major result of these reforms was to reduce voter turnout, which was lower in 1924 than it had been in 1830.[20] It is much more difficult to participate as a well-informed, independent, critical individual than as a member of a mass movement or party. The quality of public reasoning possibly improved during the Progressive Era, but the number of people who participated certainly fell as it became more difficult to mobilize citizens in support of partisan goals.

Given these complications and tradeoffs, I would not argue that civic engagement requires an overriding commitment to the quality of public life, the excellence of public deliberations, the breadth of participation, or the search for common ground. However, civic engagement does mean *considering* the impact of our political behavior on these goods. If we set the value of public participation at zero, we are not civically engaged. Someone who is civically engaged may decide to attack a political opponent, but only after soberly considering whether the attack is worth the possible damage to civility. As for a coup against a democratic state, it can never qualify as civic engagement, even if its goals are otherwise well intentioned.

1.4 "OPEN-ENDED" POLITICS

Our definition of "civic engagement" is broad: it includes most efforts to promote particular policies, ideologies, and outcomes, whether or not they are in a person's self-interest. You can be a hard-nosed political partisan or an avid supporter of an interest group and still be civically engaged, as long as you try not to degrade public institutions or undermine the political culture. In fact, politics and civil society would be inert if people and groups did not promote their own goals and interests.

Nevertheless, it is important for some people, some of the time, to be mainly concerned about the quality of public institutions and debates. While most citizens engage politically as Democrats, Republicans, or members of another party, we also need at least a few citizens to fill nonpartisan roles, ensuring that elections are fair and government is transparent and ethical. While it is useful for editorial writers and bloggers[21] to promote their own ideological views, we also need relatively neutral and factual reporters. While it is appropriate for people to form and support organizations that promote their own economic and legal interests, we also need some organizations to worry about the overall political process and culture.

Consider, for example, the West Virginia Center for Civic Life. Its founder, Betty Knighton, has sponsored public conversations about many issues of importance to her state and has taught college students to convene and manage such discussions. She says, "We have defined the Center for Civic Life as aggressively neutral."[22] The center has a reputation for not taking the side of Democrats or Republicans, environmentalists or business interests, or any other participants in the state's debates; instead, it is an honest broker. Knighton is willing to launch a good democratic and deliberative process and let the chips fall where they may.

"Open-endedness" is perhaps a more precise term for this kind of work than "neutrality." After all, Knighton surely has some goals for her state; she is not completely neutral. And her interventions may at times happen to help Democrats or Republicans, because one side or the other may benefit more from a public dialogue. Likewise, even the most nonpartisan, independent journalist must decide which facts are important and how to describe them. How she presents the news may have effects on various parties and interests. Registering young voters sounds like a neutral act that can only benefit our democracy by increasing the level of participation. However, if one registers students on my campus, experience suggests that 70 percent will vote Democratic—a partisan consequence. Even in a simple public discussion, someone must issue an invitation that may somehow shape the ensuing conversation.

In short, neutrality is something of a myth. Nevertheless, there is surely a difference between trying to inspire, persuade, or manipulate people to adopt a view, versus helping them to form and promote decisions of their own. For example, many newspaper editors believe that their job is to provide information and forums for discussion so that their readers will be better informed and more effective. Even if there is no such thing as a politically neutral news source, a newspaper can be open-ended: it can provide multiple points of view and facts favorable to more than one position and avoid shaping its readers' opinions. Likewise, some community organizers bring adult residents together (thereby magnifying their political power), while allowing them to set their own agendas.[23] It is worth identifying open-ended politics as a valuable and undersupplied form of civic engagement, without denigrating participation that happens to be partisan, ideological, or self-interested.

1.5 CONCLUSION

The definition of "civic engagement" that has emerged so far is any action that affects legitimately public matters (even if selfishly motivated) as long as the actor pays appropriate attention to the consequences of his behavior for the underlying political system. In turn, "public matters" include the commons, the distribution of goods in a society, and all the laws and social norms that prohibit or discourage particular behaviors. We need *some* citizens to be concerned about our political system and culture and to try to improve it in an open-ended way, without favoring any particular ideology. Yet ideological and even self-interested participation is also civic engagement and is essential to the system.

I do not anticipate that readers will agree about the details of this definition, but its overall structure seems unavoidable. In order to define "civic engagement," one must first define legitimately public matters. Civic engagement then consists of all behaviors that can reasonably be expected to affect those matters, minus any forms of behavior that are morally illegitimate (terrorism being a clear example).

Nothing in the argument so far explains why large numbers of people ought to be engaged. Even if there is a public interest, couldn't it be managed quite well by a few elected representatives or professional managers? In short, we need reasons to favor broad civic engagement. These reasons, to which I turn in chapter 2, will help us decide what specific skills, habits, knowledge, and values most citizens should possess.

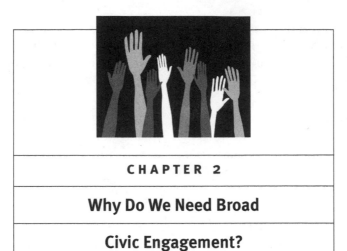

CHAPTER 2

Why Do We Need Broad

Civic Engagement?

2.1 DEMOCRACY SHOULD NOT DEPEND ON CIVIC VIRTUE ALONE

It has been very common in the history of political thought to assume that good government depends on many good citizens: people with virtues who can be counted on to act appropriately. Aristotle regarded his *Politics* and his *Ethics* as part of the same subject. In his view, a city-state could not be just and strong unless its people were virtuous; and people could not exercise the political virtues (which were intrinsically admirable, dignified, and satisfying) unless they lived in a just polity. Likewise, Confucius emphasized the close relationship between the behavior of rulers and that of the ruled. "How true is the saying that after a state has been ruled for a hundred years by good men it is possible to get the better of cruelty and do away with killing [i.e., capital punishment]. . . . Even with a true king it is bound to take a generation for benevolence to become a reality [among the people]."[1]

People do not seem to be automatically virtuous in their attitudes and actions toward their communities. Therefore, if justice and good government depend on the virtue of both rulers and subjects, perhaps the state must *make* people altruistic, responsible, brave, deliberative, and kind. Rousseau wrote in 1762, "He who dares to undertake the making of a people's institutions ought to feel himself capable, so to speak, of changing human nature, of transforming each individual, who is by himself a complete and solitary whole, into part of a great whole from which he in a manner receives his life and being; of altering man's constitution for the purpose of strengthening it." It was a legislator's job, Rousseau argued, to improve the state of "morality, of custom, and above all of public opinion." Ordinary laws are "only the arc of the arch, while manners and morals, slower to arise, form in the end its immovable keystone."[2]

Governments traditionally supported quite ambitious programs of moral and political education, often connected to an official state religion. When, for the first time, some European thinkers began to lose faith in traditional Christianity, several developed plans for "civic religions" that might fulfill the same educative goals. Few thought that a society without the functional equivalent of a national church could flourish.

There are serious drawbacks, however, to making good government dependent on widespread civic virtue. First, any demanding and universal system of moral education is incompatible with individual freedom. If the state forces people to serve in the military, to swear civic oaths, or even to enroll their children in public schools in order to create good citizens, those requirements may conflict with individuals' freedom of conscience. This is not to say that dissenting individuals are always right; only that there is a tension between mandatory moral instruction and personal freedom.

The second problem is more practical. States are not very good at producing moral virtue in rulers or subjects. Hundreds of years of mandatory church membership, state-subsidized education, and even public spectacles of torture and execution did not prevent corruption, sedition, and other private behavior injurious to the community. Nor have gentler modern methods been overwhelmingly successful.

For these reasons, some philosophers of the seventeenth and eighteenth centuries began to argue that governments should not be dependent on widespread virtue. From Locke to Madison, these political thinkers defended and (especially in Britain and the new United States) actually implemented a series of reforms that would make government proof against the various vices that seemed to be "sown in the nature of man."[3] Their tools included constitutional limitations on the overall power and scope of government; independent judges with power of review; elections with relatively broad franchise; and above all, checks and balances.

Madison explained that republics should be designed for people of *moderate* virtue, such as might be found in real societies. "If men were angels, no government would be necessary. If angels were to govern men, neither external nor internal controuls on government would be necessary." Unfortunately, neither citizens nor rulers could be counted on to act like angels; but good government was possible anyway, as long as the constitution provided appropriate controls.

The main "external controul" in a republic was the vote, which made powerful men accountable to those they ruled. However, voting was not enough, especially because the voters themselves might lack virtue and wisdom. "A dependence on the people is no doubt the primary controul on the government; but experience has taught mankind the necessity of auxiliary precautions." In general, Madison's "auxiliary precautions" involved dividing power among separate institutions and giving them the ability to check one another. "This policy of supplying by opposite and rival interests, the defect of better motives, might be traced through the whole system of human affairs, private as well as public. We see it particularly displayed in all the subordinate distributions of power; where the constant aim is to divide and arrange the several offices in such a manner as that each may be a check on the other; that the private interest of every individual may be a centinel over the public rights. These inventions of prudence cannot be less requisite in the distribution of the supreme powers of the state.[4]

The "auxiliary precautious" of separation of powers, judicial review, and federalism have been enormously valuable. The American republic has been fairly durable, prosperous, and efficient for most of the last two centuries despite frequent bad behavior by American individuals. Citizens have been relatively free because the state has not tried to shape people's characters through onerous programs of moral education, yet the government itself has been comparatively just.

Despite this record, there are reasons to suppose (as the American framers did) that our constitutional system is not a machine that will run smoothly and well *regardless* of public virtue. Through the Northwest Ordinance of 1787, Congress set aside land for public education, arguing that "schools and the means of education" should be "forever" encouraged, because "religion, morality, and knowledge" are "necessary to good government and the happiness of mankind." Even if we reject the assumption that good government necessarily requires *religious* values, there are reasons to believe that it depends on public virtue. Separation of powers and other institutional safeguards make the state capable of ruling well even when the people are not angels. Nevertheless, citizens must be considerably better than devils or idiots. Americans must be actively and responsibly engaged, for reasons described in the following sections.

2.2 CIVIL SOCIETY IS A NECESSARY COMPLEMENT TO THE GOVERNMENT

First of all, civic engagement is necessary because no democracy—indeed, no reasonably just regime of any type—can manage without private, voluntary, nonprofit associations. In turn, these associations need citizens who have certain relevant skills, habits, and virtues.

"Civil society" is the whole set of voluntary associations (formal and informal) that are outside both the state and the market. It includes churches and other religious congregations, clubs, lobbying groups, parties, unions, nonprofit corporations, and even informal networks of friends. A civil society will emerge wherever people have the freedom to associate. Why, however, are nonprofit groups and their associated virtues and skills necessary for the maintenance of a just regime? Why are they politically necessary?

To understand the importance of civil society for a regime, consider an imaginary government that managed to solve all legitimately public problems without any help from nonprofit voluntary associations. There are two imaginable ways to accomplish this feat. The first is to define very few problems as "public." Libertarians hold that almost all goods that we need or value can be provided by a market. If market exchanges are fully adequate, then the state deserves very little power and civil society has no necessary role. Individuals in a pure market society have the *right* to associate voluntarily in nonprofit groups, but it is not essential for them to do so. Nor do they need virtues other than those required by a market.

However, sophisticated libertarians have always recognized that a self-sufficient, self-sustaining market is unworkable. Markets cannot exist at all unless laws regarding property and personal freedom are defined and effectively enforced. Modern markets also require laws that permit corporations to form and that define intellectual property rights. If there are laws, then there must be some power to enforce them. That power must be prevented from turning corrupt or incompetent and from expanding its authority into illegitimate areas. Good government, even if it is very limited, requires vigilant citizens. Unfortunately, it is difficult for a private individual to learn principles of justice and to collect and interpret current information about the performance of the state. Even if a lone citizen is able to discover some abuse of governmental power, she will have difficulty remedying the problem alone. This is one reason that advocacy groups, parties, and venues for discussion are crucial, even in a society with a maximal market and a minimal state. These associations collect and disseminate information, employ independent critics and watchdogs, file lawsuits, and teach their members to understand and promote rights for all.

Further, even in a libertarian's ideal society, citizens must hold essential offices competently and responsibly. Most libertarians believe that state positions should be filled through elections, which means that some citizens must vote and a few must run for office. Almost all libertarians support courts and the jury system. It is difficult for individuals to be good jurors or voters if all their experience comes from private life and the marketplace. For example, jurors are unlikely to deliberate well unless they have previously considered weighty issues with strangers, but this is not part of most private-sector jobs. And unless citizens have experience managing associations that operate for the good of all their members, they will not know how to judge the performance of their government, which is a not-for-profit institution with high ideals.

Although libertarians distrust political power (because it can be used to restrict freedom), such power arises whenever people band together to demand what they want. Therefore, libertarians cannot ignore public opinion, but must find ways to make most people reasonably satisfied with a libertarian society. A market alone will not make most people satisfied: it will not protect their rights or their security; it will not give them all enough education to make them economically self-sufficient; it will not protect people from the negative effects of others' free exchanges; and it will not enforce the laws that underpin the market itself. Depending on the state to solve these problems is dangerous, according to libertarian theory. The best alternative is a robust civil society through which people can voluntarily assist with education, pollution control, security, and other functions that the public demands. By working together in voluntary associations, citizens will also experience liberty and learn to prize it.

Thus, even though libertarians want to maximize the scope of the market, we find that they must value civil society and public participation. Diametrically opposed to libertarians are those who are enthusiastic about the state, believing that a competent, well-organized, centralized government can resolve most or all public problems. Like libertarians, proponents of a strong state may be tempted to dispense with civil society. In fact, some classic political thinkers argued that the state should handle all public matters because it alone had legitimate authority. These writers feared that if self-selected and self-governing groups of citizens worked in private, they would become "factions," liable to conspire against the legitimate sovereign state.[5]

In modern times, strong proponents of state power have included authoritarians: militarists, leftover monarchists, fascists, and Leninists. But there have also been *democratic* enthusiasts of the state, people who believe that a powerful government, subject to popular control through elections, should regulate or even nationalize the market. Indeed, the best examples of strong states are the modern social democracies, countries like Sweden and Canada that have attained high levels of public health, literacy, security, and civil rights along with high voter turnout and frequent, meaningful elections. These countries pride themselves on good government, which requires high-minded public deliberation in their elected legislatures as well as efficient, ethical, and competent public administration. While most European countries devote a higher proportion of their wealth to the public sector and have more powerful central governments than the United States, America also took steps toward a stronger national state during the Progressive Era, the New Deal, and the Great Society of the 1960s.

Is it possible to have a strong, effective, efficient, and democratic state without civil society? Experience suggests that the answer is no. The Nordic democracies, with their powerful governments, also have the world's highest rates of membership in voluntary associations and impressive "civic literacy."[6] To be sure, there are strong states around the globe that exist without robust civil societies. However, every one is corrupt, tyrannical, or both.

It stands to reason that strong and powerful governments require civil societies. First of all, the citizen's watchdog role, mentioned earlier during the discussion of a libertarian society, is even more important if the state is powerful. There is great potential for abuse of governmental power in a country like Sweden or Canada; nevertheless, those regimes have performed reasonably well because they are held to account by populations that gather information from multiple channels (including parties, activist churches, advocacy organizations, and civic associations). Compared to other people, the citizens of the Nordic democracies show extraordinarily high levels of concern for environmental protection, social equality, and civil rights. They probably learn to care about the public interest (as they define it) in their private associations, their churches, youth groups, and unions. In turn, their concern for the public good motivates them to follow the news and act when the government seems to need their assistance or when it behaves corruptly.

Even in a society with an expansive government, the state should not be asked to handle every issue. No matter how much of the gross national product it absorbs through taxes, it will collapse if it is made responsible for everything. Social democracies work well to the extent that many public goods (from religious education to athletic events to hiking trails) are provided by independent voluntary associations.

It appears, then, that both libertarians and social democrats need civil society and its associated virtues and skills. The same is surely true of everyone who stands between them on the political spectrum. Mainstream American liberals and conservatives differ only modestly in the amount of power that they want to invest in the state versus the market. Both ultimately favor a mixed economy with a federal government that manages roughly 15 to 20 percent of the gross domestic product. Such a polity certainly needs private nonprofit associations for the reasons mentioned so far: to collect and disseminate information about public issues, to host discussions, to teach people the skills and virtues they require as voters and jurors, to organize effective resistance to the state when it is corrupt or repressive, and to address certain public matters so that the state can manage other problems that are assigned to it.

Although we disagree about which problems should be managed by the state and which ones are better handled by nonprofit groups or the market, it seems likely that states are better at relatively impersonal tasks, such as defining and enforcing general rules and rights, collecting taxes, and distributing entitlements in the form of checks and vouchers. Voluntary associations are often better at highly personalized and morally complex tasks, such as caring for the sick, creating works of art and culture, and providing religious instruction. When governmental money is spent for these purposes, most of it is (and always has been) disbursed to companies and nonprofit associations. Whether secular education is best handled by the state or by firms or associations is a matter of debate, although almost everyone agrees that the government should *fund* universal education through the twelfth grade, and almost everyone believes that there is some role for private associations in *delivering* education, at least at the college level.

Some definitions of "civil society" encompass only voluntary, independent associations, plus the virtues, skills, and habits that they require. However, most of the arguments for civil society that I have mentioned so far are really arguments in favor of dividing power among numerous institutions and allowing many people to participate voluntarily and directly in matters of public concern. Those goals can be advanced by for-profit companies as well as nonprofits. For instance, a good newspaper serves to check the power of the state, to inform voters, to teach concern for the public good, and to promote deliberation. These are classic purposes of civil society, even though a newspaper may be a highly profitable enterprise traded on the stock exchange whose employees work for paychecks.

By the same token, the state sector encompasses an enormous array of participatory bodies. We sometimes think of the "sovereign state" as a unit with a single organizational chart. In the United States, however, governmental power is divided among three levels, each with three branches. Moreover, the three levels of government have spun off innumerable commissions, public corporations, advisory boards, public/private ventures, charter schools, and other public bodies on which citizens may serve.

If the core of "civil society" is the art and practice of participation, then it takes place in all three sectors. The nonprofit sector is crucial, but we should also prize and defend profitable enterprises and governmental bodies that provide venues for deliberation and work on public matters. In fact, two of our biggest civic problems today are the decline of private enterprises that support civic engagement (for instance, newspapers, publishing houses, and law firms with strong traditions of pro bono work) and the overconsolidation of government. Opportunities to serve on a public board have declined by about 75 percent since the mid-twentieth century.[7]

To summarize this section: a reasonably successful state—whether a libertarian utopia, a Scandinavian-style social democracy, or something in between—requires "civil society," defined as an array of institutions in which citizens can inform themselves, deliberate, and address public problems. These institutions, in turn, require virtues and skills that people learn through experience.

2.3 EQUITY REQUIRES BROAD PARTICIPATION

A second argument for broad civic engagement relies on the principle of equity. Although some degree of economic inequality is inevitable in a free society, all citizens should be equals before the law and government; otherwise, those who have more clout will get unfairly better outcomes. In practice, however, people with more money and education tend to be more politically effective and to dominate civil society. For instance, of those who have ever received a federal small business loan (mostly people of some means), 100 percent said they "always vote." In contrast, of those who have received welfare or public assistance, just 56.1 percent claim always to vote. These turnout estimates are probably inflated, but the gap of 44.4 percentage points is consistent with other research.[8] Perhaps in part because welfare recipients do not vote, the federal government cut welfare payments per family by 57 percent (after inflation) between the peak year of 1969 and 2003.[9]

In the United States, there are striking correlations between most forms of civic engagement and individuals' education and wealth. Giving money, contacting public officials, working informally on community problems, even protesting—all are more common among the affluent than among the poor.[10] Table 1 shows self-reported levels of participation for those who say they belong to the working class and who have a high school diploma or less, versus those who call themselves middle-class and have a college degree or more. The more privileged group is between two and five times more likely to participate in all categories (except that *none* of the working-class respondents volunteered for a party or candidate).

In principle, there could be an equitable political system with low levels of participation, so long as every demographic group and social stratum participated at the same rate. Then the participants would be a representative sample of the whole population. There are even democracies in which the poor and weak outvote the powerful: for example, in India, where the "untouchable" or Dalit class has higher turnout than the high-caste Brahmins.[11] That is because the poor outnumber the wealthy in India, and political parties have persuaded them that they can benefit tangibly from influencing the state by voting. It seems rela-

TABLE 1 Civic Engagement by Education and Class

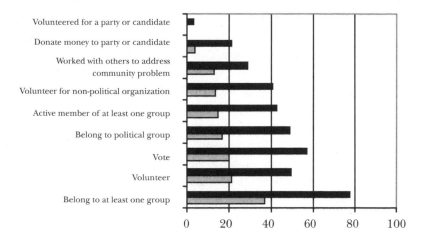

☐ = working class, high school graduate or less, not in school
■ = middle class, college graduate
Source: National Survey of Civic Engagement CIRCLE 2002

tively difficult to mobilize the least advantaged in a country like the United States, where the median family is reasonably well-off and well educated, and the poor form an electoral minority, incapable of winning elections even if their turnout is high. Also, a sophisticated, media-rich society with a strong independent voluntary sector and a high degree of political freedom rewards people who have resources—money, skills, energy, or time—to contribute.

Thus the best method for increasing political equity in a country like the United States is to raise the *total* number of people who participate in politics and civil society. When total numbers rise, the poor and poorly educated are better represented. This idea is not utopian. Voter turnout among male citizens reached 81.8 percent in 1872—far higher than it is today.[12] There is no essential reason why basic forms of participation such as voting couldn't again become near-universal.

Several reasons have been proposed to explain why wealthy and highly educated Americans are more likely to participate in politics and civil society. In particular, because they support different responses, two competing reasons deserve careful consideration. First, it could be that citizens' skills and money are *political resources* that make them effective participants. We might think, for example, that better educated people are more likely to vote because they know more. You cannot cast a ballot unless you know which candidate to prefer, and that requires a fair amount of information that may have to come from sources like newspapers, which are challenging to read. Surveys find that voters know more about politics than nonvoters. Furthermore, people with more years of education are more likely to participate in politics and civil society; in fact, that is the "best documented finding in American political behavior research."[13] A plausible explanation is that people who spend more years in school and college learn more about politics and current events, and their knowledge assists them in voting and otherwise engaging.[14]

If this theory applies, then we should try to enhance everyone's knowledge of politics so that turnout will rise. Similarly, educating everyone about health will increase participation in health-related nonprofits; teaching more people about environmental science will boost the number of people who volunteer for conservation groups; and so on.

Like knowledge, time is a resource that is in short supply. In 2002, some 30 percent of self-described nonvoters told the census bureau that they had not participated because they were too busy, they didn't have enough time, they had transportation problems, the polling place was inconvenient, or the lines were too long.[15] Those who advocate making Election Day a national holiday are essentially trying to provide harried people with a resource (time) that is scarce and inequitably distributed. On a larger scale, there is a positive correlation between the size of a country's welfare state and the level of participation in its nonprofit groups. Perhaps people who can retire securely have more time for volunteering and group membership. In that case, distributing modestly more money to retirees and unemployed people would make political and civic participation more equitable.

So far, I have discussed theories about political resources. The alternative is a *status* theory. Consider the following facts: (1) the most educated Americans have always been the most civically engaged; (2) mean levels of education have substantially increased since 1900; *yet* (3) levels of participation are flat. This pattern seems strange: Why didn't rising rates of graduation from high school and college boost voter turnout, if knowledge is a key political resource?[16] One explanation is that education is partly, or mostly, a marker of social status. Americans who have the most money and power are identified not by hereditary titles but by educational degrees. Politicians and major nonprofit institutions are most eager to recruit this governing class and to promote its interests. Institutions pursue members of this elite because such people have money, connections, and power. Nie et al. find: "The greater the educational attainment *relative to others*, the more likely it is that the citizen will be pushed or pulled into joining" voluntary associations.[17] Thus what matters is a person's position in the social hierarchy, not her specifically political resources. Even if she has no knowledge of politics and no time to vote, she will be avidly recruited to participate.

If institutions compete to win the support of an elite, then elite citizens are most likely to participate in politics and civil society. Even if the aggregate level of education and knowledge in a society rises dramatically (as has happened in the United States since 1900), the political system and major nonprofits will still ignore those at the bottom of the social hierarchy and will avidly compete for those at the top. In that case, to improve public education is not, by itself, necessarily a way to make the political system more equitable. It may simply raise the bar. Today you need an M.B.A. or a law degree to get the same status advantage that a B.A. provided in 1920. If we did a better job of teaching everyone about government and politics, then average levels of knowledge would rise. Nevertheless, some would be more successful than others in school, and the *relatively* more successful would participate at a higher rate in politics and civil society.

The resource theory and the status theory have different implications. Improving the quality of civic education seems more promising if the resource theory applies. If the status theory is true, then political institutions must be reformed so that they pay more attention to people at the lower end of the status scale. Nevertheless, both theories imply that we should try to increase the rate of political and civic participation in our whole population if we want to achieve political equality.

A third theory is compatible with the other two. It emphasizes the need to cultivate a *sense* of political equality. Our constitutional system honors two major values—freedom and equality—that are often in tension. Many Americans have strong positive feelings about freedom. They know what it is, they know when and to what extent they possess it, and they have opinions about politicians and policies that might enhance or undermine their individual liberty. Political equality is a much more abstract concept, rarely invoked in speeches or policy proposals, and rarely experienced. Most people feel that it does not prevail. For instance, in 2006, 53 percent of those surveyed said that politics was a way for the powerful to keep power for themselves—versus 35 percent who said that it was a way for the less powerful to compete as equals. Only 23 percent said that the political system was "responsive to the genuine needs of the public."[18] As Nick Bromell writes, people need to gain a taste for political equality through concrete experiences of politics: "It is increasingly clear that equality must be given some substance because it has so little force as an abstract principle. To resonate with Americans, equality must be something they feel, something they believe in because they sense its presence within them. This means that what we might call the 'subjective' dimensions of democracy must be excavated. Democracy is not just a set of institutions, a cluster of marble buildings, and a collection of laws. Democracy is about self-government, and therefore the nature of the self stands at its center."[19] Bromell implies that if people had concrete experiences of political power and efficacy, they would demand more of it. This is an additional argument for increasing the rates of civic engagement.

There is a fourth plausible explanation for the link between educational success and civic engagement—one that should hearten and encourage civic educators. Alberto Dávila and Marie Mora find that young people who participate in student government or community service (whether it is required or voluntary) are much more likely to succeed in school and to complete college than their peers who are less engaged. The reason (discussed in more detail below) may be that civic engagement increases students' attachment to their schools and their sense of purpose, thereby helping them to succeed in learning. Dávila and Mora use longitudinal data and are able to control for civic attitudes measured at eighth grade as well as a host of other factors. Thus their model estimates the impact of civic engagement when isolated from other experiences. The impact appears to be universally positive, but to illustrate it with an example, young men are 29 percentage points more likely to graduate from college on time if they have engaged in service to fulfill a class requirement during high school. We also know that habits of service and leadership in adolescence last for many decades afterward (see section 4.3). Thus it is possible that teenagers who are encouraged to participate civically do better in school, which partially explains why better educated adults are more engaged in civil society.[20]

2.4 INSTITUTIONS AND COMMUNITIES WORK BETTER WHEN PEOPLE PARTICIPATE

People get more from government and major voluntary associations when they participate. Such was the argument of the previous section. The converse is also true: public institutions work better when many people participate.

We all know individuals whom we would rather exclude from public meetings, institutions, and voluntary organizations because of their poor ethics or their lack of sense. We also know particular people whose contributions are far *better* than average, and we might wish that we could limit participation to them while excluding the worst of our fellow human beings. Nevertheless, we are much better off seeking everyone's participation—for several significant reasons.

First, it is an ethical imperative to give everyone who is affected by a decision a voice in it; and people obtain a voice not only by voting but by attending meetings, signing petitions, joining organizations, and making speeches. The principle that all should participate reflects our sense that human beings have equal dignity, which means not only the right to be treated equally well, but also the right to help *make* the rules (moral, conventional, institutional, and legal) that will govern them. This equal right to participation is "autonomy," in the root sense of "making one's own law." Only a political system that provides rule-giving power to all is worthy of full respect, according Immanuel Kant and others in his tradition.[21]

However, not everyone is convinced by the core Kantian idea that we must do right regardless of the consequences. They want to know whether the *effects* of including everyone in politics and civic life will be beneficial. In theory, we might get optimal effects if we excluded or discouraged at least a few of our fellow citizens—the truly obstructive and selfish. But screens for civic virtue tend not to work and can easily be abused. For example, the common pattern of preferring aristocrats, clergymen, or credentialed experts has usually been a smokescreen for class interest. Thus the question is whether it is better to have broad, active participation or to settle for small numbers of participants in the hope that the few will be better citizens. Samuel Huntington argued for the latter view in 1975 when he wrote that "the effective operation of a democratic political system usually requires some measure of apathy and disinvolvement on the part of some individuals and groups." An "*excess* of democracy," Huntington argued, was responsible for bad government in the United States.[22]

The empirical evidence mostly suggests that Huntington was wrong: more participation is better for social outcomes. Communities, schools systems, and whole nations seem to perform better when political participation is broad and robust.

For example, consider figure 1, which plots scores for 62 nations on two axes. (Some countries' names are hidden to make the graph more legible.) The *y*-axis shows the level of "human development" as measured by the United Nations Development Programme (UNDP) in 2005. The UNDP's Human Development Index is composed of measures of longevity, educational attainment, and gross domestic product per capita. A higher index score is assumed to reflect a better society. Along the *x*-axis, I show a composite of average voter participation in all post-1945 elections and the percentage of people who say they have signed a petition, boycotted a product, or joined protest. This composite is an attempt to measure the breadth of political participation with one indicator.[23] It correlates with socioeconomic development, especially if we omit some exceptional cases discussed below.

Very similar scatter-plots can be generated from other data. For example, Gregory B. Markus and colleagues surveyed 5,626 residents in a diverse set of fourteen American cities. Overall, they found powerful correlations between the amount of civic participation, on the one hand, and residents' approval of local government, education, crime, and community, on the other. High approval could simply reflect a contagious form of boosterism in cities that have broad participation. However, a glance at the list of cities reveals that political and civic participation is highest in those places (Madison, Seattle, and Portland) where social outcomes are best, and lowest in communities where schools are poor and crime is high.[24]

Finally, Robert Putnam uses the same kind of scatter-plots to show that the level of adult participation in communities correlates powerfully with high school graduation rates, SAT scores, and other indicators of educational success at the state level. "States where citizens

FIGURE 1 **Political Participation and Human Development**

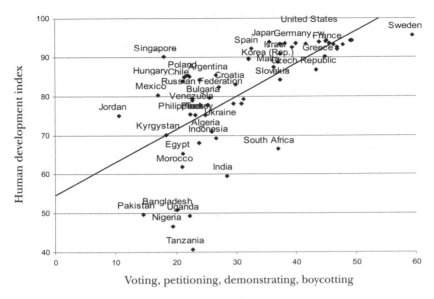

Voting, petitioning, demonstrating, boycotting

Source: See note 23, page 232.

meet, join, vote, and trust in unusual measure boast consistently higher educational performance than states where citizens are less engaged with civic and community life." Putnam finds that such engagement is "by far" a bigger correlate of educational outcomes than is spending on education, teachers' salaries, class size, or demographics.[25]

These studies do not necessarily show that we can enhance wealth, health, longevity, or educational performance by getting more people involved in politics and civic engagement. The various graphs show correlations, not causality; and the causal story is complex and controversial. It could be the case, for example, that affluent and safe communities allow people to participate: in that case, participation would be a *result* of affluence and not a cause. Or it could be that some third factor underlies both good institutions and political engagement. For instance, in some of the literature on social capital, it appears that ordinary sociability (dining with others, belonging to bowling leagues and other nonpolitical groups) is the root cause of both economic performance and political engagement. In that case, seeking to engage more people in politics might be impossible and would not improve social outcomes even if it worked.

Notwithstanding those caveats, broad political participation is present in the most successful communities: those with the highest standards of living and the best-functioning institutions. Some studies (notably Putnam's work on educational outcomes) find that the correlation between participation and institutional success remains even once we hold economic factors constant.

There are strong theoretical reasons to suspect that broad civic engagement actually benefits institutions. Many people have energy and knowledge that they can contribute if encouraged to do so. People know their own needs and interests better than anyone else. And most citizens are willing to live with decisions that they have helped to shape, whereas they resist rules and policies made by a few.

Furthermore, people must *develop* the very goals that we measure when we assess the performance of institutions and communities. Earlier, I cited the UNDP's Human Development Index, assuming that a high score reflected a good nation in which to live. That judgment could be controversial. Some people might want to give more weight to equality between the sexes, religious faith, or individual freedom. Such controversy about how to define social goals underlines the importance of political participation. If there were one obvious indicator of success (such as GDP/capita or aggregate happiness as measured in opinion polls), then it would be possible to imagine a blueprint for socioeconomic development that could simply be imposed by the government (or even by a computer). But, if people disagree about what is most desirable, then political participation becomes an intrinsic aspect of economic development and not merely a means to achieve it.

Before leaving this section, I would like to discuss two complications. First, I have argued that people should be civically engaged because their engagement (as measured by a handful of survey questions) correlates with desirable social outcomes. But there are many forms of participation, and we find some that do not show this relationship. For example, the World Values Survey asks people whether they take "local community action on issues like poverty, employment, housing, racial equality" and whether they do unpaid work on such issues. Answers to these questions correlate *negatively* with the Human Development Index. Such "local community action" is most common in the poorest countries (for example, Bangladesh, Tanzania, and China) and is quite uncommon in Western Europe.

We do not want to conclude that local community work is bad for economic development. Yet that is as valid an inference as my previous claim that voting is good for development because the highly developed nations have strong turnout. The truth is probably more complicated: some forms of civic engagement probably arise to mitigate suffering when a government and economy are failing. Hence their negative correlation with economic development.

If our fundamental commitment is to a Kantian moral principle of equal autonomy, then we should not rely on statistics to defend a right to participation. Statistical relationships may prove to be complex, ambiguous, and variable. There is nothing wrong with a pure moral principle, as long as it doesn't lead us into folly. I would interpret the studies described above as evidence that we need not be afraid to follow our moral instincts and encourage broad participation, because the economic effects will, at worst, not be bad.

The second complication involves countries and communities where social outcomes are poor but civic engagement is strong. In the graph shown above, Tanzania, India, and South Africa are among the democracies that show much more civic engagement than we would expect from their relatively low levels of economic development. All three countries are famous for democratic political leaders and grassroots democratic movements. Yet authoritarian countries like China have higher human development indices. One conclusion is that India and South Africa will ultimately be better off, because their strong traditions of democratic participation will provide sustained and balanced growth, whereas China could collapse.[26] But there is an alternative thesis: perhaps a popular movement can raise participation *without* producing better social outcomes, even though the two indicators are correlated.

Closer to home is the West Side of Chicago, one of the communities whose civic participation Markus and colleagues studied. This is a poor area: 40 percent of households had less than $15,000 in income in 1996; some 86 percent were people of color; only a third had education beyond high school. According to Markus's survey, residents tend to distrust "other people" and the local government. That is understandable, as—with a few bright spots—Chicago's City Hall has been corrupt, unjust, and even brutal. Citizens there are highly unlikely to believe that they can understand government or that officials care about people like them.[27]

Yet levels of civic and political participation on Chicago's West Side are extraordinarily high. Once you control for demographic factors, the West Side is first among the fourteen communities in both electoral and civic participation. What's more, residents of a particularly poor district within the West Side are more engaged than those in a more middle-class enclave. The most highly engaged group of all are African American residents of the particularly poor southwestern part of the West Side.[28]

The explanation is fairly evident: deliberate community organizing. Chicago has been an extraordinary laboratory for such work ever since the days of Jane Addams and then Saul Alinsky. It is the national headquarters of the Gamaliel Foundation, the Industrial Areas Foundation (IAF), and National People's Action. There are famous community development corporations like Bethel New Life; powerful religious congregations; neighborhood associations; and engaged colleges and universities.[29] There are countless links among these groups; activists in IAF, for example, spend their time launching other associations and persuading institutions to be more engaged.

One-quarter of all West Siders (and more in the poorest district) are members of a block club or neighborhood association. Almost one-fifth have served on a nonprofit board. Those who participate explain their reasons as: making the community a better place to live (71 percent), influencing policy (51 percent), being with people they enjoy (43 percent), and meeting new people (40 percent). Especially in the poorest district, a substantial group claims that participation is "exciting." These statistics reveal a neighborhood in which people are used to *political group membership*, which they see as both powerful and enjoyable.[30]

For those who value civic participation, the results from Chicago and India are heartening. They imply that even under adverse economic conditions, residents can build traditions of participation by deliberately organizing their fellow citizens. If we want to argue, however, that a good way to improve schools, reduce corruption, and achieve growth is to enhance political participation, Chicago's West Side and India become problematic examples. Despite a century of political organizing in both places, neither scores well on social indicators. Perhaps they would score *lower* without the democratic organizing. For example, Chicago has fared better than some of its peers—Saint Louis, Detroit, and Cleveland—and the difference could be attributed to strong neighborhood-level politics. But that would be a subtle thesis and not as inspiring as the claim that engagement leads directly to prosperity and good government.

2.5 EVERYONE HAS CIVIC NEEDS

I will argue here, as a corollary to the previous section, that everyone has problems that can only be addressed through voluntary, collective action. Our problems vary a great deal, often as a result of differences in our economic and social status. Yet, even privileged people have needs that they must address collaboratively.

This thesis is demonstrated clearly in Annette Lareau's book *Unequal Childhoods: Class, Race, and Family Life,* a careful, qualitative study of working-class, middle-class, and poor households in the same American metropolitan area. For the most part, the problems of the poor and working-class families involve dysfunctional public institutions or a lack of resources and opportunities. For example, one girl in the study has learning disabilities. She is receiving no special help at school. According to the rules of her school district, it would take a minimum of 120 days after her application to reassign her to special education.[31] These rules—at least as Lareau describes them—must be changed; but it takes collective action to change bureaucratic procedures.

In general, the problems that face middle-class suburban families result from competition among themselves, not from underperforming or underfunded institutions. Middle-class parents are good at obtaining excellent services from schools, doctors, and other organizations. If their schools were unresponsive, they would simply move. (In the terminology of Albert O. Hirshman, they would use "exit" not "voice" to address perceived institutional failure.)[32] Nevertheless, their lives are not idyllic. They rush from activity to activity. The children are so used to being provided with stimulating organized activities that they become bored or quarrel instantly when left alone. In the fiction that suburban kids read, the young protagonists always decide what to do from hour to hour. But only working-class kids actually have that kind of independence.

Families also feel unable to control their time. If a parent refuses to take her child to an inconvenient soccer practice, the child will be cut from the team. And if the child is cut from the team, she will lose access to peer networks and learning experiences. One parent says, "There's something arrogant about soccer. I mean, they just assume that you have the time, that you can get off work, to lug your kids to games. What if you worked a job that paid an hourly wage?"[33]

One middle-class family struggles with an unmanageable load of homework. As the father says, "I don't think I did that much homework in college."[34] This burden could be the fault of teachers; but I suspect the underlying cause is pressure from other middle-class parents. It would take counterpressure from many families to lower those demands. Lareau cites "Family Life First," an excellent collective effort by parents in Minnesota. Participating parents ask coaches to reduce demands on all kids at once. The project was started, although Lareau doesn't explain so, by William Doherty, a family counseling professor who realized that his clients' stress arose from competition and required a political response rather than a therapeutic one.

The conclusion I want to draw is that community organizing—usually seen as a way to enhance the political capacities of poor people and racial minorities so that they can address profound injustice—is also needed in middle-class, suburban, predominantly white communities. Even relatively affluent people have problems that cannot be solved by money, but only by voluntary collective action through groups and networks.

2.6 CIVIC ENGAGEMENT IS LINKED TO CULTURE

We often think of a democracy as a political system in which "the people" are ultimately in control of their government's budget, important laws, and relations with foreign nations. But it is at least as important for a people to control its own identity and self-image. In order to be self-governing, a community or a nation must be able to illustrate and memorialize its values and present its identity to outsiders and future generations of its own people through works of art and literature, rituals and traditions, forms of entertainment, public spaces, and prominent buildings.

No free community will have a single, harmonious cultural identity, because people are diverse and will inevitably express conflicting values. For example, at the time of writing, there is a heated debate about whether individuals and private companies should use the secular phrase "Happy Holidays," or the religious expression "Merry Christmas." Those phrases appear in cultural products, such as cards, signs, and broadcasts. Americans debate which greeting to use because they care how their common culture develops. Our goal should not be consensus about this or any other matter of cultural identity. Rather, all the citizens of a free community should have opportunities to create and share cultural products, and the community as a whole should support a robust and independent cultural life.

At the beginning of the twenty-first century, there are new opportunities for cultural production. It is cheaper than ever before to create a movie or a music recording; and the Internet enables people to collaborate in new and interesting ways. On the other hand, books, movies, images, and music now move easily across borders and look the same everywhere. Globalization thus threatens the capacity of local communities to shape their own identities through culture.

In nature, when unlike things become more alike through contact, we say that entropy has increased, leading ultimately to bland inertness. The only way to reduce entropy is to apply intelligence. For example, by sorting objects into separate piles, an intelligent being can make a heap less entropic. Likewise, "globalization" means an increased rate of interchange among diverse cultures. This interchange tends to make them more similar, thereby threatening to create an entropic, homogeneous world. Nevertheless, it is possible to fight cultural entropy through intelligence, in this case by deliberately creating distinctive cultural products for each community.

Unfortunately, cultural products produced by celebrities seem to generate the greatest demand. Talented and beautiful performers and highly trained experts (such as producers, sound engineers, and designers) are responsible for the world's most popular cultural products. People do not want to hear amateur music if they can easily listen to the world's most famous singer on a digital recording that costs less than one dollar. People do not want to watch a live theatrical production if they can turn on their television set and watch famous actors in an expensively produced movie. The easy availability of commercial culture reduces demand for ordinary people's creativity and makes the world more homogeneous, thus frustrating local communities (and even whole nations) that want to govern their own cultures. The more that slick, professional products penetrate the international market, the less scope exists for ordinary people to create cultural products that others will value.

To some extent, the popularity of celebrity culture is a function of corporate investment, which purchases talent, technological support, and advertising. Corporate power varies and can be influenced by public policy and technological innovation. For example, the Internet has reduced the power of corporate media by adding millions of alternative voices.[35] Even so, there may be an *intrinsic* tendency for democracies to produce mass cultures, quite apart from corporate influence. We have seen such concentration emerge on the Internet, where a few blogs have attracted enormous audiences despite a complete absence of corporate backing.[36]

In a democracy, we tend to assume that popularity is evidence of quality. Just as we choose leaders by voting, so we are encouraged to purchase movies because they are "blockbusters," songs because they are "hits," and books because they are "best sellers." The equating of popularity with quality is not universal. In aristocratic cultures, an elite caste that has disproportionate influence over the culture abhors popular taste. It is thus a special problem for democracies that people flock to whatever other people have flocked to. As Alexis de Tocqueville observed:

> Among aristocratic nations every man is pretty nearly stationary in his own sphere, but men are astonishingly unlike each other; their passions, their notions, and their tastes are essentially different: nothing changes, but everything differs. In democracies, on the contrary, all men are alike and do things pretty nearly alike. It is true that they are subject to great and frequent vicissitudes, but as the same events of good or averse fortune are continually recurring, only the name of the actors is changed, the piece is always the same. The aspect of American society is animated because men and things are always changing, but it is monotonous because all these changes are alike.[37]

In an age of celebrities and scandals, Tocqueville's vision seems prophetic. He warned that true freedom suffers when mass culture dominates, because individuals have fewer genuine choices. Worse, an increasingly homogeneous population may demand a centralized, uniform state that will obtain dangerous power. It is difficult to imagine fascism or Stalinism without mass-produced popular culture.

Fortunately, Tocqueville offered not only a diagnosis but a cure. When people associate in communities and voluntary organizations, each group takes on a distinct character. Many groups choose to display their identities through music, statuary, graphic design, narrative history, and other forms of culture. Members of groups are interested in work created by fellow members, not just mass-produced culture. To build those associations requires civic skills and engagement. Thus a robust democracy will have a diverse culture, and vice versa.

2.7 CIVIC PARTICIPATION IS INTRINSICALLY VALUABLE

So far, I have explored the beneficial *consequences* of civic engagement for prosperity, equity, institutional performance, and cultural development. However, participation can also be seen as an end in itself, an intrinsic good. This position counteracts a widespread assumption that we derive from the classical liberals (Locke, Madison, Adam Smith, Friedrich von Hayek, and others), who believed that civic participation was a cost; it was the price people had to pay for good government. These classical liberals realized that government would not protect liberty or provide essential public goods unless citizens participated— taking the time to vote, follow the news, and join voluntary associations. Even so, they considered a government to be well designed if it required *relatively little* participation. The best state left its people maximally free to conduct their own private pursuits.

An alternative to classical liberalism is the view that we now call *civic republicanism*. Civic republicans see participation as intrinsically good, as a benefit and not a cost to those who participate. For example, whereas classical liberals believe that the purpose of politics is to make private life safe and sustainable, Hannah Arendt announces in *The Human Condition* that "politics is never for the sake of life. . . . Household life exists for the sake of the 'good life' in politics."[38]

It seems incredible that we would live as workers, parents, and consumers only so that we could participate in politics—especially if political participation mainly means casting a vote once a year. However, Arendt (following Aristotle) defines "politics" much more broadly, as the interaction of people who are different on a common subject.[39] Thus we are engaged in "politics" when we debate and make decisions in religious congregations, schools, community associations, and theater groups (and perhaps, although Arendt does not say so, inside certain corporations). Arendt sees this work as essentially dignified and valuable, more so than our activities as producers and consumers. Whereas labor is mostly a matter of implementing orders, political interaction occurs among rough equals who are free to initiate unpredictable processes of their own volition. Politics also permits individuality: "In acting and speaking, men show who they are, reveal actively their unique personal identities and thus make their appearance in the human world."[40]

Politics generates memorable stories, because interesting conflicts arise when each citizen's goals are partially frustrated by others. To be part of a story is to have true "character."[41] We admire such heroes as George Washington and Martin Luther King because they had opportunities to play roles in great political dramas. Without politics, there would be no such characters. To be sure, civic participation is not the only activity that generates stories; for example, we also participate as "characters" in individual and team sports. But sports stories tend to recur; they follow stereotyped patterns and fade fairly quickly in observers' memories once a new season begins. Deep down, everyone knows that the activity is just a game. In contrast, political participation is serious and allows us to create and preserve memories and institutions that last beyond our death. Thus, Arendt argues, politics can overcome the "futility" of human life.[42]

Arendt observes that for humans, fully experiencing something requires displaying it. Unless other people notice an experience that I am having, it may not seem real even to me. In particular, to experience a *virtue* requires displaying it so that it can be recognized in public. Thus another advantage of politics is to allow us to develop virtues and to feel them from the inside as others recognize them.

In a famous speech delivered in 1819, Benjamin Constant distinguished between the "liberty of the moderns" (which most Americans value and demand on their own behalf) and the liberty of the ancients (which everyone except civic republicans tends to forget). The liberty of the moderns is a lack of constraint on individual choice. It is, writes Constant,

> the right to be subjected to nothing but laws, to have no possibility of being arrested, detained, executed, or maltreated in any way as a result of the arbitrary will of one or many individuals: It is for each the right to state his opinion, to choose his business and work in it, to dispose of his property, to take advantage of the same; to come and go without obtaining permission, and without explaining his reasons and itinerary. It is, for each, the right to associate with other individuals, whether to confer about their own interests, to profess the religion that he and his associates prefer, or simply to pass days

or hours in a manner that fits his inclinations, his fantasies. Finally, it is the right, for each one, to influence the administration of the Government, whether via the nomination of some or all officials, or via representations, petitions, demands that the authority is more or less obligated to take into consideration.

These rights are enshrined in the United States Constitution. For the most part, they are limitations on the power of government, which is seen as the greatest danger to individual choice. But there is also a kind of liberty that we can only exercise as part of a group. That is what Constant called "the liberty of the ancients." It consists, he said, "of exercising collectively, but directly, many parts of absolute sovereignty, [and the right] to deliberate, in a public space, about war and peace, to ratify treaties of alliance with foreigners, to vote laws, pronounce decisions, examine the accounts, actions, and management of officials, to compel them to appear before the whole people, to accuse them, to condemn or acquit them."[43] Someone who values the liberty of the ancients would rather lose a political struggle and live under laws framed by the opposite side than not have that struggle at all, because we can exercise political freedom only in politics. The state must be limited (else it will have the power to suppress public participation), but there must *be* an active state that people can freely and collectively influence.

Like the classical republicans before her, Arendt developed a hierarchy of pursuits and behaviors, and political participation was at the very top of her list. Aristotle had counted politics as the *second*-best human pursuit—the best being "philosophy" (which would today include science and mathematics). Christian republicans in the late Middle Ages and Renaissance generally ranked politics immediately below spirituality on their list of excellent forms of life.

I am unconvinced by arguments for the superiority of any single human pursuit. There is no common coin or single criterion by which to compare the relative merits of politics, pure scholarship and science, artistic creativity, religious worship, appreciation of nature, and care for loved ones.[44] Thus I would depart from classical republicanism because I would not claim that political participation is the best (or even the second-best) pursuit for all human beings. Nevertheless, the great civic republican authors were correct that political participation has intrinsic merits. It has potential dignity that is absent in many other forms of life.

It is certainly better than a life devoted to shopping or using up consumer goods.

Civic engagement can be especially rewarding in youth. Wordsworth captured that feeling when he recalled his youthful experiences in the French Revolution: "Bliss was it in that dawn to be alive / But to be young was very Heaven!" It was the combination of being new to the world and being able to change it that made his experience "blissful." He recalls that both "the meek" and "the lofty"

> Were called upon to exercise their skill,
> Not in Utopia, subterranean fields,
> Or some secreted island, Heaven knows where!
> But in the very world, which is the world
> Of all of us,—the place where in the end
> We find our happiness, or not at all![45]

Similarly, the columnist Jonathan Yardley treasures his memories of being a student journalist who supported the civil rights movement: "It was my enormous good fortune to be at the right place in the right time: to be young, to have found a great cause, to be doing nothing of moment on its behalf, but to be doing it with all my heart." Youniss and Yates add: "Grassroots social activism is as alive and appropriate today as it was in the past. Youth today are as talented as they were during the civil rights era. Thus, it is appropriate that [a school] resolutely encouraged students to think of themselves as being *at the right place in the right* time to find their cause and build their identity."[46]

If we count participation as a potential benefit and not always a cost, then we must make sure to provide opportunities for argument, deliberation, advocacy, and collaboration. It ought to concern us that the number of school board seats has shrunk by 86 percent since 1930, even as the population has more than doubled.[47] This is just one example of a general decline in opportunities for Arendt's kind of "politics." On the other hand, civic republicans should endorse certain recent reforms and proposals. For instance, whether or not charter schools produce better educational outcomes for their students, they allow citizens to band together, innovate, and serve the public. They thus promote the intrinsic good of political participation (see section 10.1).

In addition to providing actual opportunities for participation, we should also make sure that people are aware of the value of politics (broadly defined). A market system generates plenty of advertising for consumer goods, thereby constantly reminding people that they need money. Markets do not advertise the intrinsic merits of political participation. Politicians and parties vie for popular support, often by claiming that they can provide better services than the competition. They rarely present participation as a good. Religious congregations compete to persuade people that faith and worship are important; they have no motivation to depict politics positively. Only nonprofit groups have a clear self-interest in advertising the value of civic participation— but they have inadequate budgets and must meet other needs. Besides, many nonprofits are run by professionals who do not themselves value public engagement. Thus one purpose of civic education is to make young people aware that "politics" (in Arendt's broad sense) can be fulfilling and dignified. When they are adults, it will be their *choice* whether to participate or not, but they ought to understand the potential advantages of being engaged.

2.8 DEMOCRACY AS LEARNING

Related to the argument of the previous section (that civic engagement is an intrinsic good) is the idea that democracy is educative. At the end of *On Liberty* (1859), after John Stewart Mill has argued for many pages that people should be left alone so that they can learn the truth through free inquiry and uncensored debate, he notes the educative advantages of learning *together,* through participation in bodies that make binding, public decisions:

> In many cases, though individuals may not do the particular thing so well, on the average, as the officers of government, it is nevertheless desirable that it should be done by them, rather than by the government, as a means to their own mental education—a mode of strengthening their active faculties, exercising their judgment, and giving them a familiar knowledge of the subjects with which they are thus left to deal. This is a principal, though not the sole, recommendation of jury trial (in cases not political); of free and popular and local municipal institutions; of the conduct of industrial and philanthropic enterprises by voluntary associations.[48]

This insight then became the basic theme of Mill's *On Representative Government* (1861). A half century later, John Dewey pushed the argument still further. He defined "democracy" as any process by which a community collectively learns, and he defined "education" as any process that enhances individuals' capacity to participate in a democracy. Although these definitions pose some difficulties, they constitute an insightful theory—especially for those concerned about civic education.

A conventional definition of "democracy" is a system of government that honors equity and freedom. In a democracy—or so we are taught—every adult has one vote, and all may speak freely. For Dewey, however, such rules were merely tools that happened to be in current use. No institution (including free elections and civil rights) could claim "inherent sanctity." There were no general principles, no "antecedent universal propositions," that distinguished just institutions from unjust ones. The nature of the good society was "something to be critically and experimentally determined."[49]

As described so far, Dewey's theory of democracy gives no guidance and makes no distinctions. If we reject all "antecedent universal propositions," then we cannot know that a system of free elections is better than a tyranny. However, Dewey had one profound commitment: collective learning. Thus he valued the American constitutional system, not because all human beings were truly created equal, and not because elections would generate fair or efficient outcomes, but because democracy promoted discussion; and discussion was educative. "The strongest point to be made in behalf of even such rudimentary political forms as democracy has already attained, popular voting, majority rule and so on, is that to some extent they involve a consultation and discussion which uncover social needs and troubles."[50]

If learning is our goal, then we could spend our time reading books or observing nature. The kind of learning that Dewey valued most, however, was social and experiential. A democracy was a form of social organization in which people realized that they were interconnected and learned by working together. "Wherever there is conjoint activity whose consequences are appreciated as good by all singular persons who take part in it, and where the realization of the good is such as to effect an energetic desire and effort to sustain it in being just because it is a good shared by all, there is in so far a community. The clear consciousness of a communal life, in all its implications, constitutes the idea of democracy."[51]

It might seem strange to evaluate societies and institutions largely as opportunities for collective education. But that approach emerged from Dewey's beliefs about the purpose of life itself. In *Democracy and Education* (1916), he argued that individual life had value as experience; and the richer the experience, the better. The value of a society was to permit individuals to share and enlarge their experiences by communicating. "The ulterior significance of every mode of human association," he wrote, is "the contribution which it makes to the improvement of the quality of experience." It followed that a "democracy is more than a form of government; it is primarily a mode of associated living, of conjoint communal experience."[52]

I think that Dewey's rejection of universal propositions in favor of continuous collective learning was problematic. As he noted, "every social institution is educative in effect."[53] However, not every educative institution is democratic. Consider science, which Dewey valued very highly. Science is a collective enterprise and an excellent means of learning. But when it works as advertised, it is meritocratic, not democratic. If we equate democracy with collective learning, then we may weaken our commitment to equality and try to organize the government on the same principles as science (as Dewey recommended in *Liberalism and Social Action* [1935]), or we may try to democratize scientific research. Both reforms are mistakes, in my view.

Or, consider any society in which some oppress others and deprive them of rights. Such arrangements are consistent with "learning": the oppressors learn to dominate, and the oppressed learn to manage. Indeed, the two classes learn *together*, and they may learn continuously. I would deny that such a system is democratic, because it violates antecedent principles of equality. But Dewey's deep pragmatism prevented him from endorsing such external principles.

In *Democracy and Education,* Dewey recognized that "in any social group whatever, even in a gang of thieves, we find some interest held in common, and we find a certain amount of interaction and cooperative intercourse with other groups. From these two traits we derive our standard. How numerous and varied are the interests which are consciously shared? How full and free is the interplay with other forms of association?" In a "criminal band," Dewey thought, the shared interests must be narrow ("reducible almost to a common interest in plunder") and the group must isolate itself from outsiders.[54] In a good society, by contrast, everyone has everyone else's full range of interests at heart and there are dense networks connecting all sectors. Using modern tools of network analysis, we could map a community by asking people to name individuals with whom they collaborate on common problems and depicting those connections as links among nodes. A good community, according to Dewey's principles, would be one in which we could move from any individual node to any other by following a small number of links.

This ideal seems more satisfactory than a simple commitment to "learning," but it relies on the kind of abstract moral principles that Dewey elsewhere rejects. For example, concern for the holistic well-being of all fellow human beings is a strong moral commitment, characteristic of Kantianism. It does not derive logically from the concept of communal learning, but is a separate principle. It is not clear to me how a Deweyan pragmatist can embrace it.

Notwithstanding this qualification, there is much of value in Dewey's theory. For those who promote public deliberation, a theory of democracy-as-learning is inspirational. It explains why adults should be, and are, motivated to gather and discuss public problems: discussion is virtually the purpose of human life. (One Australian who participated in a formal citizens' deliberation said afterward, "It's the most important thing I've ever done in my whole life, I suppose."[55]) Dewey's theory also provides a response to those who say that deliberation is "just talk," that it lacks sufficient impact on votes and policies. Dewey would reply that the heart of democracy is not an election or the passage of a law, but personal growth through communication. "There is no liberal expansion and confirmation of limited personal intellectual endowment which may not proceed from the flow of social intelligence when that circulates by word of mouth from one to another in the communication of the local community."[56]

Dewey's endorsement of verbal communication does not mean, however, that speech should be disconnected from action. "Mind," he thought "is not a name for something complete by itself; it is a name for a course of action in so far as that is intelligently directed."[57] Likewise, deliberation (which is thinking by groups) should be linked to concrete experimentation. Public deliberation is most satisfying and motivating—and most informed and disciplined—when the people who talk also act: when they argue from personal, practical experience and when their decisions have consequences for their individual and collective behavior. This is "public work," in Boyte's phrase. A common example for youth is any program in which young people decide on a social issue to tackle, conduct research, and then take some action. That approach is typical in the best current programs of civic education, which have a Deweyan inspiration. Such programs illustrate the educational value of democratic participation—a final reason that we should prize participation for people of all ages.

CHAPTER 3

Measures of Civic Engagement

Having defined "civic engagement" and investigated several reasons why it is valuable, we are now in a position to ask which civic characteristics should be widespread in a democratic society. We can then measure those characteristics (with varying degrees of reliability) using surveys and other data.

3.1 PARTICIPATION IN ASSOCIATIONS

First, I have argued that all polities need widespread participation in their "civil society," defined as venues for deliberating and solving problems directly. Many of these venues are private voluntary associations; thus the rate of assocational membership is an important civic indicator. However, people can participate in venues that happen to be created by the state, for example, as members of local school boards and advisory commissions. They can also work on public problems as employees of a company, such as a newspaper or a law firm. The following survey question begins to capture these forms of participation: "Have you ever worked together informally with someone or some group to solve a problem in the community where you live?" In 2006, about 19 percent of young adults and 20 percent of adults over the age of twenty-five answered that question affirmatively.[1] The DDB Life Style survey asks people whether they have worked on a community project in the preceding year. The proportion who answered yes fell from 43 percent to 27 percent between 1975 and 2005 in a slow but steady decline.

Participation in civil society is a set of *behaviors* that require certain *virtues* and *predispositions*. Members of voluntary groups must know how to discuss issues civilly and on terms of mutual respect, without recourse to violence. They must enjoy participation; else they will not be motivated to join in the first place. At least some of them must know how to manage budgets, write agendas, and run meetings.

Finally, participants must have the capacity to manage certain problems that are endemic to human interaction. For instance, anyone with any experience in civil society knows that some group members will try to benefit from others' hard work without contributing as much themselves. Groups may fail to provide adequately for their own future or invest enough resources in recruiting and training new generations. Social networks often struggle with the awkwardness that arises when members have conflicting values. If they put a contentious issue to a majority vote, the minority may quit; but if they try to reach consensus on every point, they risk stalemate. These problems are predictable, yet they can be solved. Through the exercise of social virtues and the use of wise organizational mechanisms and traditions, some voluntary associations have thrived for centuries. Cumulative experience has generated an impressive range of solutions, including (among many other examples) Robert's Rules of Order, bylaws and regulations, potluck suppers, bake sales, awards for donors and volunteers, newsletters, and e-mail lists. In a good society, many people understand and have experience with these techniques.

In the literature on civil society, much attention has been devoted to social trust, which is measured as people's willingness to say that they generally trust other individuals. Social trust is a primary ingredient of what Robert Putnam (following James Coleman and others) calls "social capital."[2] Social trust correlates with membership and participation in associations, although it is controversial whether trusting causes people to participate or whether participants become trusting as a result of their experiences in associations. Trust also correlates with economic success, probably because people who trust others are more willing to undertake business partnerships; such partnerships are (with some exceptions) a path to prosperity.[3]

There are two main interpretations of social capital theory. The *political* interpretation says that people deliberately develop organizations and networks in order to solve public problems. Trust is a byproduct of this work; it is also something that people deliberately enhance by developing personal relationships and by raising children as members of communities. It is good to develop social capital because it enhances a community's capacity to solve problems in the future.

The *apolitical* interpretation assumes that social capital goes up or down because of large social forces and trends, such as suburbanization, the work environment, and exposure to television. (TV makes people less trusting and less sociable.) The reason we should care—according to this interpretation—is that social capital correlates with mental health, longevity, and good educational outcomes. Therefore, if we can, we should tinker with big institutions to increase social capital.

For the purpose of the argument in this chapter, the political theory is more relevant. It raises the question of whether, how much, and in what ways people can enhance trust through deliberate collaboration on civic issues.

To some extent, social capital is a proxy measure. We really want to know what human ties exist in a society and how people use them to address collective problems. As Coleman wrote in his pioneering article, "Social capital is defined by its function. It is not a single entity but a variety of different entities, with two elements in common: they all consist of some aspect of social structures, and they facilitate certain actions of actors—whether persons or corporate actors—within the structure." Later he observes that the network of relationships among parents and between parents and institutions represents social capital that benefits children.[4] We can get a rough sense of these ties by asking people whether they participate in associations, trust their fellow citizens, and work on local problems: the usual ingredients of social capital. However, people could participate in associations that were highly segregated; their trust could be limited to people like themselves; or they could join associations that had no problem-solving purposes. Thus it is very helpful to go beyond standard surveys of representative individuals and also map the networks of relationships that exist within a community (or a school) and the purposes that these serve. Ideally, such networks will form a dense and interconnecting lattice.

3.2 POLITICAL PARTICIPATION

Civic engagement encompasses behavior that involves the state as well as that which occurs in civil society. Such behavior includes direct, personal involvement in the government itself (for example, running for and holding an elected office, serving as a juror, serving on an official board, and working as a civil servant). Political participation also includes efforts to influence the state by, for example, voting, organizing or persuading other people to vote, petitioning or lobbying the government, and suing for changes in policy. Finally, political participation includes open-ended efforts to influence the state by, for example, organizing public deliberations or educating young people to be effective participants.

Some measures of political engagement are percentages of the whole population who engage in desirable behaviors. For example, the turnout rate tells us what proportion of the people vote. Other forms of political engagement cannot be measured that way. We do not necessarily want to see more people serve on juries, nor is a society more civically engaged if the number of civil servants increases. More appropriate are measures of interest, responsibility, and awareness. For instance, the percentage of citizens who say they would be *willing* to serve on a jury is a civic indicator.

Political participation requires skills. Even the act of voting is fairly complicated and intimidates some novices; winning a change of policy is more complex still. Political participation also requires virtues, even when one participates largely in one's self-interest. Any effective participation requires discipline and patience; altruistic participation also requires a concern for others' interests.

Voting is by no means that alpha and omega of political engagement. It is rarely an effective way to influence voluntary associations, which are essential to democracy. It is not a form of deliberation. It does not give people much scope for creativity and learning. It does offer an individual some leverage over the government—but not much leverage, especially when 100 million others also participate. It is a form of expression, but an imperfect one. Walter Lippman observed in 1925: "We go into a polling booth and mark a cross on a piece of paper for one of two, or perhaps three or four names. Have we expressed our thoughts on the public policy of the United States? Presumably we have a number of thoughts on this and that with many buts and ifs and ors. Surely the cross on a piece of paper does not express them. It would take hours to express our thoughts, and calling a vote the expression of our mind is an empty fiction."[5] Instead of voting, wearing a sticker or maintaining a website may seem a better form of political expression.

Despite these caveats, it is important for people to vote. First, although an individual's vote counts for little, social groups (including whole age cohorts) receive benefits depending on the number of votes they cast. For example, if youth do not vote but elderly people do, the government may borrow to cover current retirement costs, leaving the rising generation to pay the bill. Second, political parties and lobbies court demographic groups that vote, giving them information and encouragement. Being courted is a good thing; it probably encourages confidence, a reasonable sense of entitlement, and a willingness to participate in many ways beyond voting.

In the 1990s, fewer than 10 percent of all actual voters were young, thanks to a relatively small age cohort that voted at a low rate. Political parties, social movements, and organized lobbies began to ignore youth altogether, producing a downward spiral that probably had negative effects on young people's group membership, interest in the news, and other matters beyond voting.

As implied in the last sentence, voting correlates with many other forms of political participation. It is relatively easy to vote if you talk about issues, feel a sense of membership in civil society, and gather information about public affairs. Those who do not belong to any associations and who do not follow the news have a much more difficult time knowing for whom to vote; they are more likely to stay home. Voter turnout is thus a proxy for overall civic engagement. To be sure, the correlation between voting and other forms of participation is not perfect. Some people are heavily engaged in volunteering or protest movements but deliberately shun elections because they dislike the available options or the overall political process. However, polling data provides no evidence that their response is typical. More common is a positive relationship between voting and other forms of engagement, which suggests that turnout is an acid test of overall participation.

Political participation also has a strong relationship with "efficacy," the sense that one can have an impact or make a difference through politics or civic engagement. Political scientists sometimes distinguish between *internal* efficacy (confidence in one's own political skills, knowledge, and ability) and *external* efficacy (the belief that major institutions are responsive, accountable, and fair). One needs a degree of both forms of efficacy before political participation will seem worthwhile. This is probably why surveys usually find that people who are more efficacious are more likely to vote and otherwise participate.[6]

3.3 POLITICAL VOICE

Closely related to the previous category is behavior that expresses a point of view. The ultimate purpose of such expression may be to influence the state. For example, some people who submit letters to the editor of a newspaper or who call a radio talk show want to influence public opinion so that the government will change its policies. However, it is possible and reasonable to express one's political views without wanting to shift laws or policies. One may be more interested in changing prevailing corporate or private behavior. Or, one may find the act of expression intrinsically valuable.

Means for expressing "voice" have proliferated recently. Thus, when we measure civic engagement, we should include displaying a sign, bumper sticker, or button or wearing a T-shirt with a social or political message; using a credit card that gives some of its profit to a social cause; operating or participating in a political blog; contributing time or money to an advocacy group or think tank; and boycotting or "buycotting."

In focus groups, young people who are asked for examples of their own civic engagement often cite times when they have challenged friends who were using racist or other immoral language and stereotypes. A young white woman said that her friends from high school "make racial comments and slurs and things like that, and I'm sitting there like, 'No, you're wrong'; and I had never told any of my friends that they were wrong before."[7] Prompted by such stories, we asked the following question in our 2006 omnibus survey: "Have you ever confronted someone who has said something that you consider offensive, such as a racist or other prejudiced comment?" Two-thirds of young people (ages 15 to 25) and virtually the same proportion of older people claimed that they had. Even if they exaggerated, this is a sign that people believe they ought to intervene to challenge other people's language. Such everyday "micropolitics" was crucial to several important social movements, including second-wave feminism. It is a form of "voice" that should be counted when we measure civic engagement.

3.4 KNOWLEDGE AND "COGNITIVE ENGAGEMENT"

We would like citizens to have a base of factual knowledge about politics, law, and public affairs and issues, and to update that knowledge throughout their lives by absorbing news, commentary, and analysis, and by discussing their own views with other people. It seems a safe assumption that individuals cannot process timely and relevant information unless they already possess some fundamental knowledge about matters like the Constitution and the two major parties. But if their knowledge is limited to such perennial matters, they cannot apply it to immediate, practical purposes. Hence the need for core knowledge plus constant updating.

Important public issues are intrinsically worth trying to understand. Even if one never takes action or makes decisions relevant to great matters of policy, to study them seems part of a good life. It reflects a breadth of horizon, enlarged sympathies, and openness to ideas. For example, I think we should know about the condition of human rights in countries like Iran and Burma, over which our nation has little leverage, because to ignore those places means not to care about some of our fellow human beings. There is, however, plenty of room for debate about which particular issues are most important to know. No short list of important facts enjoys consensus as the best measure of adults' knowledge. The National Assessment of Education Progress (NAEP) civics assessment has been constructed on several occasions by diverse panels who agreed about the items to include. But that instrument only measures general political and civic knowledge (rather than up-to-date understanding of current events).

Not only is some knowledge of politics intrinsically valuable; it also correlates with such behavior as voting and joining associations.[8] Presumably, people cannot participate unless they have some threshold knowledge, even if they only know the date of the next election or the name of a group they have been asked to join. Once they do participate, they are likely to deepen their knowledge, at least a bit.

A principal advantage of being informed is that one can then act in such a way as to advance one's own goals and interests. Delli Carpini and Keeter find that Americans with very little political knowledge answer questions about domestic policy more or less randomly. Those with a great deal of knowledge, however, diverge into two groups: the well-off, who generally prefer conservative policies, and the economically troubled, who choose liberal solutions. Similarly, for the well-informed, there is a strong correlation between conservative policy preferences and voting Republican; well-informed liberals vote Democratic. But poorly informed people seem to choose between Democrats and Republicans more or less irrespective of their own policy preferences.[9]

Voting itself is one of the least educative forms of civic engagement, although one can learn while waiting on line at the polling place. Some other forms of engagement are intensely instructive, to such an extent that knowledge may be a reliable proxy measure of participation. For example, it is common to ask survey respondents whether they can name the vice president of the United States. In 2006, an American who does not know that Dick Cheney is the vice president probably has not talked or *done* much about national or international issues.[10]

Few recent surveys have combined good measures of knowledge with useful questions about civic participation, thereby allowing us to explore the relationships between the two. It is nonetheless interesting to contrast daily readers of a newspaper (people who must be quite attentive to the news) with those who do not read any newspaper in a typical week. The 2000 American National Election Study found strong, statistically significant relationships between people's frequency of reading a newspaper and their likelihood of volunteering, working on a community issue, attending a community meeting, contacting public officials, belonging to organizations, and belonging to organizations that influence the schools (but not protesting or belonging to an organization that influences the government). To illustrate these relationships with an example: 42.4 percent of daily newspaper readers belonged to at least one association, compared to 19.4 percent of people who read no issues of a newspaper in a typical week.[11] These relationships do not control for background factors, such as education, which might increase both community participation and newspaper readership. But the most carefully controlled studies do find that residents who engage in their communities also seek information from a high-quality source, and vice versa. It seems likely that having information about current events gives one relevant facts and motives to participate; and that participation leads one to seek information.[12]

Once again, Tocqueville's impressionistic observations of America nearly two centuries ago remain relevant. Newspapers were the main news organs of his day, and he wrote that "hardly any democratic association can do without" them. "There is a necessary connection between public associations and newspapers: newspapers make associations and associations make newspapers; and if it has been correctly advanced that associations will increase in number as the conditions of men become more equal, it is not less certain that the number of newspapers increases in proportion to that of associations. Thus it is in America that we find at the same time the greatest number of associations and of newspapers."[13] There is nothing sacrosanct about a printed daily newspaper. But people need it *or its functional equivalent* to participate in politics and civil society.

Some of the founders assumed that public participation was desirable, but only because the people could be informed. For example, Jefferson said, "I know of no safe repository of the ultimate power of society but the people. And if we think them not enlightened enough, the remedy is not to take power from them, but to inform them by education." In a defense of public schooling, Madison wrote, "A popular Government, without popular information, or the means of acquiring it, is but a Prologue to a Farce or a Tragedy; or, perhaps both. Knowledge will forever govern ignorance: And a people who mean to be their own Governors, must arm themselves with the power that knowledge gives."[14]

During the 2004 election season, an outright majority of Americans believed (erroneously) that Saddam Hussein's Iraq had provided substantial support to al Qaeda, that Iraq had weapons of mass destruction or a major WMD program on the eve of the invasion, and that world opinion was largely favorable toward the war.[15] Perhaps those misconceptions contributed to voters' decisions in the presidential election. Or perhaps not: many people said that they voted in 2004 on moral issues and the economy. The most sophisticated election model predicted that the incumbent slate would win because real per capita disposable income had risen.[16] In any case, when there are more than 100 million voters, and everyone must cast a ballot based on many issues and values, it is not obvious that it is worth the trouble for each person to inform himself fully about Iraq.

Likewise, in the 2006 CIRCLE omnibus poll, two-thirds of respondents said that the federal government spends more on foreign aid than on Social Security. In reality, Social Security consumes at least 25 times as much money. But maybe such misapprehensions are not worth correcting, given the small influence that each citizen has on federal policy through a biennial vote.

I believe that following the news and understanding policy is worthwhile, but not mainly because of the impact on voting behavior. It is also the way that we refine and test our general outlook or ideology. We may see the world as threatening, or divided between Islam and the West, or full of needless suffering, or stricken by Western imperialism, or united by a common humanity. We may see our own nation as a land of opportunity, a divided and unequal society, or a culture in moral crisis. Each significant news story helps us to revise and develop that worldview. In turn, our ideology shapes numerous consequential decisions: not only about federal elections, but also about where we live, what groups we join, and what we expect from schools.

Journalism itself is never free from ideology. Many people say that they do not read or watch the news because they believe that it has been shaped by values with which they disagree. When David Mindich interviewed young people about their attitudes toward the news, "a common theme . . . was that the news is bought and paid for by big corporations." His interviewees said: "it's just so biased and packaged," it's "run by . . . Sony, cigarette companies," or simply, it's "all crap." Most of these young respondents would be identified with the Left and were critical of the corporate media. But President George W. Bush also says that he does not read beyond the front page because he detects a hostile ideological bias in most reporting. He says: "My antennae are finely attuned. . . . I can figure out what so-called 'news' pieces are going to be full of opinion, as opposed to news. So I'm keenly aware of what's in the papers, kind of the issue du jour. But I'm also aware of the facts . . . It can be a frustrating experience to pay attention to somebody's false opinion or somebody's characterization, which simply isn't true."[17]

To the extent that the press is biased, it is wrong to blame *readers* for disengaging: the media must change, not the audience. For ideas on how the press should evolve, see section 10.3. It seems to me, however, that citizens cannot simply be absolved from the responsibility to read news that they regard as biased. You cannot be a responsible observer of the world unless you use the raw material that the mainstream press provides. Sometimes the quality of coverage is poor. But to reject it all is to walk in that absolute night when all cows are black. If you despise the most detailed sources of information, then you can make no distinctions except on the basis of your original prejudices.

In short, appropriate measures of civic engagement include measures of people's knowledge and attentiveness, including their scores on the NAEP civics assessment or its equivalents, rates of using high-quality news sources such as metropolitan daily newspapers, and answers to factual questions about current events.

3.5 WHAT ABOUT RESISTANCE?

Jane Junn notes that if Rosa Parks had been asked standard survey questions about her civic engagement, she would not have been able to mention her most famous political act: sitting in the front of a segregated bus.[18] This was not a case of volunteering, voting, or joining a group; it was a deliberate violation of the law. It so happens that Parks was an exemplary citizen according to standard measures: a leader in several secular and religious community groups. Martin Luther King called her "a well-known community activist" and "one of the most respected Negro women in Montgomery"—her reputation having arisen from her civic engagement.[19] In fact, Parks succeeded in desegregating Montgomery's bus system *because* she belonged to groups; a lone act of civil disobedience never would have worked. Nevertheless, her law-breaking encourages us to ask whether and when such acts of resistance should be counted as civic engagement. Perhaps even violent resistance is appropriate on occasion; otherwise we must deny that General George Washington was civically engaged.

We could also ask about everyday noncompliance and foot-dragging. Consider the African American adolescents in Philadelphia whom Michelle Charles observed doing a lackluster and unenthusiastic job cleaning up their neighborhood as part of a service-learning program.[20] According to conventional measures, their service learning would be a form of civic engagement, and their failure to do it well would count against them. But what if the clean-up project was fundamentally misconceived, because the streets were immediately strewn with garbage after the students finished their work? What if poor African American urban students were being asked by well-meaning but ill-informed middle-class white people to do pointless work without pay and without real educational value? In that case, the students were perhaps wise to drag their feet until someone canceled the program. Its closure would represent positive social change.[21]

At this point, it is important to note a gap in the relevant research. Very rarely do scholars of civic engagement ask what kinds of political action (or deliberate inaction) *work* for people in various circumstances. There are theories of social change that ascribe it to macrolevel factors, such as innovations in technology, crises of rising expectations, cracks in the dominant institutions, or shifts in populations. Often these theories imply that deliberate action by individuals is insignificant—but surely that is too pessimistic a conclusion. There is very little theoretical or empirical work that asks whether a person in a particular situation, having particular political objectives, would be wise to vote, to form an organization, to protest, to petition, to make a documentary film, or to act in various other ways. In chapter 6, section 6.4, I will argue that there is no academic discipline of civics or citizenship. If such a discipline existed, one of its chief tasks would be to analyze the effects of various forms of political action by individuals and by small groups. Absent such knowledge, we tend to give advice based on the typical strategies of the dominant class, on the assumption that they know how to get what they want. For example, we tend to advise poor and marginalized teenagers to emulate middle-class adults. Thus we recommend voting, petitioning, following the news, and forming associations— and engaging in organized, disciplined civil disobedience only under extraordinary circumstances. We assume that skipping school, loitering during a service-learning class, "tagging" a wall with graffiti, illegally downloading copyrighted music, or burning buildings during a riot will only harm the individual who takes these actions and will not produce the change that he or she desires. I suspect that this is sound advice, but I acknowledge the lack of research into the efficacy of various forms of political action for variously situated Americans. Lacking such research, I cannot prove that resistance is always a bad strategy or that it should be omitted from measures of civic engagement. It is worth noting that many young protesters of the 1960s evolved into "ideal citizens" who voted, worked full-time for the government or schools, and trusted public institutions.[22] In that instance, at least, protest was a path to conventional engagement.

3.6 COMMITMENT TO PURELY CIVIC GOALS

As noted in chapter 1, most civic engagement is directed at substantive goals, such as obtaining more money for a particular cause or changing law and policy. Even so, we need some people, some of the time, to be committed to the health of our civic institutions in a way that, if not perfectly neutral, is at least open-ended. When people act in an open-ended civic way, they encourage participation in a political process without trying to move it toward any particular conclusion. For example, a person acts in an open-ended civic way if she convenes citizens to discuss a public issue, informed by neutral and unbiased background materials, as is done in National Issues Forums, Study Circles, and Citizens Juries. Journalists (paid and unpaid, professional and amateur) help by collecting basic information relevant to public deliberations. Those who volunteer or work for nonpartisan watchdog groups are engaged in open-ended politics when they monitor the government to make sure that its procedures are transparent, participatory, and equitable. And community organizers in networks such as the Industrial Areas Foundation, People Improving Communities through Organizing (PICO),

TABLE 2. Core Indicators of Civic Engagement

Core indicators	2002		2006	
	15–25	26 and older	15–25	26 and older
Civic indicators				
Active member of at least 1 group	22%	33%	20%	26%
Regular volunteer for non-political groups	22%	24%	19%	24%
Volunteered in the last 12 months (any type)	44%	32%	36%	34%
Community problem solving (last 12 mos.)	21%	22%	19%	20%
Ran/walked/biked for charity (last 12 mos.)	16%	13%	18%	15%
Raised money for charity (last 12 mos.)	28%	32%	24%	29%
Electoral indicators				
Regular voter (for those 20 and older)	32%	54%	26%	56%
Tried to persuade others in an election	36%	32%	35%	40%
Displayed a campaign button or sign	20%	28%	23%	28%
Donated money to a candidate or party (last 12 mos.)	4%	15%	7%	14%
Regular volunteer for political candidates or groups	1%	2%	2%	3%
Member of a group involved in politics	19%	32%	16%	26%
Political voice indicators				
Contacted an official (last 12 mos.)	10%	19%	11%	22%
Contacted the print media (last 12 mos.)	10%	11%	7%	11%
Contacted the broadcast media (last 12 mos.)	7%	8%	9%	8%
Protested (last 12 mos.)	7%	4%	11%	5%
Signed an e-mail petition (last 12 mos.)	14%	12%	16%	21%
Signed a paper petition (last 12 mos.)	20%	23%	18%	26%
Boycotted (last 12 mos.)	38%	38%	30%	38%
Buycotted (last 12 mos.)	35%	34%	29%	33%
Canvassed (last 12 mos.)	2%	3%	3%	2%

Source: CIRCLE omnibus surveys.

and Gamaliel try to build civic organizations that will, over time, define and address local problems.

It is difficult to quantify the degree to which people perform such work, but we should at least measure skills and habits of public deliberation.[23] We should track membership in nonpartisan civic groups at all levels of government. We should assess the numbers and diversity of people who consider careers in journalism. And we should be interested in case studies of people who have devoted their lives to open-ended civic work.

3.7 CONCLUSION

This analysis has supported a list of civic indicators much like the one developed by Keeter et al. in 2002. But now we have a more explicit rationale for the list. Table 2 shows the percentage of Americans who said in April–May 2002 and April–May 2006 that they had performed the actions listed by Keeter et al.

As noted already, this list omits some variables that may be quite important. The missing indicators include the density and diversity of social networks; acts of political "voice," such as operating blogs and giving money to think tanks; commitment to open-ended politics, which would be reflected in activities such as organizing public meetings and running online discussion groups; and acts of resistance, which range from organized, nonviolent civil disobedience to quiet foot-dragging, absenteeism, and noncompliance. Nevertheless, the list shown here is a useful compendium of indicators that are sufficiently frequent, respectable, and concrete that they can be detected in national surveys. In subsequent chapters, I will be mainly concerned with finding ways to raise these indicators among youth.

CHAPTER 4

Why Do We Need the Civic

Engagement of Young People?

In the United States in the mid-1990s, many foundation and institutions that traditionally had been interested in civic culture turned their attention to youth and the development of citizens between ages fifteen and twenty-five. In this chapter, I explore six reasons for this new focus.

4.1 YOUNG PEOPLE HAVE DISTINCT INTERESTS

Any generation is diverse in ideology, values, and socioeconomic status and prospects. Thus it was no surprise in 2004 to see voters under the age of twenty-five split their party registrations almost equally among Democrats (39 percent), Republicans (32 percent), and Independents (22 percent).[1] This is not a monolithic group.

Nevertheless, young people *as a category* have interests that conflict with those of older generations.[2] When the government borrows money, young people pay most of the interest over the course of their lifetimes. Interest currently constitutes 8 percent of annual federal spending.[3] If the borrowed money is spent on Medicare, Social Security, or other programs targeted at retirees, young people get little direct benefit. Eighty percent of people in the military are younger than thirty-six; thus higher military salaries would benefit youth, but combat deployments disproportionately harm them.[4] Cutting down a hardwood forest generates goods and jobs now, but denies the forest to later generations. On the other hand, government subsidies for college tuition (unless they are poorly structured) should lower costs for young people and increase their lifetime earning capacity.

There is always a temptation to take benefits now and pass the costs on to later generations. Gokhale and Smetters calculate that if current policies were sustained, Americans who are now older than fourteen would (over the course of their lives) reap $11 trillion more from Social Security than they pay in, whereas today's children and subsequent generations would pay $1.5 trillion more in Social Security taxes than they received from the program. Current policies, however, would leave Social Security in an enormous deficit. That projected gap will have to be closed by increasing taxes and cutting benefits by a total of about $8 trillion.[5] Unless those painful changes start soon, Gokhale and Smetters argue, they will be entirely borne by people who are now younger than fifteen.

These estimates rely on various assumptions about growth, productivity, and policy; they are by no means precise. But they reflect a reasonable guess that today's adults are taking trillions of dollars from today's children and future generations by borrowing instead of paying for their own benefits. Such a transfer of wealth might be acceptable if it were a fair and public decision, perhaps grounded on the argument that future generations will be so much better off—thanks to improving technology and bequests from their parents—that they *should* pay for today's retirees. However, this rationale is rarely acknowledged or fairly debated. Young people vote at such low rates that their interests are simply overlooked.

More political participation by youth would not solve the problem of generational injustice. Today's young adults cannot speak for their younger brothers and sisters, let alone for unborn generations. Besides, younger people—who will be especially harmed by shortsighted policies—also have the shortest time horizons and tend to discount the value of delayed rewards more steeply than older people do.[6] Therefore, they tend to be insufficiently concerned about ways in which current policies will harm them in decades to come. Nevertheless, when young people organize politically, they often do so around issues of generational equity, such as obtaining adequate funding for education or resisting a military draft. Thus more youth voting and political activism would shift the balance somewhat. Perhaps the biggest effect would not be on federal fiscal policy but on decisions within religious congregations, neighborhoods, and voluntary organizations. Like the government, small groups also face questions of generational fairness and may be more amenable to argument.

4.2 CIVIC ENGAGEMENT IS GOOD FOR YOUNG PEOPLE

The previous section was about the potential effects of youth participation on equality. I now move to the psychological and developmental benefits that young people may reap from civic engagement itself. It is clear from survey results that young people who are civically engaged (those who volunteer and belong to and lead voluntary associations and extracurricular groups) also tend to develop in healthy ways. They are less likely than those who are civically disengaged to use illegal drugs, to drop out of school, to be violent, and to have unprotected sex. For instance, using three national longitudinal surveys, Nicholas Zill and colleagues found: "Compared to those who reported spending 1–4 hours per week in extracurricular activities, students who reported spending no time in school-sponsored activities were 57 percent more likely to have dropped out by the time they would have been seniors; 49 percent more likely to have used drugs; 37 percent more likely to have become teen parents; 35 percent more likely to have smoked cigarettes; and 27 percent more likely to have been arrested."[7] These relationships remained statistically significant even after the researchers controlled for other measured characteristics of families, schools, and students (such as parents' education levels).

There is some debate about causality. Civic engagement could improve educational and health outcomes; or the reverse could be true; or both outcomes could arise from some third factor, such as personality type or religious faith. In one longitudinal study, the correlation between volunteering and success in school was explained by the fact that the more successful students chose to volunteer (not the reverse). Even in that study, however, volunteering increased participants' interest in pursuing meaningful careers, rather than simply making money.[8] In general, the evidence makes it at least plausible that civic engagement enhances adolescents' health, psychological well-being, and educational success—what Richard Lerner calls their "thriving."[9] Perhaps the most convincing study is by Dávila and Mora, who (using longitudinal data) find that experiences with community service and student government substantially increase the odds that students will stay in school and attend and complete college. Those relationships hold even after many background factors are controlled, even when the authors look separately at various demographic groups, and even when they limit their analysis to *mandatory* service programs.[10]

The most ambitious theoretical explanation comes from the movement known as "positive youth development." Proponents of this view note that adolescence has traditionally been defined as a deficit state. The very word "adolescence" means becoming adult. Thus teenagers are conventionally seen as similar to adults, except that they are not equally mature, sensible, cautious, informed, or responsible. When things go well, teenagers are on a direct course to adulthood, as revealed by their *lack of serious problems* such as illegal drug use, premarital sex, pregnancy, crime, gang-membership, and depression. Those problems should be prevented or deterred if possible; when they occur, they should be treated as pathologies. Institutions conventionally use discipline, surveillance, punishment, and various kinds of persuasion and exhortation to alter teenagers' behavior so that it becomes more adultlike. An adolescent who makes it through the teenage years without exhibiting problems is counted as a success.

Proponents of positive youth development note several drawbacks to this "deficit model." It encourages us to invest heavily in surveillance and control, but not to provide sufficient opportunities for exploration, creativity, and sociability. When the deficit approach succeeds, it produces young adults who lack pathologies but who are not necessarily ready to flourish. As Karen Pittman writes, "Adolescents who are merely problem-free are not fully prepared for their future."[11] The deficit model also encourages institutions to isolate various pathologies and dangers and to assign them to separate adult specialists: thus the police and school administrators work on discipline; school nurses and pediatricians try to reduce sexual activity and bad eating habits; teachers intervene to prevent academic failure. No one is responsible for the whole child, and no one talks to adolescents themselves about their overall goals.

Furthermore, it can be profoundly alienating to treat adolescents as potential problems or threats who have nothing to offer a community until they grow up. Jane Addams fell into a profound depression when she found (as a young woman with a college education but no career prospects and no family of her own) that she lacked a useful social role. She recovered when she created the Hull-House Settlement as an experiment in social action. Addams always sympathized with adolescents who felt that they were social deficits. She wrote, "We have in America a fast-growing number of cultivated young people who have no recognized outlet for their active faculties. They hear constantly of the great social maladjustment, but no way is provided for them to change it, and their uselessness hangs about them heavily. [Julian] Huxley declares that the sense of uselessness is the severest shock which the human system can sustain, and that if persistently sustained, it results in atrophy of function."[12]

The alternative to a deficit approach is to provide positive opportunities for adolescents to display and cultivate the assets that they possess disproportionately: energy, creativity, resilience, independence, and fresh thinking. Some of the opportunities that they need are aesthetic or athletic, but some are civic. Asking adolescents to be leaders, to serve, to deliberate, and to address problems collaboratively can help them to "thrive" and develop in healthy ways. This may be why a positive correlation is observed between civic engagement and healthy youth development.

Voluntary civic engagement may be especially valuable in a culture such as that of modern America, which offers most adolescents very little responsibility until they leave their families, when they suddenly become completely responsible for their welfare. Most high school students have little scope for "initiative," a key word in Erik Erikson's developmental theory that Reed Larson defines as "self-directed attention over time."[13] While schoolwork and play *can* encourage initiative, usually they do not. The activities that consume most of adolescents' time are either forced upon them (most school assignments, including service projects) or they involve no cumulative effort and planning (most leisure and social activities).

No wonder most adolescents describe themselves as bored: "'I feel bored like all the time, 'cause there is like nothing to do,' said Shannon Carlson, 13, of Warren, Ohio, a respondent who has an array of gadgets, equipment and entertainment options at her disposal but can't ward off ennui."[14] Video games, audio players, and the like do not provide the compelling challenge that comes from planning and sustaining work over time with other people. However, Larson cites evidence that students who work in community organizations learn new ways of speaking about projects that reflect longer time horizons, greater cognitive complexity, and more psychological investment.[15] These changes will serve the youth well in the workforce and may help to explain the correlation between extracurricular participation and healthy development.

Erikson's developmental theory offers additional clues as to why it might be especially valuable for adolescents and young adults to participate in voluntary groups that take on useful community functions.

In adolescence, Erikson believed, the main task was to develop an *identity* that would be the basis of career aspirations. Young people explore identities by joining groups that define insiders and outsiders. They are more likely to form healthy, ethical identities if they have opportunities to join groups that define their membership in ethical terms: for example, service groups that enroll anyone who is truly willing to help, in contrast to cliques that are defined by "skin color or cultural background" or by "petty aspects of dress and gesture." Further, adolescents are better off joining groups that take on worthwhile and satisfying functions and that connect their members to other institutions and types of people. These are typical features of civic, service, religious, and political organizations.

Then, in young adulthood, once people move away from their birth families, a major task is to avoid isolation by committing "to concrete affiliations and partnerships and [developing] the ethical strength to abide by such commitments, even though they may call for significant sacrifices and compromises." Although Erikson had (heterosexual) marriage in mind as the main partnership, he explicitly mentioned work as another opportunity for developing human "affiliation." But entry-level jobs are not ideal for overcoming isolation. Voluntary organizations and social movements play important roles in combating the anomie of young adulthood.[16]

These arguments in favor of positive youth development have had relatively little impact on mainstream public schooling. In fact, public education often responds to problems in almost the opposite way that would be recommended by proponents of positive youth development. Consider, for instance, the issue of high school dropouts. Many powerful constituencies, such as the Business Roundtable, are concerned about the dropout rate. They address that pathology by isolating discrete causes located inside the heads of adolescents. Consultants tell them that "reading proficiency in third grade [as measured by test scores] is the single strongest predictor of high-school dropout rate."[17] They therefore try to prevent illiteracy at third grade. Under the No Child Left Behind Act of 2001, schools are required to make "adequate yearly progress" toward uniform success on reading exams. At the third grade, those tests emphasize phonics and decoding skills. Therefore, teachers—encouraged by consultants and companies that sell tools for diagnosis and instruction—spend a great deal of instructional time teaching decoding skills, often using meaningless passages.

This response to the dropout problem is a perfect example of viewing students as problems, isolating discrete causes, and applying interventions developed by experts. However, the emphasis on phonics probably does not work, even for the advertised purpose of raising reading test scores at third grade. Learning to read also requires motivation, cultural knowledge, and comprehension skills.[18] Even if current strategies did produce higher reading scores, they probably would not mitigate the high-school dropout problem. Literacy at third grade and completion of high school are correlated, but that does not mean that the former causes the latter. Recent evidence finds that many high school students who drop out can manage the academic curriculum but are profoundly bored or alienated in school.[19] Again, the alternative would be to provide high school students with constructive opportunities, including projects in their communities. Schools find this alternative difficult for a variety of reasons, not least their reliance on standardized tools and methods. Whereas a phonics program can be purchased from a national company and implemented in any school, providing civic opportunities requires deep local knowledge and flexibility.

Positive youth development encompasses arts and athletics programs. For the purpose of this book, the important subset of positive youth development programs are those that emphasize constructive *civic* opportunities, such as service, community-based research, journalism, or political organizing and advocacy. Such programs are often classified under the rubric of "community youth development" (a term coined in 1994).[20] Existing empirical research does not permit direct comparisons between positive youth development or community youth development, on the one hand, and deficit-reduction strategies, on the other. It is sometimes said that narrow prevention programs "are not in the main successful in promoting [positive] behaviors."[21] This claim implies that positive youth development has the potential to be much more successful than prevention or therapy. In fact, quite a few programs that take a preventive or therapeutic approach toward violence, drug abuse, and teen pregnancy have been shown to have statistically significant positive effects in controlled studies.[22] Not many programs that focus intensively on positive or community youth development have been evaluated in equally rigorous ways; it is thus premature to declare that approach more effective.

Besides, few measures have been developed to assess either the degree to which a program focuses on asset development or the degree to which youth gain civic assets in such programs.[23] In the real world, many programs that focus on prevention actually provide opportunities for youth participation, service, and creativity; and many programs that advertise a commitment to positive youth development actually spend their time preventing specific problems. A National Academies study proposes "that much of the tension between these two perspectives derives from competition for funding and the changing trends in public policy and rhetoric."[24]

In general, the existing research is not designed to test the relative efficacy of positive youth development versus prevention and therapy, but to address different questions, such as whether major existing programs (which generally combine several strategies) are effective overall; whether after-school programs are in the main useful; or which form of positive youth development will work best for particular groups (such as poor youth of color and gay/lesbian and bisexual youth).[25]

Despite the dearth of clear, head-to-head comparisons between positive youth development and prevention or therapy, I believe we should bet on positive youth development as a promising approach. First of all, the few directly relevant studies have been positive. For example, in a rigorous experiment with a control group, the Teen Outreach Program (TOP) significantly reduced teen pregnancy, school suspension, and school failure. TOP was successful despite focusing "very little attention on the three target problem behavior outcomes." In other words, the staff did not directly address pregnancy or school-related problems. Instead, youth in the program were enrolled in service projects and asked to discuss their work in classroom settings. (They also discussed youth development.) The cost per student was a reasonable $500–$700 for an entire academic year.[26]

People who start with a deficit model would not expect 45.8 hours of community service (the average observed in the TOP experiment) to cut teen pregnancy, disciplinary problems, and academic failure. Yet that is precisely the outcome that the full theory of positive youth development predicts. By tapping young people's civic assets, TOP redirected them from harmful behavior. While more studies are important, the combination of an elaborate theory (which is anchored in developmental psychology) plus some experimental evidence is promising.[27]

Perhaps more important, the positive youth development approach is normatively appealing: it meets some of our core moral intuitions. Kant crystallized a long tradition of ethics when he argued that we have two fundamental duties in life: to develop our own character and virtues and to help others pursue reasonable ends of their own choice.[28] To corral other people into behaviors that *we* find desirable would violate their autonomy. But if we fail to support their development into autonomous, reasonable decision-makers, we shirk a duty. To be sure, children lack full autonomy and can be *directed* toward desirable outcomes in the interest of their own freedom as adults. For example, to prevent a child from becoming addicted to tobacco is a way of enhancing her autonomy rather than restricting it; therefore, a parent should take a cigarette away from a twelve-year-old without feeling that her freedom has been violated. We should also enroll all children in schools (or other forms of structured education) even if they would prefer not to attend. Yet we have a duty to children and adolescents to help them develop as autonomously as possible. This attitude is always the most ethical way to treat other human beings, so long as our efforts to respect their autonomy do not backfire for practical reasons.

At this point, we might ask what constitutes desirable human development. There are several definitional pitfalls to avoid. If we define successful human development as progress toward subjective satisfaction, well-being, or happiness, then we make it relative to people's preferences, which may be mistaken. Some people are not aware of the goods (spiritual, aesthetic, or political) that they should value. Individuals can want completely bad things, (for example, crack cocaine). Or they can want too much, as in the case of Hollywood actors who want to have six Hummers. Or they can want too little—a common problem among the world's very poor. A deeply deprived person can be made happy by small acts of kindness, whereas an affluent person can be depressed despite living in plenty. It is a mistake to see the former as better-off than the latter. As Amartya Sen has written: "The hopeless beggar, the precarious landless labourer, the dominated housewife, the hardened unemployed or the over-exhausted coolie may all take pleasures in small mercies."[29] But even if they are subjectively satisfied with modest assistance or mere expressions of goodwill, their *rights* have not been met.

If we reject subjective reports of happiness, then it is tempting to list a series of behaviors (Sen calls them "functionings") that everyone who is developing successfully should exhibit. That approach, however, violates our sense that cultures and communities may legitimately value different behaviors, not to mention that individuals ought to have choices about what to do. For example, a person who fasts for religious reasons is exercising a free choice *not* to exhibit the function of eating.[30] However, to say that each culture can simply define its own measures of success is to endorse all existing norms. Some may be objectionable. For example, girls may be expected to function in limited ways, with no opportunities for public roles.

Facing this dilemma directly, Sen and the philosopher Martha Nussbaum have developed what they call the "capabilities approach." They have proposed lists of capabilities (rather than functions) that they believe every human being should possess. While Nussbaum and Sen are open to dialogue and deliberation about their lists, they believe that our goal is to develop an objective and universal set of human capabilities. A society is successful insofar as everyone develops those capabilities.

Capabilities are inherently good things, yet increasing one's capabilities does not restrict one's freedom, because one can choose whether and how to use a capability. Furthermore, capabilities are defined loosely enough so that they are compatible with various forms of diversity. For instance, I would say that there is a valuable capability of "raising children." Increasing this capability does not compel anyone to participate in raising any actual children. And people can choose to express it in diverse ways, from parenthood within a nuclear family, to participation in a peasant village where everyone raises all the kids, to employment in a convent orphanage.

Applying the capabilities approach to adolescent development would mean saying that we want (and will help) teenagers to develop a list of capabilities: providing for themselves financially; loving others; expressing themselves creatively; developing spiritually; understanding nature; raising the next generation; and participating politically. Whether and how they choose to exercise these capabilities is up to them, but it is our job to develop them. In this conception, the capability for civic or political engagement is an intrinsically or objectively good thing (as argued in section 2.7). It is also good for communities, because through broad-based deliberation people can decide fairly how to achieve the other capabilities (see 2.4). Finally, as noted earlier in this section, the development of civic capabilities correlates with other good outcomes and may help to produce them.

4.3 IMPROVING YOUTH CIVIC ENGAGEMENT IS THE MOST EFFECTIVE WAY TO ENHANCE CIVIL SOCIETY

A mass of empirical evidence suggests that we are "dyed in the wool" as citizens.[31] Sears and Levy define "the impressionable years" as the "period up to one's late twenties, roughly."[32] During these years, some people develop lifelong identities as active, responsible, ethical participants. Others become lastingly alienated or apathetic. Many factors have been identified that can change these outcomes in adolescence, whereas there are hardly any experiences that reliably change the civic identities of adults over thirty.[33]

It would be immoral to write off adults because they are much less "plastic" (to use Dewey's term) than adolescents and less susceptible to deliberate civic education. But it is crucial to invest in the development of young people. They will be permanently shaped by the way they first experience politics, social issues, and civil society.[34]

Two main streams of evidence support the argument of the previous paragraphs. First, *generations* share durable civic and political characteristics attributable to the political and cultural situation that prevailed when they were young. Second, particular experiences during adolescence have been found to influence *individuals'* civic values and behaviors many decades later. These two streams of evidence are compatible. The one emphasizes the common experiences of people who are born around the same historical moment; the other examines individual experiences, which vary among individuals at any time in history. Both findings suggest that early experiences are formative.

There is a theoretical explanation for these results, first proposed by Karl Mannheim in the 1920s. Mannheim observed that we first become seriously aware of a world of government, politics, law, policy, and ideology at the point in our lives when we emerge from the sheltered environment of our families and become sufficiently literate to follow the news (whether in print, oral, or electronic forms). That moment occurs at different times for different people. Child soldiers in Africa are no doubt aware of current events by age seven. At the opposite extreme, there is evidence that some modern Americans and Europeans are delaying their transition to adulthood by continuing their education, and often living with their parents, well into their twenties. They may also be able to delay their awareness of politics and related matters.[35] In Europe when Mannheim wrote, most people first encountered the broad political and civic world around age seventeen; this may still be typical in the United States.

When we first become aware of politics, government, and ideology, we must decide what we think of it. Our stance can be one of contempt or neglect. Or, it can be some kind of engagement, whether critical or conservative. At stake is our identity; we either see ourselves as efficacious, obligated, critical members of a community, or we do not. Our civic identity, once formed in adolescence, is hard to shake. From then on, the psychic cost of reevaluating one's views is not worth the price, unless a major event (such as a war or revolution) forces a review. Mannheim wrote, "even if the rest of one's life consisted in one long process of negation and destruction of the natural world view acquired in youth, the determining influence of these early impressions would still be predominant."[36]

Mannheim wrote in the 1920s, after one of history's most obvious "generation gaps" had opened up. Victorian gentlemen in whiskers and top hats had sent millions of young men to die in trenches. For the rest of their lives, those who fought did everything they could to distinguish themselves from their forebears, as did women of the same generation. Because wars usually affect youths more directly than older people, it is not surprising that they sometimes cause young people to coalesce into recognizable generations with civic identities. Of course, not every cohort faces a war, certainly not one as murderous and revolutionary as World War I. Baby boomers, who experienced the Vietnam War and the draft in their youth, display more of a generational identity than do the subsequent group (born between 1965 and 1984), who came of age in comparatively tranquil times. The novelist Douglas Coupland coined the phrase "Generation X" for that latter group, alluding to a *lack* of identifiable characteristics and epochal events.[37] In a 2002 survey, half of the "Boomer" generation agreed that "my age group is unique," compared to just 42 percent of the Generation Xers who followed them.[38] Still, even the Xers seem to have a prevailing civic character: one of mild alienation and ennui caused by the sense that they missed the dramatic events that occurred just before they came of age.

This example shows that Mannheim's theory of generations does not have equal relevance for all cohorts. Nevertheless, it is an important theory for at least three reasons: (1) it illustrates the potentially powerful and lasting impact of events experienced in adolescence; (2) it explains why some generations possess distinctive civic characters (for better or worse); and (3) it may help us to understand the newest generation of young Americans. While it is too early to tell the full story of the Millennials, "Dot-Nets," or "echo-Boomers" (three names for the generation born after 1985), they appear to have gone through a dramatic sequence of events: first a period of peace and rapid economic growth fueled by technological innovation (1994–2001), and then the terror attacks on September 11, 2001, and a protracted war in the Middle East. I will say more below about what this sequence may mean for their civic development. For now, it is worth noting that the Millennials—like the Boomers, but unlike the Xers who immediately preceded them— are a large cohort that has a strong sense of a generation gap. In 2002, some 69 percent said that their generation is unique.[39] That rate was the highest by far, and it was not simply a result of their being young. (There is no linear relationship between age and strength of generational identity).

A second stream of evidence concerns individual experiences rather than the grand events that shape whole generations. James Youniss and Daniel Hart have summarized more than a dozen longitudinal studies that follow young people into adulthood and repeatedly ask questions about their civic engagement and values.[40] The basic pattern is consistent: those who participate in politics or community affairs or leadership roles at age fifteen or twenty-two are much more likely to be involved at age thirty or fifty. Probably the longest study is by Kent Jennings; it finds a relationship between participation in high school groups in 1965 and participation in community groups by the same people in the 1990s.[41]

One possible explanation is that some people have a personality trait, moral value, or other internal characteristic that predisposes them to participate when they are young and still applies when they are older. In that case, the correlation between civic experiences and civic values, skills, and habits does not reflect causality; it results from some underlying psychological characteristic of an individual. Then it does not matter very much whether young people are given opportunities to participate in civil society. Those who have the right predispositions will participate as soon as they find an opportunity, even if they must wait for adulthood. Our best hope, then, is to change hearts and minds: to make people feel more civically responsible. Civic education is mostly a matter of moral exhortation or exposing youth to role models.

If this theory applied, then we would have to understand historical events as the result of shifts in values. For example, we know that tens of thousands of people took direct action against racial segregation in 1965, but not in 1935. If values are the underlying factor, then people's norms and priorities must have shifted between 1935 and 1965 to favor participation in the civil rights movement. Today, we should worry about certain *negative* trends in values, such as the substantial increase in materialism and decrease in trust among youth (discussed in section 5.2).

The evidence, however, tends to suggest a very different view. Based on surveys of participants and nonparticipants, it does *not* appear that young people engage in service or politics because they hold particular values beforehand. It seems to matter much more whether there are opportunities for political engagement or service and whether individuals are recruited to participate.[42] People who are asked to volunteer, vote, join an association or protest movement often do so. Although values do not cause people to participate, participation changes people's values and habits. When we compare participants who appeared similar *before* a civic opportunity, we often find that they behave quite different afterward. A similar gap emerged between comparable people who did and did not participate in the Freedom Summer campaigns of 1964. Such profoundly moving and terrifying work might be expected to leave a lasting mark.[43] But the same is true to a lesser extent of young people who participate in student government or school newspapers. Even forty years later, they remain more civically engaged.

Participants in civic life could have some disposition or character trait that was not measured in the surveys given before they chose to engage civically. That unobserved disposition could be responsible for their civic participation. But it is much more straightforward to assume that most people will participate if they are given the opportunity.[44] The variation in their characters and values matters little; the opportunity is more important. Once people begin to participate, they obtain skills to engage civically; they get satisfaction from doing so; they enter networks that inform them about other opportunities and cause them to be frequently recruited; and their identity begins to shift. They begin to see themselves as citizens or participants, rather than as isolated individuals.

Some seventy-five highly engaged students at the University of Maryland participated in focus groups in 2004. Many told stories of recruitment that led to habits of participation. Several acknowledged that they only began to serve in high school because of pressure from parents or to improve their college prospects, but they found they liked it. "I became addicted to service," one student said. Another observed, "You tend to see the same pattern, where people who were active in high school are the same people who come to college and are active." Many students explained that they had become involved in a first campus group or program almost by accident, but then were recruited to join other groups and activities. They suspected that if they had missed the initial invitation, they never would have become campus leaders and engaged citizens. One student whose personal career had taken her from student government into peer counseling said, "Everything builds on itself." Several students said that they had participated in groups, projects, and events because they were *asked* to do so. Personalized invitations from faculty, staff, or peers were much more effective than mass mailings and e-mails. As student leaders, participants in these focus groups also *issued* many invitations to peers. One said, "In the committees I run, I take people who have the qualities of leaders, and expose them, bring them along in meetings with the Administration."

If this theory of recruitment followed by habit formation applies widely, then the most important goal is to make sure that many people are recruited and encouraged to participate in meaningful ways. We should be less concerned about shifts in values as measured by opinion polls (although those might be symptomatic of changes in available opportunities). And we should be more optimistic that if we provide extracurricular groups, service projects, and other civic opportunities, young people will sign up and benefit lastingly.

4.4 YOUTH HAVE AN "AUTONOMOUS CULTURE" WITH POWERFUL EFFECTS

To varying but significant degrees, young people live in a world of their own, influencing one another and making decisions without their parents and other adults even being aware of what they decide. At one extreme, some youth have no parents at all, or their parents are unable to exercise any influence on them. (One subset of detached parents consists of certain new immigrants who have great difficulty understanding the American institutions, opportunities, and networks that their own children quickly master.) At the opposite extreme, guidance counselors now complain of "helicopter parents" who hover low over their children, observing and influencing all the choices they make, from courses to friends. Despite this range, however, adolescents generally live in a youth sphere that is at least somewhat autonomous. It is a characteristic and novel feature of modern societies to establish "parallel institutions that are designed specifically for [young people]. . . . Contemporary youth, then, spend much of their lives outside the formal economic and political spheres, but in a milieu that reflects the larger structure and is designed explicitly for them. It is marked by clothes, food, music, entertainment, and the like, and is recognized as belonging to youth but excluding adults."[45]

Young people's behavior within this autonomous sphere is enormously consequential. If an adolescent joins a gang and commits a crime, he can easily ruin his whole life as well as that of his victim. If he joins the debate team, then he and his friends can substantially increase their chances of attending a competitive college and thereby boost their longevity, income, health, political power, and capacity to serve their communities.

It is important not to jump to the conclusion that peer effects are usually bad and that teenagers should be prevented from creating their own social networks. On the contrary, research finds more positive effects than negative ones: usually, friends help friends *not* to get into trouble. Furthermore, today's adolescents are closer to their parents than their predecessors were. They take their parents' cues on the most important matters, deferring to peers about relatively superficial issues; and they tend to select friends who reinforce their families' values.[46] Nevertheless, there is a great deal of *variation* in the effects of teen cultures and networks. Even if the average (that is, the mean or modal) effects are positive, there are some youth for whom peer networks are catastrophically bad.

Eccles and Barber asked Michigan tenth-graders to identify themselves with one of the characters in *The Breakfast Club*, a 1985 movie that was popular then. Ninety-five percent of the students were willing to identify themselves as just one of the following: a "princess," a "jock," a "brain," a "basket case," or a "criminal." (They were asked to overlook gender; significant numbers identified with a *Breakfast Club* character of the opposite sex.) Students of each type spent much of their time with peers who were similar. Follow-up surveys found that these self-descriptive identities were strongly predictive of college attendance and success in school and of alcohol and drug use. If you were a "princess" in tenth grade, for example, you were relatively likely to attend college and to drink. If you were a "brain," you would likely complete college and not abuse drugs or alcohol. Although the word "criminal" was applied humorously, the "criminals" had distinctly poor developmental outcomes.[47]

We would like to make young "criminals" into "brains"—or at least "jocks" or "princesses." Parents, other adults, and institutions should certainly try to influence identities and peer networks by providing some mix of guidance, positive opportunities, and penalties for bad decisions. Many programs have been implemented to improve youth culture, sometimes with significant positive effects. To mention just one example, rigorous evaluations of the Big Brothers Big Sisters mentoring programs find that they improve grade point averages and lower violence, alcohol and drug abuse, truancy, and lying to parents.[48]

However, there are limits to what adults and institutions can accomplish, given the opacity of youth culture and young people's resistance to being manipulated. Therefore, it is important that young people *themselves* have the skills and values they need to make their own sphere as constructive as possible. If they know how to create and sustain positive voluntary associations, they may be less likely to join criminal gangs for support and fellowship. If they have skills for conflict resolution, their conflicts are less likely to turn violent. If they have the skills necessary to influence schools, police, and other authorities with good arguments, they may be able to change policies that are counterproductive.[49] All of these skills and values are civic. They are the same characteristics that will later make youths effective citizens of the adult polity.

CHAPTER 5

How Are Youth Engaging Today?

In chapters 1 through 4, I argued that society needs broad civic engagement, and that the best way to achieve such is to focus on youth. I now ask how well we are preparing today's young people for civic engagement. The available data paint a mixed picture. There are positive trends as well as grounds for concern. In this chapter I summarize the major evidence.

5.1 TRENDS IN BEHAVIOR

One reason that youth civic engagement attracted renewed interest in the late 1990s was a set of troubling trends in young Americans' civic behavior.

Voting

Voting (an important form of engagement and a relatively easy one to measure) is the most widely followed statistic. Compared to the baseline year of 1972—when those between the ages of eighteen and twenty-one first won the right to vote in federal elections—youth turnout fell by about one-third during the 1980s and 1990s.

In most states, election officials do not record the age of voters. Therefore, all measures of youth turnout come from surveys that ask people whether they voted (and we know that surveys produce inflated estimates). Furthermore, researchers have various choices about how to measure self-reported turnout. How, for example, should one treat the many young Americans who are ineligible to vote because they are noncitizen immigrants or because they have been convicted of a felony and stripped of their voting rights? Some scholars exclude them from

FIGURE 2 Turnout (ages 18–25)

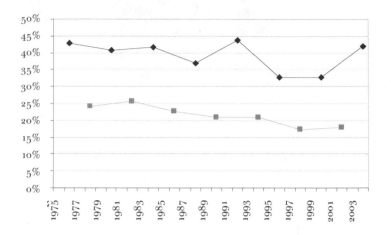

—◆— = presidential years
—■— = mid-term elections
Source: Census Current Population Surveys, per resident population

the turnout calculation; others count them as nonvoters on the ground
that the laws could be changed to enfranchise them. Given these meth-
odological problems, there is no single, obviously correct turnout figure for youth in any year. However, the decline between 1972 and 2000
was about the same regardless of how it was calculated. Using any reasonable method produced a smooth downward trend broken only by a
spike in 1992 (see fig. 2). Meanwhile, there was no decline in turnout
among Americans over the age of twenty-five. The decline in overall
voter participation appeared to be strictly a youth phenomenon.[1]

At the time of writing, it is unclear whether this trend is continuing
as the Millennial generation takes its place in the electorate. In 2004,
the self-reported turnout of Americans between the ages of eighteen
and twenty-four rose by eleven percentage points, to 47 percent. This
level was typical of the 1970s. Although all age groups registered increases in 2004 (when the turnout of the whole population reached levels last seen in 1968), the youngest cohort recorded the biggest increase of all compared to the previous presidential election. Early 2006
estimates (based on exit polls, not census data) suggest young adults
increased their turnout by two to four percentage points compared to

the previous off-year election of 2002, whereas those over thirty saw almost no increase at all in 2006. It is possible that 2004 and 2006 represent a temporary spike in youth turnout, like that of the early 1990s; it is also possible that the long downward trend has ended.[2]

News Consumption

Voting is closely correlated with attention to the news. That finding makes sense: you cannot vote unless you know whom you will support, and you cannot know *that* unless you are aware at least of the candidates or parties and a few fundamental issues. As noted above (section 3.4), attention to the news also correlates closely with community participation: joining groups, volunteering, and attending local meetings.

Thus it is not surprising that the long and deep decline in youth voting between 1972 and 2000 was accompanied by a similar decline in news consumption (see fig. 3). Higher Education Research Institute (HERI) surveys of incoming college freshmen found that the proportion who considered it "important" or "essential" to "keep up-to-date with political affairs" fell from 60 percent in 1966 to about 30 percent in 2000, although it recovered by six points between 2000 and 2005

FIGURE 3 Attentiveness to News (ages 18–25)

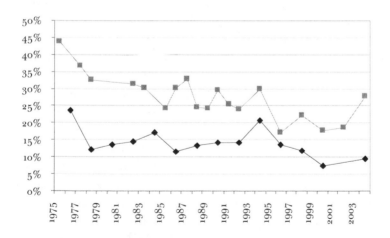

—■— = read daily newspaper (General Social Survey, by the National Opinion Research Center)

—◆— = follow public affairs (American National Election Study) (while turnout also rose.)[3] Likewise, in the National Election Studies, the percentage of Americans between the ages of eighteen and twenty-five who consistently followed the news fell from 24 percent in 1960 to 5.1 percent in 2000, but popped up to 9.6 percent in 2004. Newspaper readership among young people was cut in half between 1975 and 2002, according to the General Social Survey, although again there was some recovery in 2004.

These declines in regular attention to the news cannot be attributed to the rise of media such as the Internet. First, questions about "following the news" are phrased to include all forms of media consumption, including the Web. Second, the dramatic decline occurred during the 1970s and 1980s, before the Internet reached large scale. Third, even once the Internet arrived, it probably did not increase the total amount of information that young people obtained. Between 2000 and 2004, young people's use of the Internet for campaign news rose by seven percentage points, but their use of newspapers for the same purpose fell by nine points, to 23 percent. The biggest single source for youth remained local television news, which is almost content-free.[4]

For as far back as we can track the trends, young people have been less interested in the news than their elders. They have other things to think about (school, courtship, and entertainment), relatively light attachment to their communities, and relatively little of the background information that enables one to follow stories. Nonetheless, the gap in news consumption by age has dramatically widened. As the Times Mirror Center for the People and the Press noted in 1990, young citizens were as interested as older ones in the Army-McCarthy hearings of the 1950s, the Vietnam War, and Watergate. Compared to their elders, however, they were much less likely to follow major news events of the 1980s and 1990s.[5] The attacks of September 11, 2001, caught young people's attention, but youth still lagged far behind their elders. In a survey that CIRCLE conducted two months after the attacks with the Pew Research Center for the People and the Press, middle-aged people (ages 50–64) were twelve percentage points more likely than young adults (ages 18–25) to be following the terror attacks against the United States, and twenty-five points more likely to be following the war in Afghanistan. Of those over age fifty, more than 60 percent said that they were highly attentive (closely following three or more unfolding news stories). Just one-third of young adults were paying that much attention.[6]

To make matters worse, it does not seem to be the case that people are delaying their interest in the news until later in their lives, and then catching up with previous generations. On the contrary, several careful studies of the historical data show that each recent generation has entered adulthood with less interest in the news than its predecessors had, and has never closed the gap. For example, those who were young adults in 1982 have remained about twenty percentage points behind the children of the 1960s in news consumption as the two cohorts have moved through their lives.[7]

Given the close correlation between civic participation and newspaper reading, one explanation for the drop in readership would be the decline in civil society, as revealed by negative trends in group membership, attendance at local meetings, and participation in communities (see below). People who are not recruited to join local associations may be less likely to subscribe to a newspaper or use other news sources of equivalent value. Of course, part of the problem may be just the reverse: some people may have first stopped using newspapers and other high-quality sources, and *as a result* they withdrew from civil society.[8]

We also know that people who *trust* the press are much more likely to read a newspaper.[9] But confidence in the press has fallen along with news consumption (alike for younger Americans and older ones; see fig. 4).

FIGURE 4 News Consumption and Confidence (ages 18–25)

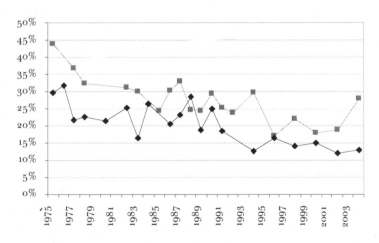

—■— = read daily newspaper (General Social Survey [NORC])

—◆— = confidence in the press (GSS)

Group Membership

As noted above, membership in organized groups is a third major area of decline. Most of the traditional voluntary associations of civil society have seen big drops in their youth membership since 1970. In 1975, according to the General Social Survey, two thirds of young people (ages 18–25) belonged to at least one group. (Respondents were prompted to think of several kinds of associations, including church groups, unions, and sports clubs, and were also given the opportunity to say that they belonged to a kind that had not been listed.) In 1994 and 2004, only half said that they belonged to any group at all. In DDB Life Style surveys conducted during the 1970s, some 40 to 50 percent of young people said that they had attended a club meeting at least once within the previous year. In the same survey conducted between 2000 and 2006, only 15 to 22 percent of young people recalled attending a club meeting.[10] These declines are particularly disturbing because there is no reason to believe that the 1970s were a golden era of group membership. I have compared the 1970s with the 2000s because GSS and DDB data are available for that span of time. If we could start the trend line in the 1950s, I am confident that it would show deeper decline. (There was, however, no significant decline in the percentage of young people who told DDB that they had worked on a community problem.)

A similar pattern applies to religious participation. Although young people are just as likely to express faith in God today as in the past, surveys have found that regular religious attendance among high school seniors declined from 41 percent in 1976 to 33 percent in 2000 (see fig. 5).[11] In the DDB Life Style survey, the question is different but the decline is bigger. Half of young people in the DDB sample reported "regular" church attendance in 1975, down to one-third in 2002 and 2004.

Extracurricular school groups have also lost membership, perhaps because they receive less support (funding and adult attention) or because consolidation of schools reduced the sheer number of student organizations. The longitudinal study that Kent Jennings began in the 1960s allows us to compare high school seniors in 1965 with their own children (who were asked in 1997 about their past high school experiences). Athletic participation was up sharply, probably as a result, at least in part, of Title IX and increased opportunities for female athletes. Musical groups and speech and debate teams had grown modestly. But overall rates of membership and leadership were down sharply.[12]

FIGURE 5 Measures of Community Participation from the DDB
Life Style Survey (ages 18–25)

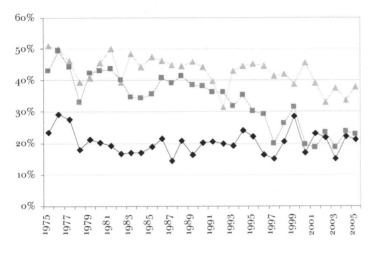

-◆- = attend church often

-■- = attend a club meeting

-◆- = work on a community project

In a subsequent section, I ask whether new forms of association are beginning to form that will replace the old ones measured in our existing surveys. For the time being, however, it is clear that young people are less likely than in the past to participate in associations that give them practice in deliberating and solving problems collectively.

Protest

Between the 1960s and the 1990s, there was a striking decline in the frequency of protest, especially involving young people. According to data collected by Sarah Soule and Ann Marie Condo from newspaper archives, the United States saw more than twice as many "protest events" per year between 1964 and 1974 than during the 1980s. In 1970, more than half of all protests were initiated by youth, whereas only 10 to 20 percent had youth leaders in the eighties. In other words, youth protests were an important part of the national political scene in 1970 but either rare or unnoticed fifteen years later.[13]

On college campuses, the rate of demonstrations fell by two-thirds between 1967 and 1978, but it almost fully recovered by 1997.[14] Thus the most consistent decline seems to be among *noncollege* youth. Today, there are many fewer urban protests dominated by young people than there were forty years ago. Some of the means of political expression that have become increasingly common among college students (such as e-mail petitions, lawsuits, and media campaigns) are difficult for non-college youth to manage.[15] Meanwhile, strikes have become much less frequent, both on campus and in the workforce. The general trend is away from protests, pickets, strikes, and disruptions and toward sophisticated "white-collar" forms of politics.

To set a baseline in the 1960s could be misleading: that was an unusual time of ferment on college campuses, in high schools, and in urban neighborhoods that had high proportions of youth. The wrenching political issues of the day (such as the draft, school desegregation, and the sexual revolution) disproportionately affected young people. In all the industrial economies, a large cohort of babies was born between 1945 and 1955, and many of them became politically rebellious in their late teens and twenties. Some people do not regret the decrease in the number of youth-led protests since the 1960s, especially since students have discovered other means of changing policies and challenging institutions. Nevertheless, the decline relative to 1964 has been steep, and it is part of the story of youth civic engagement.

Volunteering

There is one major respect in which youth civic engagement has strengthened in recent decades. Volunteering is increasingly common. For example, the HERI annual survey of first-year college students (which primarily measures their experiences in high school), finds a substantial and continuous increase in volunteering since the 1980s, when the question was first fielded (see fig. 6). That result is corroborated by the Monitoring the Future survey of high school students.

The increase in volunteering is an important trend, but it requires some caveats. First, by rephrasing survey questions about volunteer activity, one can produce wild variations in the number of people who say that they volunteered. I suspect that this is because volunteering is a catchall category that can include everything from giving a neighbor a hand with her groceries to spending a year helping in a refugee camp. People think of different activities depending on how they are prompted. It is reasonable to worry that the meaning of the word "vol-

FIGURE 6 Two Measures of Youth Volunteering

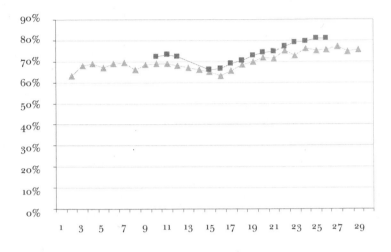

-◆- = at 12th grade (MTF)

-■- = incoming college students (HERI)

unteering" has broadened since 1976, creating a false impression of actual growth.

Second; much youth volunteering is episodic. For example, in the CIRCLE 2006 omnibus survey, more than half of young people reported having volunteered for a civic or community organization. But of those, 56 percent described the frequency of their volunteering as "just once in a while," and only 10 percent said that they had volunteered "to address a social or political problem." (Seventy-seven percent said "to help other people.") Not many volunteers (of any age) believe that they can change the world in any fundamental way. In a qualitative study of Minnesota citizens (completed in 2000), respondents said that volunteering often consigned them "to positions of mediocrity with the assumption that they lacke[ed] the capacity to work on big issues that impact the community."[16]

Finally, the upward trend may result, in part, from the imposition of volunteering requirements in many schools and a widespread sense that one should be able to list volunteer experiences on one's college application.[17] But those explanations do not negate the trend in behavior. It is possible that volunteering because of a requirement builds habits of participation.

5.2 TRENDS IN VALUES

As I noted in chapter 3, there is a debate about whether changing young people's values would increase their participation. For example, some assume that if adults persuaded young people to be more altruistic, public-spirited, tolerant, trusting, and patriotic, they would become more likely to participate. The contrary argument is that young people will comply if (but *only* if) they are recruited to participate in activities; and once they participate, their values will change for the better. In that case, providing opportunities is more important than exhorting people. This debate remains important, but both sides are interested in trends in values over time. They see them either as a cause or a symptom of the changes in participation.

The good news about values should come first. Young Americans are the most tolerant since polling began. On average, individuals become somewhat more tolerant as they age, but the big change in attitudes has occurred because each generation has entered adulthood more tolerant than the preceding one. For example, the percentage of Americans who favor a ban on interracial marriage has fallen steadily. If we look separately at the trend for each generation, we find that most cohorts have not changed their attitudes much as they have moved through life. (The exception is people born before 1906, many of whom *did* change their minds about miscegenation laws during the 1970s.) Even so, each new generation has entered adulthood with more positive attitudes toward interracial marriage, causing a gradual but inexorable change in public opinion.[18]

Only 4 percent of young Americans (ages 18–25) say that they favor segregated neighborhoods. That is down from about 25 percent in the 1970s and is lower than the rate among people over age twenty-five. This change is almost entirely attributable to the arrival of new generations: again, individuals do not seem to change much over their lifetimes.[19] Still, this change in values has not accompanied a big change in behavior. More than half of young churchgoers still say that their congregations have members of only one race—the same rate as among older people, and not much different since 1975. In the Social Capital Benchmark Survey (2002), some 66 percent of young white people who belonged to participatory groups said that all the other members were also white. This rate was not much different for older whites. In the same survey, just 20 percent of young people claimed that they had invited a friend of another race to their house—better than the 6 percent rate among adults over age fifty-six, but still hardly common. We should ask whether tolerant answers to survey questions will translate into real social change if people remain quite segregated in their daily lives.

A similar pattern is evident in attitudes toward allowing an "admitted homosexual teacher" to speak. People born before 1906 were extremely unfavorable when they were first asked the question in 1973, but some become more tolerant as they aged. The subsequent generations have changed less, but in the same direction. Each generation is more favorable than the older ones (see fig. 7). (Too few Millennials were surveyed in the 2004 General Social Survey to be included.)

In theory, a rise in tolerance for gay teachers could result from several causes: people could be more accepting of homosexuality; they

FIGURE 7 Free Speech Rights for Gay Teachers

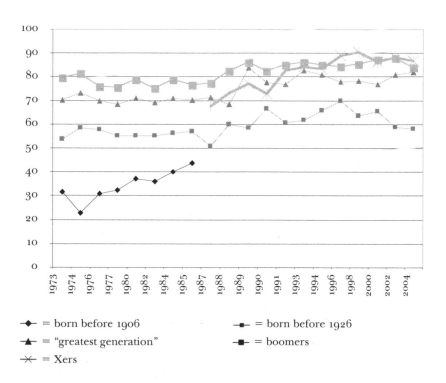

—♦— = born before 1906   —■— = born before 1926
—▲— = "greatest generation"   —■— = boomers
—✕— = Xers

Source: General Social Survey (NORC)

could be more likely to support First Amendment rights (even if they do not accept gays); or conceivably they could be less concerned about education and hence less interested in banning teachers whom they disparage. We cannot tell for sure which explanation is the most important, but there are hints that acceptance of gays is the root issue. A 2002 survey found that young people were the most likely cohort to accept "homosexuality as a way of life."[20]

The pattern is a little different when people are asked whether a racist should be allowed to speak in their community. According to General Social Survey data, each generation is more willing to permit hate speech than the previous ones, except that Xers are slightly *less* favorable than Boomers. It may be that rising support for free speech conflicts with declining racism (and tolerance for racism) to generate this result. Tolerance for the intolerant is a subtle and controversial position, and it is not surprising that the Xers have not fully embraced it

Young Americans are also highly patriotic and idealistic.[21] Many believe that they can and should make the world better, especially by directly serving their fellow human beings. Even so, there have been some disturbing trends in values over the past twenty years. For example, there has been a 50 percent decline in the proportion of young people who trust others.[22] Wendy Rahn and John Transue explain the erosion of young people's social trust as a result of the "rapid rise of materialistic value orientations that occurred among American youth in the 1970s and 1980s."[23] Eric Uslaner explains trust as a function of optimism. People who believe that the world will get better (that there will be more public goods for all) are willing to trust others and cooperate. People who believe that the pie is shrinking adopt a zero-sum, "me-first" approach.[24] Whatever the cause, a decline in trust spells danger for civil society, because trust correlates with participation in voluntary associations.[25]

The rise of materialism that Rahn and Transue cite is itself troubling. Figure 8, derived from surveys of American college freshmen, shows that "developing a meaningful life" and "becoming well off financially" traded places during the 1970s as priorities of college-bound adolescents. Our response to that pattern should not be to scold young people for their materialism. The underlying causes perhaps include increasing economic insecurity, mass marketing of consumer goods, or political leaders who emphasize financial success over other values. Nevertheless, the results suggest an erosion in youth commitment to the civic values described in chapters 2 and 3.

FIGURE 8 Priorities

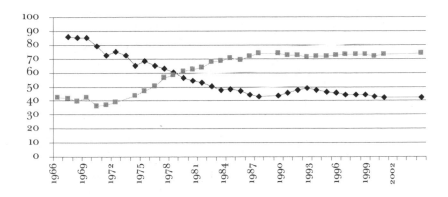

—◆— = develop meaningful philosophy of life

—■— = become well off financially

Source: Higher Education Research Institute

5.3 DIFFERENCES BY INCOME, RACE, AND GENDER

In chapter 2, section 2.5, I cited data that show striking differences in rates of civic and political participation by levels of education. I was discussing adults then, but the differences are already evident in childhood. For example, according to the International Association for the Evaluation of Educational Achievement (known as IEA) study of civic education of fourteen-year-olds in twenty-eight countries, Americans score reasonably well on average; but the disparities are more pronounced in the United States than in almost any other nation. If one compares two groups of American fourteen-year-olds—those who have highly educated parents, many books in the home, and plans to attend college, versus those without any of those advantages—the former display far more political knowledge and are three times more likely to expect to vote when they turn eighteen.[26]

To some extent, these disparities may arise because of differences in schooling. Education in such subjects as reading, writing, and mathematics is important for civic participation, but the quality of education available to poor children is often inadequate. Differences in quality are evident, too, if one looks narrowly at civic education. According to the 1998 NAEP, students of color and students from low-education families were the least likely to report experiencing interactive classroom learning activities in their social studies classes, such as role-playing exercises, mock trials, visits from community members, or letter writing. Differences in quality of instruction may contribute to differences in knowledge. In the same civics assessment, the proportions of students who scored "below basic" at twelfth grade were 27 percent for whites, 34 percent for Asian/Pacific Islanders, 56 percent for Hispanics, 56 percent for American Indians, and 58 percent for African Americans.[27]

Students gain civic skills and confidence when they have a voice in the management of their schools (see section 7.3). One way to attain that voice is by making the student government empowered and representative. Yet Daniel McFarland and Carlos Starmanns find that student governments are much more common and more empowered in affluent suburban schools than in poor urban ones.[28]

There is also evidence that child development in the home and neighborhood replicates patterns of inequality by class. In Lareau's *Unequal Childhoods*, we see differences emerging in late elementary school. The middle-class children in her qualitative study learn their rights. One fourth-grader says (jokingly): "This is America. It's my prerogative to change my mind if I want to."[29] He and his peers have been placed in neighborhoods, schools, and organizations that work. Their parents demand excellent and tailored services to meet their "specialized needs" (173). Parents exchange detailed information about schools and other institutions. They also encourage their children to advocate for their own interests, even to the point of interrupting and challenging a physician. "The incivility of interrupting a speaker is overlooked in favor of encouraging children's sense of their individual importance and of affirming their right to air their own thoughts and ideas to adults" (125).

Middle-class children develop skills that will be useful in some forms of political action. They can make speeches, marshal evidence in favor of their views, confidently address adults, work with acquaintances and strangers, and follow and criticize institutional rules. Finally, they are explicitly educated about politics. Their parents read the daily newspaper. In one family, "The African American Baptist church they attend each Sunday includes sermons on social and political issues such as the national debt, welfare policies, and poverty programs. They also discuss political issues at home over the dinner table" (119).

The middle-class children are basically being prepared for white-collar work. Although they exchange information with one another, they have no experience in organizing collective action and will usually respond to dissatisfaction by simply exiting an institution—not a solution to all their problems. In that respect, their civic education is lacking.

Working-class children, meanwhile, have low expectations of institutions and do not know how to navigate or change them. They can organize *themselves*, because they must fill hours of unstructured time. They "learn how to be members of informal peer groups. They learn how to manage their own time. They learn how to strategize. Children, especially boys, learn how to negotiate open conflict during play" (67). Poor boys "play games that they have devised themselves, complete with rules and systems of enforcement" (80). They thereby obtain "skills in peer mediation, conflict management, personal responsibility, and strategizing." These are certainly civic assets, and ones that schools and surveys usually overlook. Poor children, however, lack experience in following organizations' rules and don't know how "to pressure an organization to be responsive to . . . individualized needs" (81).

Working-class parents have great difficulty interpreting institutions. They "merge authority figures into one indiscriminate group. Thus, classroom teachers, resource teachers, librarians, and principals are usually all referred to as 'the school.'" They rarely exchange information with other parents about school policies. Above all, they feel powerless and resentful. One mother says, "I think, 'Why do you let the school do this to you time after time?'" (238, 214, and 205).

These differences are captured by the definitions of "citizenship" used in working-class and middle-class communities. In an inner-city school, the phrase "good citizenship" means "restraint . . . , avoiding fights, being respectful."[30] In contrast, a middle-class mom says she arranges music lessons because "I'm convinced that this rich experience will make him a better person, a better citizen, a better husband, a better father—certainly a better student" (113).

So far, I have emphasized class. Race and ethnicity are also powerful correlates of civic engagement, but not always in the stereotypical ways. Latinos (ages 15–25) lag behind whites and African Americans on almost all of the nineteen indicators of civic engagement listed in chapter 3.[31] They also volunteer and vote less than whites and African Americans, according to census surveys.[32] Often, when we control for differences in income, education, language, and citizenship (that is, we distinguish citizens from legal residents), we find that Latino youth remain less engaged than comparable members of the other groups.[33] The reasons may include disparities in education, a relative dearth of grassroots political organizations in Hispanic communities, a lack of outreach to Latino constituencies, or cultural norms that are less supportive of civic participation. It is also possible that important forms of Latino civic engagement, such as translating for parents and collecting money for towns in Latin America, are not captured in standard surveys. The only clear bright spot was found in June 2006, shortly after mass marches against immigration reform had occurred. At that point, Latino youth were the most likely to say they had protested. The main slogan of the marches suggests some potential for increased political engagement: "¡Hoy marchamos! [Today we march]—¡Mañana votamos! [Tomorrow we vote]."

African Americans present a very different picture. As we have seen, education and income generally promote participation, and African American youth continue to have lower average levels of education and income than whites. Nevertheless, African American youth are well ahead of whites on several measures of civic engagement: regular volunteering, raising money for charity, persuading other people about elections, displaying signs and buttons, donating money to parties and candidates, belonging to political groups, contacting the print and broadcast media, and canvassing.[34] The electoral turnout of African American youth has been very close to that of whites in most recent federal elections, even though black youth have less education on average, and even though an estimated 1.4 million African American men (of all ages) are blocked from voting because of felony convictions.[35]

In short, being young and black is currently a positive predictor of civic engagement. The reasons probably include a legacy of political organization and community-based civic education that began in the African American church under slavery and then inspired the civil rights movement. African American youth turnout first jumped to the same level as white youth turnout in 1984, the year that Jesse Jackson ran for president; no significant gap has appeared since then.

African American youth remain more likely than others to discuss current events with family and friends.[36] These discussions probably encourage voting and giving money. A particular combination of attitudes may also motivate engagement. At least for the past several decades, African Americans have expressed understandable skepticism about the fairness and responsiveness of government, coupled with a belief in their own power and obligation to take civic action. Shingles called this combination of attitudes "black consciousness."[37] Although some have argued that black consciousness diminished with the fading of the civil rights legacy,[38] we still found in CIRCLE's 2006 omnibus survey that African American youth held the most skeptical attitudes about government and politics, yet were more likely than whites to feel a responsibility to "make things better in society." The norm in favor of participation—especially voting—can be palpable in African American communities. In my experience, I often find that predominantly white groups of students are divided about whether voting is worthwhile, but almost everyone in a group of African American adolescents will declare an intention to vote at the earliest opportunity. We know that most will not actually participate in every election, but the norm is significant, and it appears to increase turnout.

Finally, gender is clearly relevant to civic and political participation. Women, for example, still constitute only 15 percent of Congress and 22.8 percent of all state legislatures.[39] Women also vote somewhat differently from men. In 2004, a majority (55 percent) of men voted to reelect President Bush, but only a minority (48 percent) of women did. And traditionally, there were differences in the civic development of young men and women. Female adolescents were more involved with community service, but male adolescents were more interested in politics.[40] Today, however, when we investigate young Americans between the ages of fifteen and twenty-five, the overwhelming impression is a *lack* of significant differences by gender. Their level of civic knowledge was the same in the IEA Civic Education Study, although girls performed somewhat better on measures of skills and expected to be more involved in politics.[41] Whether we consider raw rates of participation, rates adjusted by education, or explanations of why young people participate, the differences between men and women are very small. The most noticeable gap is a higher rate of nonpolitical volunteering among young female Americans.[42] According to the census bureau's voting survey, women under the age of twenty-five are also somewhat more likely to vote than their male contemporaries—a six-point gap in 2004 that might be partly explained by their higher rates of college attendance.

None of this means that tomorrow's Congress will be 50 percent female. Scarce and desirable positions, such as seats in the national legislature, are fiercely guarded and require power to obtain. It does appear, however, that young men and women are about as likely to engage in the ordinary forms of civic engagement that are open to volunteers, such as voting, community service, expressing views, and joining groups.

5.4 CIVIC INNOVATION AMONG YOUNG PEOPLE

The data presented so far from national surveys show declines in young Americans' civic engagement. However, most surveys measure only traditional forms of participation, such as voting, belonging to unions and organized religious congregations, and displaying signs and signing petitions. I believe that these forms of engagement remain valuable and that we should encourage young people to participate. (For example, I have offered arguments in favor of voting. Shunning elections in favor of other forms of politics would be a mistake, in my view.) Nevertheless, we should be open to alternative forms of engagement that may be more appropriate for the twenty-first century. It would be possible to exchange traditional associations—such as the Masons, Elks, and other fraternal and sororal groups—for new forms of association, some primarily online. Religious congregations could be supplanted by new types of religious community. Certainly, bumper stickers and signs could give way to blogs and other Web sites.

If a new civic infrastructure is developing at the beginning of the twenty-first century (much as the existing array of civic associations developed between 1900 and 1920),[43] young Americans are among the pioneers. For example, in 2005, the Pew Internet and Public Life Project found that 17 percent of teenagers (defined as ages 12–17) had created their own blogs, compared to 7 percent of adults.[44] When historians look back on the current period, they may pay less attention to declines in average levels of youth participation than to the exciting work of young civic innovators.

Much civic innovation involves computers and electronic networks. That domain changes so rapidly that it is risky to make predictions. Dwelling on the latest innovations can quickly make one's analysis obsolete. Nevertheless, we can detect prominent themes in the current decade's developments, including:

- blogs: frequently updated Web pages, often structured like public diaries, and usually containing many links to other blogs
- open-source software: programs that any user can edit and improve and then put back into the commons

- wikis: online documents that are written and edited collaboratively by visitors
- social networking services that provide each user with a Web page that displays her interests and shows links to other users
- podcasts: short audio and video segments, often created by amateurs, that can be downloaded to various portable devices
- social bookmarking services: databases of many users' favorite Web sites that allow people to learn from others' preferences
- digital petitions and widely circulated messages calling for consumer boycotts
- hacktivism campaigns: various forms of online civil disobedience, including efforts to shut down Web sites for political or moral reasons

Each of these activities is susceptible to rapid change; several may be passing fads. Yet taken together, they reflect a fairly profound shift. In the twentieth century, voluntary communications and problem-solving often took place within formal organizations that one had to join, committing to pay dues, follow rules, and obey the official leaders. As Dietlind Stolle and her colleagues note, the new forms of online engagement are much looser. Membership is provisional and not clearly defined. There may be no official leaders: governance is horizontal rather than vertical. These groups tend to focus on personal and lifestyle issues rather than formal politics. They mobilize people sporadically and spontaneously and allow easy exit. Finally, as Stolle notes, the "new forms of participation are potentially less collective and group-oriented":

> The actual act of participation is often individualized in character, whether this involves the decision to forward a selected e-mail as did Jonah Peretti, who subsequently triggered a world-wide response to Nike's footwear production practices, or whether it involves the decision to purchase a certain product for ethical reasons. Such individualized acts do not necessarily lead to group interaction or face-to-face meetings of the kind we typically encounter in unions, voluntary groups, regular council meetings, and so forth. . . . This leads to a certain paradox: while this form of protest and participation can be seen as an example of co-ordinated collective action, most participants simply perform this act alone, at home before a computer screen, or in a supermarket.[45]

Young people are heavily represented in innovative online activities such as blogging and wikis. The Pew Internet and American Life Project has identified a group of "Power Creators" who each create online material in an average of two different ways: for instance, maintaining a personal site and also posting on other sites. This group has a median age of twenty-five. Since the youngest people surveyed were eighteen, the real median is certainly lower.[46] (However, young adults are not the most active age group online; people in their thirties and forties are more likely to create or contribute to Web sites. Content creators also tended to be well educated: just 6 percent were adults without high school diplomas, and almost half held college degrees.)[47]

It is impossible at this stage to predict whether the civic effects of these new forms of interaction will be positive. I believe, however, that the important questions are now fairly clear. First, is it possible to overcome collective-action problems through loose, voluntary networks? For example, in an online group in which people use pseudonyms and can easily exit, can members be persuaded to take disciplined and costly steps, equivalent to going on strike in a traditional union? We see a "tragedy of the commons" online in the form of unsolicited e-mail, viruses, and other destructive behavior. Can self-organizing online groups handle such behavior?

Second, we know that the World Wide Web has enormously expanded our choices of news, opinion, and information. Does this expansion allow people to segregate into narrow interest groups (many having no connection to politics)? Or does the easy availability of countless perspectives encourage people to learn about other views?[48]

Third, can online organizing translate reliably into offline activity when the latter is necessary? Much online politics consists of mobilizing people to express their views, to donate money, or to withhold their business from targeted companies and countries. The ultimate objective is to change the policies of governments or corporations. For example, people who contributed money to the Howard Dean presidential campaign—usually over the Internet—wanted their contributions to be spent on conventional advertising so as to change ordinary voters' minds and elect a new president. But Dean was defeated by a campaign with a better offline organization and left more than $2 million of his campaign money unspent when he dropped out.[49] Can online organizing actually change offline decisions?

Fourth, the Internet is a global network that has dramatically reduced barriers to international communication and cooperation. But there are important benefits to *local* participation. Local associations are not thriving online, as evidenced by the shortage of compelling Web sites produced by voluntary groups for specific localities. Commercial sites that are intended for geographical communities are full of advertising and generic news and entertainment; they have few public contributions. Neighborhood associations, voluntary organizations, religious congregations, and other groups that do public work within geographical communities have benefited from establishing Web pages. But most of the actual sites that these groups have created amount to simple online brochures, no more valuable to their visitors than printed posters would be.

A 2001 survey by the Pew Internet and American Life project found that, of those Americans who communicated online with other members of a group, just 15 percent contacted people in their "own local communities"—compared to 43 percent who contacted others "all over the country." Asked whether "the Internet [is] more useful for becoming involved in things going on in your local community, or things going on outside of your local community," just 9 percent chose the first option. And only a fifth of those who had used the Internet to communicate with fellow members of a group had ever met those people face-to-face.[50] It is useful to be able to participate at low cost in national or international associations and to communicate with people whom one will never be able to meet in person. But if local associations have an important civic and social role, then we need to take deliberate action to support them online.

Finally, can online activities draw new people into political and civic participation? Or do citizens gain their civic identities offline and merely use the Internet as a tool? So far, those who are most likely to participate in online politics are highly educated and have strong, pre-existing political commitments. Thus online forms of civic engagement may worsen political inequality by giving those who are already engaged new tools that make them more effective, while leaving others on the sidelines.

It would be surprising if electronic interactions, simply by virtue of their format, were worse than face-to-face communication at drawing new people into politics. Still, the new digital media have the following feature in common: people select what they want to see voluntarily, out of a huge array of choices. It seems possible that only those with a pre-existing interest in politics will opt to visit political blogs or download political podcasts. The situation is different in a church or union.[51] People join those associations for complex reasons, including family backgrounds, that are beyond their control. They rarely join in order to participate in politics. Yet, churches and unions have reasons to inculcate political identities in their members. They create civic engagement.

In 2004, Representative Richard Gephardt ran for president as the representative of labor unions and the organized Democratic Party. He had paid his dues by working for both institutions for decades. His strongest supporters were people who had been politically socialized by unions and the party. Howard Dean, in contrast, ran as an independent voice and used the Internet to draw support from people who were especially angry at the Bush administration. On average, Dean supporters were considerably wealthier, better educated, and older than the Democratic primary electorate as a whole. Two major unions (the Service Employees International Union and the American Federation of State, County, and Municipal Employees) endorsed Dean, not because he had a record of supporting their agendas, but because they thought that he had drawn political momentum from his loose network of supporters, and they should get behind him. Dean defeated Gephardt handily, suggesting that a new era of politics had begun, in which motivated individuals would count for more than organizations. The question is whether people who are *not* already motivated and informed can also play a role.

CHAPTER 6

What Are the Barriers

to Civic Education?

"We must prepare students for competent and responsible participation in a democracy." "We need to tap the energies and talents of young people." "We have to provide opportunities for positive civic development." Those are exhortations aimed at an unspecified "we." That exhortatory style is very common in politics and political commentary. I believe it begs the critical questions: Who has reasons to enhance civic engagement? How are such people organized? What assets do they have? What strategies or incentives would make them act in favor of the recommendations?

There are reasons that Americans do not educate many youth for effective and responsible citizenship, even though polls show that many parents consider that an important goal. No policy proposal is useful unless it addresses these underlying reasons. Therefore, I will discuss barriers to civic education in this chapter before turning to policy proposals in chapters 7 through 9.

6.1 CIVIC EDUCATION IS A "PUBLIC GOOD"

Civic education (defined as preparation for responsible and effective participation in politics and civil society) is a *public good*. If most people become good citizens, everyone benefits. That means that each individual does not have a self-interested motivation to become civically educated and engaged. If other people turn into good citizens, then an individual can spend his time on more profitable or enjoyable pursuits, taking advantage of others' civic services. And, if most other people fail to be good citizens, no individual is able to carry the burden all on his own. Either way, the logic of self-interest argues for concentrating one's own efforts on private goods while hoping that most other people will be good citizens.

Many people strive to be civically engaged and want to raise their children to participate in civil society. In a 2004 poll, 71 percent of adults said that it was important to "prepare students to be competent and responsible citizens who participate in our democratic society."[1] These altruistic and patriotic sentiments are significant, but the problem of providing public goods should nevertheless be taken seriously. It means that when people make difficult choices about where and how to educate their own children, their commitment to civic goals may turn out to be mostly symbolic. I once heard a teacher in a focus group say that if you ask parents whether schools have a civic mission, they will agree, because they know it's the right thing to say. But they mainly want their own kids to get an education that will help them to get ahead. The teacher said, "Civic education is for other people's kids."[2]

In any case, while most adults polled in 2004 considered civic education to be important, they ranked several other goals higher (see table 3).[3]

Americans are increasingly concerned that their own children receive the skills necessary to prosper in an economy that ignores national borders and rewards certain kinds of flexibility, initiative, and competence. These skills include the four top priorities in the 2004 survey: basic academic knowledge, preparation for the workforce, preparation for college, and critical thinking. We also know from survey data and qualitative research that young people are deeply aware of the need to amass the marketable skills that economists call "human capital."[4] While a whole community or nation benefits when such skills are widespread, human capital also profits each person who possesses it. It is primarily a private good that also has public value. Therefore, parents are motivated to obtain marketable skills for their children, and youth want those skills for themselves.

Meanwhile, educational institutions at all levels are increasingly competitive with one another. Research universities fight tooth-and-nail for faculty and students, who have enormous choice about where to work or study. James Fallows notes the "insane intensity" of the college-admissions process for successful high school students; the competition for famous faculty is similar.[5] Money and status come with institutions' ability to attract these top candidates.

TABLE 3 Purpose of Public Schools

Purpose	Percentage rating it very important (7 on a 1–7 scale)
Teaching basic reading, math and science skills	81.3
Preparing students for the workforce and employment	64.3
Forming critical-thinking and decision-making skills	63
Preparing students for college and life-long learning	60.9
Developing positive character traits	54.9
Preparing students to be competent and responsible citizens who participate in our democratic society	**52.9**
Developing an appreciation for art, music and culture	34.2

Source: See note 3, page 243.

Community colleges and universities that serve local students are somewhat insulated from the market, although they compete with more distant institutions, for-profit colleges, and the workforce. At the pre-college level, independent private schools compete fiercely for students, less so for faculty. Charter schools and schools funded by public vouchers have been deliberately placed in markets in which parents are the "consumers." Finally, even a large, standard, urban public school system is in some sense part of a market. To the extent that parents have resources, they can choose to move away (often a short distance away, across a municipal border) or to enroll their children in private or parochial schools. Likewise, public school teachers often have some degree of choice about where to work.

Competition may have advantages for education. It can promote the efficient production of private goods, such as marketable skills. But competition has clear disadvantages for *civic* education. If schools, colleges, and universities compete to attract families (especially families with money or with children who appear likely to succeed), then these institutions will strive to offer private goods: marketable skills, comfortable conditions for living and learning, and opportunities for fun. They will not prosper if they put their resources into public goods, such as civic education.

At its worst, a competitive educational system need not even provide excellent training for participation in the workforce. Rational parents may be most interested in *markers* of economic value, quite apart from any actual skills that their children learn. This logic is especially evident in the most competitive reaches of our whole educational system: the elite colleges. Parents know that a college degree is worth a lot of money, especially if it is a degree from a competitive, prestigious institution. The diploma is economically valuable even if a graduate has not learned much of value. Therefore, many parents are more interested in the diploma and its pedigree than in the quality of education their children receive. The same is true of the prospective students themselves. *U.S. News & World Report,* which designs its ranking of colleges and universities for the largest possible audience, weighs heavily the reputation of each institution, the number of applications it attracts, and the percentage of admitted students who choose to matriculate: all measures of prestige but not of quality.

College students do score higher on tests of knowledge and critical thinking near the end of their undergraduate careers than at the beginning. The best estimates suggest that college exposure has a positive effect on intellectual skills—between one-quarter and one-half of a standard deviation, depending on what outcomes we measure. However, there is remarkably little evidence that the type of college matters, even though colleges differ extraordinarily in size, selectivity, and mission. When experts investigate student outcomes from very different kinds of colleges, they find differences in "career and economic attainment" after graduation, but few differences in what students actually learn. "These findings could be expected because in the areas of career and economic achievement, the status-allocating aspects of a college and what a degree from that college signals to potential employers about the characteristics of its students may count as much if not more than the education provided."[6] In other words, little of what a college does intentionally to educate students has an impact. Students grow, in part thanks to the college experience (which includes extracurricular activities and living arrangements); they do not benefit to an impressive degree from college teaching.

One benefit of the "college experience" is exposure to other students. At all stages, parents may be anxious to enroll their own children with other young people who are on track for economic success. Desirable peers can provide valuable networks and role models. Thus parents may want their students to attend selective institutions, regardless of educational quality. In short, they want admission to a well-known, exclusive club. They may also prefer homogeneous elite institutions over diverse ones. Again, the result is to favor a private good (access to prestigious networks) over the public good of social integration. This sorting is deeply unfortunate, because diversity and integration have positive effects on students' civic development.

For similar reasons, families may not care whether youth enroll in educational institutions where other students are civically engaged. In general, peers seem to influence students' civic attitudes and behaviors profoundly. When institutions bring together many young people who are civically engaged, the youth reinforce one another's civic habits and skills. When institutions concentrate young people who are not interested in civic life, however, the "peer effects" are negative.[7] We would like civically engaged students to be enrolled with others unlike themselves, so that they can have positive peer effects; but families have little incentive to make sure that happens.

In short, if an educational institution wants to meet parents' demands, its easiest course is to pay some lip service to civic education, diversity, and other public goods—most parents say they want *other* people's children to be good citizens—but to focus all of its serious resources on developing students' marketable skills. Furthermore, for some important institutions, it is easier to provide markers of economic value than actually to add value. If an admissions office can make someone wealthy simply by admitting him, then there isn't much pressure to educate him once he matriculates. Already in 1918, Thorstein Veblen saw that a "businesslike executive" in charge of a college would choose, given the "exigencies of prestige," to build a glamorous new facility of no particular value for undergraduates rather than to invest in their education.[8] The pressure to educate is greater at the primary and secondary levels—yet even there, success can be guaranteed if a school gets a reputation for exclusivity. Even a public school system can achieve high rates of success with relatively little effort if many privileged families choose to live within its boundaries.

Meanwhile, schools and colleges must try to attract the best-qualified faculty because that is a way to increase their reputations, and hence their attractiveness to potential parents and students. In a competitive market for teachers (especially at the college level), an institution can offer its faculty light teaching loads and lots of time to concentrate on research that is valued inside their disciplines. If an institution puts pressure on its faculty to enhance students' skills, then the most successful professors can avoid the pressure by simply leaving. They are especially likely to balk if they are asked to enhance students' *civic* skills, values, and knowledge, because their academic disciplines do not value these outcomes. In turn, the departure of well-known faculty can make an institution less desirable to prospective students; and a decline in the number of applicants will cause a university to fall in the *U.S. News & World Report* ranking. A vicious cycle ensues. A similar pattern can occur in any K–12 institution that must compete for students (including urban public school systems that compete with nearby suburbs).

One response to this very basic problem is to emphasize that civic education is not only a public good but also a private good for individual students. Parents should value it for their own children because (1) the same skills that are useful for civic participation (consensus building, working with diverse people, addressing common problems) are also increasingly valuable in the twenty-first-century workplace; (2) students who engage in their communities while they attend school and college may feel better about school, gain confidence and motivation, and therefore have a better chance of achieving educational success; and (3) civic participation arises from human relationships and obligations that can be intrinsically fulfilling.

On the other hand, it may prove difficult to achieve satisfactory civic outcomes as mere byproducts of pre-professional education. Unless students are explicitly encouraged to develop civic skills, they may never realize the importance of participation in a democracy or think about their political and civic responsibilities. "Convergent research from numerous studies shows that achieving civic outcomes requires intentionality on the part of those who teach and their institutions."[9]

Perhaps we can make some limited progress if we challenge ranking systems like the one published by *U.S. News & World Report,* because it uses selectivity as evidence of excellence. That method does not reward institutions for educating their students. Alternative rankings, such as *Washington Monthly's College Guide* and the Princeton Review's *Colleges with a Conscience,* at least give applicants and their parents the opportunity to consider institutions' impact on students (including their civic impact). Likewise, measuring the civic outcomes of K–12 schools might somewhat change the way that parents and taxpayers evaluate these institutions.

Nonetheless, I believe that the problem outlined here is fundamental and cannot be solved merely by providing alternative rankings and assessments (in a word, more *information* about what schools and colleges do). In a competitive market system, public goods tend to be undersupplied. Civic participation is a public good. An outside power, the government or a social movement, must apply leverage to change the priorities of schools and colleges.

6.2 THE CITIZENSHIP OF CHOICE

In the nineteenth century, citizenship primarily meant duties that one held because of the group (the geographical community, religious denomination, class, color, and nation) to which one belonged. High school textbooks and college speeches alike constantly exhorted students to do their duties.

During the Progressive Era, the model of civic duty shifted to one of choice.[10] The good citizen was now the judicious and well-informed individual who selected among candidates (or better yet, policies) in order to obtain desired outcomes. That profound change was marked by such reforms as the secret ballot, attacks on political parties (which represented identity groups), the rise of a nonpartisan, independent press, and a profound shift in education. Instead of sermonizing about duty, schools and universities began to provide arrays of autonomous academic methods and disciplines from which students could freely choose.

The new model of citizenship has flaws. First, making judicious choices among policies is very demanding. It takes time, information, and motivation. If this is what citizenship requires, many people will not participate at all. For instance, when party-line voting declines, so does turnout. In a state like California that presents its electorate with hundreds of complex initiatives and referenda, turnout is especially low.

Second, a market system creates expectations of wide choice, ease of transactions, efficiency, and customer service that cannot be met in politics, because politics involves debate and conflicting interests. There-fore, people accustomed to consumerism will tend to shun politics.

Finally, at some deep level, a life spent making instrumental choices is unsatisfying. Perhaps we can choose political parties and politicians in order to advance non-political goals, such as security. But if we choose our family ties, our neighborhoods, our religions, and everything else for instrumental reasons, what is the purpose of it all?

Nevertheless, the modernist definition of citizenship is here to stay; we cannot return to a widespread sense of ascribed duty. In a 2002 survey, 31 percent of young people said that voting was a right and 34 percent said it was a choice. Twenty percent said that it was a re-sponsibility and 9 percent said that it was a duty. These results may change a little over time, but they will not turn upside-down.[11] They represent one of the challenges that effective civic education must now overcome.

6.3 TECHNOCRACY

Technical expertise has evident value. No one can doubt that we are better off because of the specialized knowledge possessed by physicians, engineers, economists, and others. Expertise is such a fundamental or-ganizing principle that we often overlook its drawbacks and limitations—especially for democracy.

First, exceptional knowledge does not entitle anyone to special po-litical rights. Even if we could find brilliant people to govern us, they would still not understand our situations and problems as well as we do. Nor could they be trusted to act fairly, as their interests would differ from those of the people they ruled. Therefore, all citizens have the right to participate as equals in politics.[12]

According to National Election Studies conducted between 1952 and 1992, about 70 percent of the public consistently said that "politics and government seem so complicated that a person like me can't really understand what's going on." That proportion did not change much despite dramatic improvements in education for the population as a whole. In some respects, the government *is* complicated, and has prob-ably become more so. (For example, global warming, a major issue of the present, is harder to understand than government pensions, which were a salient topic of the 1930s.) Nonetheless, we would like people to have enough confidence in their own understanding of issues that they feel empowered to vote; otherwise, democracy cannot work.[13] I suspect that people *underestimate* their ability to follow politics because they see experts laying claim to specialized knowledge.

Second, experts have no special insight into right and wrong, justice and injustice. On such questions, as the great philosopher John Rawls wrote, "there are no experts: a philosopher has no more authority than other citizens."[14] But economists and other quantitative social scientists sometimes *seem* to have expertise about essentially moral questions. This appearance arises because they know something about means: about what measurable variables correlate with, and probably cause, other variables. Frequently, our public discourse submerges questions about what we *should* value and concentrates exclusively on what policies would be most efficient at achieving ends that are taken for granted. An example is the assumption that policy ought to maximize economic growth, defined as the annual change in gross national product. But GNP may not measure what we should value most.

Finally, technical expertise has intellectual biases.[15] Most of these biases are avoidable in theory but widespread in practice: I have in mind the biases toward quantifiable variables, statistically normal cases, and general rules that can be applied to many instances. Technical experts lack appropriate tools for making insightful judgments about idiosyncratic, concrete, local situations.

Technocracy in Education

Recent waves of reform in American public education typify technocracy and illustrate how it conflicts with public engagement. Almost all of today's advocates and policymakers—whether conservative, centrist, or moderately liberal—use technocratic strategies for improving education. They do not debate what goes on inside schools as much as they call for changes in the incentive structure that will motivate students and teachers. In other words, they tinker with institutions from a distance, applying general insights from economics to a process (education) that is all about culture and values.

Traditionally, Americans assumed that the important questions about education were "what?" and "who?" "What" meant the materials, teaching methods, and curriculum used in actual classrooms. Citizens felt that they had a right and duty to know what was going on in public school classrooms. Much of the debate about education from 1900 until about 1985 consisted of arguments that the content of instruction should be more rigorous or more relevant, more directive or more experiential, more coherent or more diverse. (See, for example, the *Nation at Risk* report of 1983.)[16] These arguments were explicitly normative, having to do with what children ought to know and how they should be treated. Decisions about content were made—in varying proportions—by state agencies, school districts, principals, and teachers, sometimes with considerable input from citizens (especially those who served on school boards and PTAs). Thus the education debate was mostly about what should be taught, and arguments were directed to state and local school leaders.

People also debated "Who?" meaning the identity of the teacher—how she was qualified and selected—and the composition of classes. The influential Coleman report of 1966 led people to think that the teacher was relatively unimportant but that the mix of students was crucial.[17] Poor children needed to be exposed to middle-class students; children with disabilities needed to be mainstreamed. Thus, for a generation, the main issues in federal education policy were desegregation and integration. There was also much debate about the pros and cons of "tracking" students; that is, separating them by interest or ability level. Again, this was a debate about "who?"

Despite all this attention to "what?" and "who?" education changed neither fast enough for many reformers, nor in the directions they wanted. Recently, reformers have given much more attention to "why?"—in other words, to the incentives that are supposed to motivate administrators, teachers, and students to behave in certain ways. This is (for better or worse) a detached and technocratic approach to education. It is typical of a culture that likes to measure the inputs and outputs of institutions without getting inside them to examine their values.

There exist three major proposals for changing the incentive structure in education, thus causing students and educators to answer the "why?" question differently. Some want to increase funding for schools or equalize funding among districts. Others would impose regular, standardized tests with carrots and sticks. Still others prefer to increase the degree of parental choice and allow funding to follow students.

None of these approaches is completely new. Liberals have been advocating higher teacher salaries for a long time. School choice was first defended (to my knowledge) by Milton Friedman in 1955. There were high-stakes tests before No Child Left Behind. Nevertheless, the tenor of the debate has shifted. Politicians and policymakers now seem to agree with the Nobel Prize–winning economist Gary Becker about the futility of looking inside schools: "What survives in a competitive environment is not perfect evidence, but it is much better evidence on what is effective than attempts to evaluate the internal structure of organizations. This is true whether the competition applies to steel, education, or even the market for ideas."[18] Becker is a libertarian, but liberals who want to pay teachers more to teach in inner-city schools are also interested in competition—they just want schools to compete better in the job market.

It is important to think about incentives; that is one of the main themes of modern social science. In fact, I began this chapter by noting that we must not simply call for better civic education or analyze what techniques work best for that purpose; we must also find levers that, if pulled, would encourage or compel big institutions to provide better civic education. Asking schools to educate better (or differently) without changing their incentives won't work. Nevertheless, there are democratic reasons not to ignore the internal policies and choices of schools.

Consider the strategy of imposing accountability through standardized testing. This strategy puts pressure on schools to raise individuals' factual knowledge and cognitive skills, outcomes that can be measured on exams. It is much more difficult, or perhaps impossible, to create high-stakes assessments of moral values, habits and dispositions, and collaborations. Yet a democracy needs people who collaborate and who have civic virtues and habits.

A test must be secret until it is given—so there is no opportunity for broad public participation. In principle, the public could deliberate about standards, and experts could simply create examinations that measured students' performance on those public criteria. But the process of writing standards and examinations is expensive, so in practice it tends to be done by a few expert employees of national testing firms. Their products are imposed simultaneously in many schools and districts, thereby reducing opportunities for public deliberation. Moreover, much of the work of modern test construction is highly technical, involving questions of statistical reliability and psychometrics. Although the choice of what questions to ask inevitably raises questions of value, technical issues tend to dominate, leaving the public with a marginal role.

If schools are required to prepare all their students for demanding tests of academic subjects, and if the tests are written by experts, then the only questions left for citizens to debate are hot-button issues that cannot be suppressed, such as the teaching of evolution or sexuality. I am convinced that we see rather unproductive debates about those matters (which mobilize committed partisans and often end in court) because citizens cannot deliberate about all the other moral questions that evidently concern them more. David Mathews, president of the Kettering Foundation, reports qualitative research that finds:

> Public accountability is more relational than informational. That is, citizens are looking for more than data from schools. They want a face-to-face exchange with educators and a full account of what is happening in classrooms and on playgrounds. They want to know what kind of people their youngsters are becoming as well as how they are doing academically. Americans have said that most legislated accountability measures don't do that; they still leave citizens on the outside trying to look in. . . .
>
> When citizens think about accountability, they are particularly concerned with the moral commitments of educators, not just their professional or technical competence. . . . For example, studies show that people value teachers who can encourage and inspire, who can make learning come alive, who are inventive in their classrooms, and who are patient in one-on-one relationships with students. Legal accountability standards, in contrast, emphasize teacher certification in subject matter and students' scores on tests.[19]

Elsewhere, Mathews has written of the long trend toward professionalizing education and marginalizing citizens. Starting in the 1960s, he thinks, "the public as a real force in the life of schools was deliberately and systematically rooted out. Citizens were replaced with a new group of professionals, true guardians of the public interest, there to do what it was assumed citizens couldn't or wouldn't do."[20] We can document these trends with statistics. In the 1970s, according to the DDB Life Style survey, more than 40 percent of Americans said that they worked on community projects—which often involved education—but that percentage is now down to the twenties. PTA membership rose to 45 per 100 families in 1960, but then fell to less than half that in the last twenty years.[21]

Market systems are intended to decentralize power and *curb* the power of professionals by giving parents choices among schools. Some of the arguments for vouchers are populist and anti-technocratic. Vouchers, however, do not put communities in charge of civic education. If parents create incentives for schools by choosing where to send their children, then most will seek private goods for their own offspring (such as marketable skills and membership in exclusive peer groups) rather than public goods (such as civic skills, experience with democracy, and exposure to diversity). There may not be forums in which people can discuss what public values the next generation should acquire.

Further, in a marketlike educational system, only parents who are well educated themselves will tend to choose schools that provide demanding extracurricular activities and enrichment programs that generate civic skills. According to Lareau, participation in extracurricular activities is a function of class not only because middle-class parents can afford teams and music lessons, but also because they fully understand the educational advantages of such activities. In their culture, scarce time must be invested in children's human capital. As one mom says, Saturday morning TV doesn't "contribute" anything, so she gets her son out to "the piano lesson, and then straight to choir for a couple of hours."[22] In contrast, the working-class parents regard team sports and other extracurricular activities as forms of entertainment that they will consider only if their children demand them. Thus, even if they had much more cash, they would not spend their days ferrying their children from practice to practice. They don't see the point. (One mother admits she takes her son to free football practices, at his request, but finds the process draining and "pray[s] we don't have to do it again.")[23]

Finally, all these approaches to reform (including the liberal tactic of increasing funds for teachers' salaries) involve extrinsic motivations. But people can also be intrinsically motivated to teach and to learn. Democracy needs citizens who understand the intrinsic value of working and learning together. In any case, it is offensive and alienating to treat good teachers and students as if they lacked internal goals and will only respond to carrots and sticks.

Raising teachers' salaries, equalizing school spending, mandating tests that have financial consequences, requiring that a specific percentage of education funds go to "classroom instruction," introducing vouchers—these proposals run the gamut from left to right, but all are ways of manipulating incentives. They are technocratic rather than democratic/participatory approaches to reform.

The opposite is the following ideal. Members of a community educate the community's children. They do not see education simply as a responsibility of the schools, but they do take responsibility for the schools in their area. Many adults (and some youth) play a direct role in education: serving on parents' associations or school boards, teaching Sunday school, volunteering in a classroom or a youth center, writing an education column for the newspaper, working at the local college. There is a great deal of deliberation and debate about the content and methods of education across the community. The purpose of it all is seen to be not merely getting children through a test, but also developing interests, traits of character, and civic skills.

I readily admit that this is an idealized picture of education without technocrats. Yet it contains at least a germ of truth. Nina Eliasoph has found that teachers, librarians, and parents engage in intense and morally serious deliberations about such questions as how boys should act on the playground and whether young children should be exposed to wrenching facts about the Holocaust and slavery.[24] Such conversations are important, but they have limited scope. Broader debates about educational priorities tend to be suppressed by both liberal and conservative technocratic approaches that concern themselves exclusively with incentives.

6.4 THE LACK OF A "CIVICS" DISCIPLINE

Today, there is no academic discipline devoted to questions about what people can and should do as participants in a democratic society. The lack of such a discipline has practical consequences. First, it means that questions about citizens' roles are not addressed with sufficient seriousness by academic scholars; there is not enough research about citizenship. Second, high schools emulate college curricula, because schools are under intense (and perhaps appropriate) pressure to prepare their students for college attendance. If there is no academic discipline of civics or citizenship, then high schools naturally provide classes on history and political science (under the name of "government"). These are academic disciplines for which Ph.D.s are awarded. Those who defend civics or social studies have difficulty answering Diane Ravitch's question: "What is social studies? . . . Is it history with attention to current events? Is it a merger of history, geography, civics, economics, sociology, and all other social sciences? Is it a mishmash of courses such as career education, ethnic studies, gender studies, consumer education, environmental studies, peace education, character education, and drug education? Is it a field that defines its goals in terms of cultivating skills like decision making, interpersonal relations, and critical thinking, as well as the development of 'critical' attitudes like global awareness, environmental consciousness, multiculturalism, and gender equity?"[25]

Courses labeled as "civics" and "social studies" were launched during the Progressive Era, to prepare youth for active citizenship. They grew at the partial expense of history, which some saw as an overacademic discipline. In 1915, the U.S. Bureau of Education formally endorsed a movement for "community civics" that was by then quite widespread. Its aim was "to help the child know his community—not merely a lot about it, but the meaning of community life, what it does for him and how it does it, what the community has a right to expect from him, and how he may fulfill his obligations, meanwhile cultivating in him the essential qualities and habits of good citizenship."[26] In 1928–29, according to federal statistics, more than half of all American ninth-graders took "civics." That percentage had fallen to 13.4 by the early 1970s. In 1948–49, 41.5 percent of American high school students took "problems of democracy," which typically involved reading and debating stories from the daily newspaper. By the early 1970s, that number was down to 8.9 percent.

Nevertheless, the percentage of high school students who have taken any government course has been basically steady since 1915–16.[27] Although the historical data have gaps, it appears most likely that "civics" and "problems of democracy" have disappeared since 1970, while American history, world history, and American government have either stayed constant or grown. Today, American Government is the fastest-growing Advanced Placement exam. As Nathaniel Schwartz notes, the old civics and problems of democracy textbooks addressed their readers as "you" and advocated various forms of participation.[28] Today's American government texts discuss the topics of first-year college political science: how a bill becomes a law, how interest groups form, how courts operate. Social studies arose during the Progressive Era, when philosophical pragmatists argued for a curriculum of practical relevance to democracy. Social studies and civics appear to be waning at a time when academic rigor is valued and colleges increasingly set the tone for high schools.

Certainly there is nothing wrong with studying political science in high school or college. First of all, it is a challenging discipline that deals with interesting topics. Besides, the discipline began with an explicit civic purpose. The American Political Science Association, founded in 1903, created four successive high-profile committees on civic education before World War II. John William Burgess, a major political scientist who died in 1931, saw his discipline as a way to "prepare young men for the duties of public life."[29] In 1901, President Arthur Hadley of Yale had argued for civic education that would enhance motivations, virtues, and skills as well as knowledge. "A man may possess a vast knowledge with regard to the workings of our social and political machinery, and yet be absolutely untrained in those things which make a good citizen."[30]

Today, however, political science has limited relevance to questions about what a citizen can and should do. A certain logic has led political science to focus on the most powerful forces: nations, Congress, the presidency, major lobbying groups, and social classes. In the 1950s, Harold Lasswell, reflecting a view that had by then become standard, wrote: "Political science, as an academic discipline, is the study of the shaping and sharing of power." Hence serious political scientists should not worry much about citizens as agents: "The study of politics is the study of influence and the influential. . . . The influential are those who get the most of what there is to get. . . . Those who get the most are the *elite;* the rest are the *mass.*"[31] Of course, there have since been numerous studies of local political institutions and of ordinary people's political behavior, but far fewer than one would find in a discipline devoted to citizenship.

Second, political science (as its name implies) is an empirical and not a normative discipline, which means that it says little about what citizens *should* do as opposed to what they actually do. Although political science began in the late nineteenth century with ambitions to enhance civic engagement, that aim began to seem unscientific by 1920. In 1933, University of Chicago President Robert Hutchins announced, "'education for citizenship' has no place in the university."[32]

Not only did traditional civic education seem preachy and unscientific; it also appeared naive. A 1971 report by the American Political Science Association (APSA) argued that the role of political education was to provide "knowledge about the 'realities' of political life." According to this report, most high school civics teachers imparted "a naïve, unrealistic, and romanticized image of political life which confuses the ideals of democracy with the realities of politics."[33] No doubt, it is important to give students a realistic sense of politics: they should understand shortcomings of actual institutions and tradeoffs between fundamental goods (such as liberty and equality) that make it impossible to design perfect systems. However, the kind of "realism" recommended in the 1971 report—and evident in many introductory college lectures—is basically discouraging. It suggests that reality leaves no room for civic action.

A third reason for the gap between political science and a discipline of citizenship is the problem of expertise, already treated at length in section 6.3. While political scientists differ about the appropriate role of "ordinary people" in a modern democracy, the very concept of a sophisticated, highly quantitative discipline devoted to politics suggests that expertise is important. At times, political scientists have drawn undemocratic lessons from this suggestion. For instance, the APSA Committee of Seven argued in 1914 that citizens "should learn humility in the face of expertise."[34] This form of civic education is unlikely to promote active participation.

Despite all the reasons for political science to drop its civic mission, many universities still try to enhance their own students' civic capacities by providing opportunities for service-learning, internships, foreign study, and dialogues with other students about issues and conflicts. These opportunities, however, are not tightly connected to research or included in the courses that are most highly valued in the disciplines. Separating service from teaching and research has hurt all three activities.

Things may be changing. The APSA's Strategic Planning Committee recommended in 2000 that the central purposes of the association should again include "preparing citizens to be effective citizens and political participants." It remains to be seen, however, how much impact that unmistakable shift in the association's rhetoric will have on actual research and teaching in political science.[35]

Political science is not the only discipline that first arose with the explicit purpose of enhancing citizenship, only to abandon that goal. In ancient Greece, the more responsible Sophists founded the rigorous study of literature as an education for participants in republican self-government. Protagoras, for example, invented the study of grammar through his careful, analytic reading of literature. He claimed a moral and civic purpose for this work. In Plato's dialogue that bears his name, Protagoras says, "The works of the best poets are set before [children] to read on the classroom benches, and the children are compelled to learn these works thoroughly; and in them are displayed many warnings, many detailed narratives and praises and eulogies of good men in ancient times, so that the boy may desire to emulate them competitively and may stretch himself to become like them."[36] Protagoras defended literature for its moral benefits, but the moral virtues he had in mind were also civic, useful for participation in the polis.

Many centuries later, in Italian republics that somewhat resembled Protagoras's polis, people who called themselves "humanists" began to teach literature as a form of civic education (in preference to theology and moral philosophy, which were seen as otherworldly and nonpolitical—more for clergy than for citizens). Humanists argued that stories depicted virtuous actions in concrete situations, while story-*tellers* exemplified eloquence, which was an essential skill for civic participation. As Francis Bacon observed, "it is eloquence that prevaileth in an active life."[37]

Today, however, mainstream modern literary criticism is not a discipline devoted to civics. Some critics consider political and social themes in their courses and writing, but that is not the same as asking what citizens ought to do to define and address public problems. Modern critics are unlikely to endorse "eulogies of good men in ancient times," because the values of citizens from distant times and places do not seem directly relevant to the issues of our own era; critics are historicists who are aware of cultural and social change. Besides, in an effort to become professional, many critics have abandoned the practice of looking for explicit moral value in stories and are instead interested in issues more amenable to expert judgment, such as influence, genre, form, and rhetoric. As R. S. Crane wrote in the 1930s, "The essential thing about the understanding to which the literary critic aspires is that it is understanding of literary works in their character as works of art. It is not criticism but psychology when we treat poems or novels as case books and attempt to discover in them not the art but the personality of their authors. . . . It is not criticism but ethical culture when we use them primarily as a means of enlarging and enriching our experience of life or of inculcating moral ideas. . . . Criticism . . . is simply the disciplined consideration, at once analytical and evaluative, of literary works as works of art."[38]

History has also been advanced as a civic discipline. Like literature, it provides examples of virtue and vice and eloquent narration. Leibniz thought its purpose was to "teach wisdom and virtue by example," a commonplace view by his time.[39] In his famous address as president of the American Historical Association in 1931, Carl Becker said, "The history that lies inert in unread books does no work in the world. The history that does work in the world, the history that influences the course of history, is living history, that pattern of remembered events, whether true or false, that enlarges and enriches the collective specious present." That is a civic justification of historical research (and Becker advocated research that was careful and rigorous).[40] Historical evidence and examples appear essential to thinking about what citizens can and should do. Unfortunately, history is not always studied or taught with that purpose in mind.

Finally, moral philosophy has sometimes been seen as civic discipline. However, modern professional philosophers mostly work at the largest or the smallest scale: that is, they either consider the overall structure of a society and the definition and distribution of fundamental rights and essential goods; or they consider decisions and dilemmas faced by individuals in private (for example, whether abortion is moral). They also produce important work on professional ethics, including the ethics of politicians and judges. But there is much less philosophical work on the ethics of participation in civil society or political movements—the topics of most relevance for citizens.

It is intriguing to imagine a formal academic discipline of "civics." It might combine philosophical investigations of citizens' role in communities, historical research into changing forms of civic participation, empirical studies of political behavior and political development, formal study of rhetoric, and analysis of the frequent challenges that confront active citizens (such as free-rider problems in voluntary associations). Creating departments of civics in prestigious universities would have a trickle-down effect on curricula in high schools and below.

However, it seems unlikely that such a discipline will develop in the near future. The alternative is to try to infuse many (or all) existing academic disciplines with civic themes and to organize educational institutions so that they draw their members' attention to the study and practice of citizenship. But that, too, is a tall order. There is a risk that civics, if diffused across the curriculum and research programs of a school or university, will never amount to much.

6.5 IMPLICATIONS

It is not in the self-interest of individuals or of most institutions to promote civic learning. Put another way, it is not in their interest *as they understand it,* which is partly because Americans have been influenced by technocracy and a dominant ideology of individual choice, both of which divert our attention from citizenship. It doesn't help that we lack an intellectual discipline devoted to civic engagement.

Given these realities, one way to enhance civic education is to make it work for the interests that individuals and institutions *do* recognize. In the subsequent chapters, I will present arguments that organized service opportunities can keep students in school and that studying history and social studies can improve reading test scores. These are outcomes that powerful people care about.

There is a grave risk, however, that if we take a purely tactical approach to civic education—trying to make it fit into other agendas—our progress will be halting and incremental. Further, when we succeed in implementing civic education, it may be shorn of its democratic purpose and become a way to adjust young people to an unequal and alienating political system. Therefore, in chapters 10 and 11, I turn from educational interventions to political reform.

CHAPTER 7

Civic Learning in School

Schools are not the only venues for civic development, but they are vital. They alone reach everyone, including disadvantaged students and students who would not be inclined to volunteer or participate in civic projects. Joseph Kahne and Susan Sporte studied the impact of civic education in Chicago, using a longitudinal panel of about 3,800 public school students. They found that students gained commitment to civic participation if they experienced service-learning in school, were required to follow the news, or participated in open discussions of current events in their classrooms. After-school and community-based programs also had statistically significant, positive effects, but the impact was much smaller. This contrast may be surprising, because Chicago is a hotbed of excellent community-based civic projects, whereas the Chicago public schools do not have a reputation for general excellence. However, the community-based projects draw volunteers who are already committed to civic engagement before they sign up; they are hard-pressed to *increase* commitment or engagement. In contrast, even when school-based civic education is of mixed quality, it can have strikingly positive effects—presumably because even disengaged students are exposed to civic and political ideas and opportunities.[1]

Schools have inadequate funding in many communities. Nevertheless, they have enormous resources that they can use for civic education: 3.7 million teachers, 116,000 school buildings, and 78,411 libraries in the public sector alone, not to mention countless hours of time that children are required to spend in their care.[2] They have a civic mandate going back to their foundation in the nineteenth century. Finally, deliberate education for democracy in K-12 schools *works:* "If you teach them, they will learn."[3]

7.1 COURSES

Until recently, it was the "accepted wisdom in the political science profession" that courses on civics, government, current issues, law, and American history had "little or no effect on the vast majority of students."[4] That conventional wisdom was based on a few small-scale empirical studies from the 1960s, plus a widespread assumption that political participation was a function of social class or other large social forces, not amenable to direct intervention in the classroom.

However, several far larger empirical studies have been conducted since the 1980s, including the National Assessment of Education Progress (NAEP) civics assessment, which is a testlike instrument created by the federal government and taken by twenty thousand students; the IEA Civic Education Study, a detailed survey of fourteen-year-olds conducted simultaneously in the United States and in twenty-seven foreign countries; and several polls of young adults that ask them about their own civic education as well as their current civic activities. Consistently, these studies find positive correlations between taking a class on civics, government, or American history, on the one hand, and possessing civic knowledge, confidence,[5] and attitudes, on the other.

For example, Niemi and Junn carefully analyzed the NAEP civics assessment, which measures factual knowledge and cognitive skills (such as interpreting political speeches and news articles). They found that course taking has a positive relationship with knowledge and skills even after other factors were controlled.[6] Using their own Metro Civic Values Survey (conducted in Maryland in 1999–2000), Gimpel and colleagues found that taking a government course raised students' habits of discussion politics by 5 percent, their political knowledge by 3 percent, and their "internal efficacy" by 2 percent. (Internal efficacy is a person's confidence in his or her own political skills.) Taking a government course lowered students' confidence in the responsiveness of government by about 2 percent.[7]

Others have found correlations between classes and behavior, perhaps because people need knowledge in order to take action, or perhaps because students are inspired by their courses to participate later in life. By statute, the NAEP basically cannot investigate behavior, only knowledge. The IEA study involved fourteen-year-olds, who were too young for many optional forms of engagement, such as voting, contributing money, and serving on boards. However, in a poll conducted in 2003, young people who said they had taken a civics class were twice as likely to vote, twice as likely to follow the news, and four times as likely to volunteer for a campaign than those who had never taken civics courses.[8]

That finding does not prove that a single course doubles voter turnout; the relationship is more complicated than that. People might choose to take courses because of a preexisting interest in politics; or they might learn in a class that civic engagement is valued and therefore become prone to exaggerate how much they participate; or they might be more likely to *remember* taking a class because they are involved in politics or civic affairs. These explanations (among others) would undercut the theory that courses increase participation. Nonetheless, when CIRCLE controlled for all the other factors that were measured in the survey (such as race, family income, geographical location, and ideology), we still found very strong positive relationships between course taking and behavior.[9] That result is evidence that courses increase engagement as well as knowledge.

Similarly, Melissa Comber used the United States portion of the IEA Civic Education Study to examine the link between course taking and civic skills, for ninth-graders. Using a statistical model that controlled for numerous observed factors, she found that taking courses had a substantial positive effect on interpreting political texts, following the news, and discussing politics with parents.[10] A large survey of California students also found that courses had positive effects on students' political knowledge and commitment to participate in politics and civil society.[11]

One might assume that students gain information from courses but then gradually forget what they have learned (much as I have forgotten the content of my high school chemistry course). However, there is another reasonable hypothesis: perhaps obtaining a foundation of knowledge in adolescence allows a person to understand news articles and broadcasts and to participate in political conversations. By following and discussing the news, the citizen who starts with a base of knowledge gradually increases his or her understanding. This is a theory of education as investment instead of a theory that knowledge is a temporary response to a stimulus.

I am not aware of longitudinal studies specifically about political knowledge that would allow us to test this investment hypothesis. However, there is suggestive evidence that supports it. For example, two years after they completed the Kids Voting program (which combines discussions of current issues with a mock election), students who participated were still more likely than their counterparts to discuss issues outside of class and to follow the news.[12] Eric Plutzer has used longitudinal data to show that voting follows an investment or "latent growth" model: that is, various factors can increase the likelihood that an individual votes. Once a citizen casts a first vote, a habit forms. Even if the positive stimulus is removed, the citizen tends to vote in subsequent elections.[13] A third piece of suggestive evidence comes from Highton and Wolfinger's study of the political life cycle. They find that people become more likely to vote as they grow older, quite apart from any specific events that take place, such as getting married, graduating from college, having children, or buying a home. They suggest that political knowledge gradually accumulates and makes it easier to vote.[14] In that case, politics is different from subjects like chemistry, our understanding of which tends to decay over time unless we deliberately renew it.

David Campbell has found that students' anticipated level of political involvement, measured in high school, "correlates highly" with their actual political participation several years later.[15] In turn, course taking raises anticipated levels of political participation—further evidence that the effects of courses may persist or even accumulate, rather than fade away.

Thus the data argue that students should study some combination of civics, government, and social studies because that will make them more knowledgeable and engaged later in life. This finding raises two further questions: What topics should students study? And how should the material be presented to them? At least since 1900, strikingly similar debates about the content and pedagogy of social studies have recurred. Some people think that civics should be patriotic and affirm the value of American institutions; others, that civics should help students detect and oppose injustice. Some people think that civics should focus on issues of immediate relevance to students, especially problems in their local communities and opportunities for direct action; others believe that the core of civics ought to be perennial themes, such as liberty, equality, and rule of law. Some argue that civics class should be highly interactive, with opportunities for students to debate, conduct research, and go out into the community. Others emphasize the need to impart core knowledge, including challenging facts and concepts that the teacher has and the students initially lack.[16] Some believe that teachers should be rigorously neutral on all controversial issues; others think it is useful to demonstrate that teachers, as thoughtful adults, hold and defend positions.

Much has been written about these debates, which are inevitable in a pluralist democracy. Because civic education is intended to reproduce and improve our democratic culture, it will always be controversial. I will return to several of the most contentious questions below. It is important, however, not to let arguments about content overwhelm the evidence that civics classes are useful. Chester Finn is so angry about what he takes to be the typical social studies class that he is almost ready to throw the baby out with the bathwater. Finn claims that students emerge "from K–12 education and then, alas, from college with ridiculously little knowledge or understanding of their country's history, their planet's geography, their government's functioning, or the economy's essential workings." And the reason, he asserts, is that social studies teachers have bad values. By the year 2001, he writes,

> in the field of social studies itself, the lunatics had taken over the asylum. Its leaders were people who had plenty of grand degrees and impressive titles but who possessed no respect for Western civilization; who were inclined to view America's evolution as a problem for humanity rather than mankind's last, best hope; who pooh-poohed history's chronological and factual skeleton as somehow privileging elites and white males over the poor and oppressed; who saw the study of geography in terms of despoiling the rain forest rather than locating London or the Mississippi River on a map; who interpreted "civics" as consisting largely of political activism and "service learning" rather than understanding how laws are made and why it is important to live in a society governed by laws; who feared that serious study of economics might give unfair advantage to capitalism (just as excessive attention to democracy might lead impressionable youngsters to judge it a superior way of organizing society); and who, in any case, took for granted that children were better off learning about their neighborhoods and "community helpers" than amazing deeds by heroes and villains in distant times and faraway places.[17]

Finn believes that leftist professors in schools of education make their students into relativists or anti-Americans; those students then take up teaching jobs; and their victims exit school with poor values and little knowledge. Although I have not found a similarly passionate statement from the Left written within the last thirty years, I know from informal conversations that some hold a mirror-image theory. They believe that colleges whitewash American history and law and make it boring, preparing their graduates to teach civics in a way that profoundly alienates and misleads their students. Youth of color and disadvantaged kids especially are turned off by a sanitized presentation of American government.

James Murphy argues that political education is so intrinsically controversial that it always prompts divisive debates that harm educational institutions. He thus warns against civic education.[18] Yet, when either liberals or conservatives decry the content of social studies classes, they usually do so innocent of any statistical evidence about what is actually taught and discussed in schools. There are anecdotes about egregious teaching that can incense people across the spectrum, but no one knows how common these stories are. In 2004[19] and again in the omnibus survey of 2006, we asked national samples of young Americans to recall two major themes from their social studies classes (see table 4).

Asking people to recall major themes is an imperfect method, but these survey results at least hint that most civics teaching is fairly traditionalist and patriotic. That finding should mollify conservative critics

TABLE 4 Major Themes

Major themes that 15–25-year-olds recall from their classes on government, civics, or American history in middle school and high school (two responses accepted from each respondent)	2004	2006
"Great American heroes and virtues of the political system"	29.8	23.3
"The Constitution or U.S. system of government and how it works"	38.6	32.5
"Wars and military battles"	14.8	16.2
"Racism and other forms of injustice"	7.8	8.7
"Problems facing the country today"	5.2	5.6

Source: See note 19, page 246.

of the social studies profession. Leftist critics of mainstream social studies will not be cheered, but I believe that they should prefer politics to be taught than to be dropped altogether, because the average effects of classes is to increase participation. There is little evidence that students are permanently influenced by the philosophical or ideological presuppositions of their teachers, but asking them to study political and civic topics in school seems to make them more active and informed.[20]

Because education about politics and issues is intrinsically controversial and ideological, it would be improper and counterproductive to try to impose a single model on all communities. Inevitably, government and politics will be taught differently in Philadelphia, Pennsylvania, and Philadelphia, Mississippi. A broad framework for factual knowledge can attract national consensus, as shown by the NAEP civics assessments, which have been written on several occasions by ideologically diverse committees. Still, many controversial questions about what young citizens should learn and do should not be settled at the federal level.

Despite the need for pluralism, many experts propose two overarching principles. First, students should learn about great, perennial ideals and concepts such as those presented in the Declaration of Independence, the Constitution, and the Gettysburg Address. Those foundational concepts, however, should be connected to practical, current, real-world issues. Second, education for citizenship should be at least partly experiential. That does not mean that lectures and textbooks are useless, but it is important to avoid a scene that has been replicated in classrooms since the 1800s, in which a teacher instructs students about the mechanics of government without giving them any opportunity to debate, conduct research, experiment, or create.[21]

James G. Gimpel and his colleagues are able to derive two additional recommendations from their study. They find that students who *like* studying government and politics are (holding other factors constant) dramatically more likely to discuss politics, more efficacious, and more knowledgeable than their peers.[22] Enjoyment of the subject matter may arise from students' prior interests and temperaments, in which case it will be hard to change. But it may also be that enjoyable courses increase students' interest in politics, whereas boring courses turn them off. Given the importance of increasing civic motivations (not just factual knowledge), it is worth trying to make civics courses especially enjoyable instead of especially dull—their reputation. That approach argues for field trips, visitors from the community, debates, skits, and art projects.

Gimpel and his colleagues also find that most social studies classes "fail to develop in students an appreciation for the importance of conflictual aspects of American political history. Students often come to view disagreement and conflict as negative, as something to be avoided, and that no good can come of it." Students who disliked government and politics expressed "open contempt" for disagreement, as portrayed in news about Congress and the presidency.[23] This attitude is a problem, since the country is always divided about important matters of principle and interest, and politics is our means of resolving such differences peacefully. Other research has found that many Americans do not acknowledge that there are real public disagreements. They see clashes between liberals and conservatives in Washington as unnecessary and artificial—motivated by sheer partisan competition. This resistance to conflict alienates people from participating in politics.[24] It would therefore be helpful if students learned about disagreements and practiced taking sides without demonizing opponents.

Sharareh Frouzesh Bennett has examined the current best-selling textbooks and finds that they present American government as a well-organized system for implementing what the people want. Voting is by far the most commonly mentioned form of civic engagement—which makes sense if the government is basically satisfactory; majority rule is the essence of democracy. Because the existence of profound disagreement is not acknowledged in any of the leading textbooks, little is said about tools available to electoral minorities, such as "boycotts, lawsuits, protests, and civil disobedience." And because the government is portrayed as capable of handling public issues, virtually nothing is said about citizens' roles in social movements, voluntary associations, and (more generally) civil society. "The Holt text refers to civil disobedience during the section on the civil rights movement and indicates that the method was used in the past to defy laws that were thought to be wrong." Overall, politics is portrayed as a system or organization that offers a limited role for citizens (basically, to vote). Politics is not described as a struggle over contested issues.[25]

Bennett's findings are consistent with the survey result cited above: most students are taught about the excellence of the American political system, whereas only 5.2 percent recall studying "problems facing the country today." Contrary to the fears of conservatives (who dwell on scattered anecdotes about leftist teachers), most students receive a civic education that is "conservative" in a particular sense. Textbooks do not introduce them to right-wing ideas, such as reducing the size of government or banning abortion. That is because textbooks contain few political ideas of any kind. Instead, students are taught that the status quo is desirable and uncontroversial—a form of conservatism that both right and left should reject.

7.2 DISCUSSIONS OF CURRENT ISSUES

Good social studies teachers stimulate discussions of current public issues, sometimes using newspaper articles or other background materials as prompts. For example, each "issue guide" published by the National Issues Forums (NIF) offers three perspectives on a single national debate, to stimulate deliberation. NIF materials are used in many classrooms.

Although topical discussions are part of good civics teaching, they deserve separate consideration. They can occur in venues other than social studies courses. For example, analyzing a novel in an English class can stimulate a current-events discussion, as can certain topics in science, health, foreign languages, and even mathematics. Extracurricular clubs, schoolwide meetings, and homeroom classes can also be opportunities for such discussions.

Some believe that discussion-linked-to-action is the normative core of democratic citizenship: the behavior that we should value most.[26] If that is true, it is especially important to teach deliberation so that citizens can learn to talk constructively, freely, and with good information before they act politically. Unfortunately, according to the 1998 NAEP civics assessment, minority students were most likely to say that they had to memorize facts but were least likely to report role-playing exercises, debates, and visits from community members—all experiences that might stimulate class discussions.[27]

The IEA Civic Education study asked many questions about political knowledge, skills, behaviors, and anticipated behaviors along with questions that were intended to measure the quality of deliberation in schools. Respondents were asked "to think especially about classes in history, civics/citizenship, or social studies" and to say whether they agreed with the following statements:

- "Students feel free to disagree openly with their teachers about political and social issues during class."

- "Students are encouraged to make up their own minds about issues."
- "Teachers respect our opinions and encourage us to express them during class."
- "Teachers encourage us to discuss political or social issues about which people have different opinions."
- "Teachers present several sides of an issue when explaining it in class."
- "Students bring up current political events for discussion in class."

Using these questions, David Campbell has constructed separate measures to show whether individual students believe that there is an "open climate" for discussion, and whether their classmates, on average, sense such a climate. (In particular cases, those measures could be different. For instance, an outspoken and politically engaged student might feel that students *can* disagree with teachers and make up their own minds, but her classmates might disagree, in which case there would not actually be an open climate.)

Campbell finds—consistent with the previous section of this book—that taking a civics course has a positive effect on students' civic knowledge and skills. He also finds that individuals' beliefs about the classroom climate for discussion and their peers' average assessments of that climate have positive effects.[28] In fact, once Campbell includes these two measures of deliberation in his statistical model, course-taking no longer has a significant impact. In other words, *discussion* explains the increases in civic knowledge, skills, and anticipated political participation that appear to come from taking a civics course. This result is not an argument against civics classes; they provide important opportunities for conducting discussions. But it does suggest that the most important part of the social studies curriculum is an aspect that is not explicitly measured on standardized tests and that may even seem distracting: talking about current events. Campbell's study follows several others that have found benefits of deliberation for students' civic and political knowledge, interest, and behavior.[29]

Another kind of evidence comes from a quasi-experiment in which students who were enrolled in the Kids Voting curriculum were compared to similar students who were not exposed to that program. Kids Voting involves discussions of current issues. According to an analysis by Michael McDevitt and his colleagues, the program raised students' attention to political news, their knowledge of politics, and their likelihood of discussing politics with family and friends, while it lowered their total hours of television. The curriculum had no effect on students' party identifications or political opinions (which might mollify critics who worry that classroom discussions are manipulative). Gaps between white and minority students tended to shrink as a result of the program. Perhaps the most intriguing result is that *parents* were more likely to discuss politics and current events if their children were enrolled in Kids Voting—a "trickle-up effect."[30] One participant recalled, "I told my dad, 'Dad, you need to vote.' I got him interested in what is going on and told him to vote."[31]

Campbell finds that the more racially heterogeneous a school's student body is, the *less* likely its students are to report an open climate for discussions of current issues. "As the percentage of white students increases, black students are less likely to report that their teachers encourage political discussion in class, and as the percentage of black students increases, white students report less discussion."[32] (These results are controlled for numerous demographic factors.) Campbell proposes that as student populations become more diverse, teachers grow leery of controversial issues. That premise is certainly possible, but there is another plausible interpretation. Perhaps students in ethnically homogeneous schools *believe* that their discussions are free-flowing and open to diverse opinions, but they are not aware of perspectives truly unlike their own. As diversity increases, students become less satisfied with the degree to which classroom discussions address divisive issues.[33]

7.3 STUDENT "VOICE" IN SCHOOLS

In addition to talking about broad public issues, such as war in the Middle East or homelessness in America, students can also seriously discuss issues that arise within their own schools. For example, the institution's rules, its array of courses and extracurricular activities, and its lunch menu are almost inevitably topics of informal discussion. But schools' response to such conversations varies. At one extreme, adults could try to suppress any talk about school issues that occurred within their hearing, viewing such discussions as subversive. At the opposite extreme, students could govern a whole institution through a completely democratic process. There have been scattered experiments with truly democratic schools, such as Sudbury Valley in Massachusetts, which is an independent nonprofit corporation, founded in 1968, and governed by an assembly in which every person—whether a student, teacher, or another kind of adult worker—has one vote. These models offer welcome opportunities for experimentation and learning, but they would be difficult to implement in public school systems that understand "democracy" as governance by elected municipal, state, and federal officials.

The most fertile ground lies between democratic schools, such as Sudbury, and those that actively discourage student voice. Some schools grant formal advisory roles to selected students, such as the leaders of the student government. Some organize "town meetings" and other deliberations that have some impact on policy. In some schools, the student newspaper is an influential forum for discussing common issues, and the administration takes it seriously. Some schools have no formal structure for student input, yet youth feel that adults care what they think. The culture of such institutions encourages discussion. That norm may depend on day-to-day choices, such as whether to allow adequate time for discussion when school policies arise, whether to encourage everyone to speak, and whether to act on reasonable advice that comes from students.

Two recent projects have tried to move participating schools toward greater levels of student voice. The First Amendment Schools is a network of about one hundred schools that receive modest funding to increase students' constructive influence on their own policies. The motive for this initiative is to enhance young people's support for civil liberties, but the tactic is to make free expression *consequential* inside schools. Project 540 was a network of 270 high schools that encouraged schoolwide deliberation and action about issues that the students chose. It was most active during the years 2002–2004, when it had support from The Pew Charitable Trusts. Participating students were encouraged to consider what changes they most wanted in their own schools, their communities, and the broader society. They then formed "Civic Action Plans" to pursue these changes. For example, Project 540 students in Alabama fought a court order that they saw as a threat to African American teachers' tenure in their own schools.[34] Across the country, food and lunch policies were the most frequently chosen issues. School food may seem relatively inconsequential, but it can stimulate serious civic work. In one Minnesota high school, for example, students built and ran a café as a result of Project 540.

Data from surveys conducted a year apart and controlled for various background characteristics suggested that Project 540 had a positive impact on participants' commitment to deliberative democracy, their experience with civic action, and their sense of personal efficacy. For participants and nonparticipants alike, Project 540 seemed to increase their feelings of connection to their schools as communities.[35] Teachers seemed to have the most rewarding experiences when they saw themselves neither as leaders nor as bystanders in Project 540, but as active "coaches."[36]

However, Project 540, First Amendment Schools, and other recent informal experiments have not been structured as tests of the hypothesis that increasing student voice will improve measurable student outcomes. It would be very useful to know from more formal experiments whether an empowered student government, a student seat on the school board, or a "town meeting" has positive effects on the student population.

For now, the best evidence comes from surveys that ask students whether they *believe* that their opinions about school issues are welcomed. In the IEA study, there were positive relationships between students' knowledge of politics and interest in current events (on the one hand) and their confidence that they could make a difference in the way their own schools were run and their belief that the student council had an impact on school policies (on the other). These effects were also found in a subsample of schools where educational outcomes were generally poor. Thus student "voice" may have important benefits for less advantaged students.[37]

Other studies find correlations between students' confidence in American democracy and their belief that their own schools are equitable and tolerant communities.[38] Specifically, their confidence in democracy is higher if they think that their teachers "hold the same high standards for and respect the ideas of all students" and "insist that students listen to and respect one another." In several countries, students were more likely to commit to serving their communities and nations if they felt that their own schools were institutions "where caring transcended the borders of social cliques."[39] This research moves us beyond deliberations about schoolwide policies into the subtler but essential realm of school *climate*.[40] If, for example, bullying is treated as a problem that deserves adult attention, and if students are trained so that they can help to resolve it, then they are more likely to view their schools as equitable and tolerant institutions. As we have seen, such positive feelings about schools correlate with commitment to democratic communities. On the other hand, if schools either ignore bullying or develop "zero-tolerance" policies that turn all threats into disciplinary cases that must be reported immediately to the authorities, the school climate will be less favorable.[41] Political scientists have previously found that beliefs about police officers and other local government officials influence what people think about the president and Congress. Apparently, this "diffusion" pattern also applies to teachers, who are representative authority figures.[42]

In a Deweyan vein, some theorists argue that schooling for democracy must *itself* be democratic, that schools must embody political equality and free, empowered deliberation; else they will teach youth that democracy is a sham. As Carl Glickman puts the argument: "The public school is the primary institution for providing an educated citizenry for democracy. Yet most schools show in everyday action a disbelief in such preparation. Most operate on the basis of hierarchy, control, and power. They do not embrace equality among faculty, staff, and administrators, and they bypass any substantial contribution from students, parents, and local citizens in making important decisions affecting the school community. . . . Students every day see adults practicing a form of life diametrically opposed to what they hear espoused."[43]

The relationship between democracy in schools and democratic outcomes is an empirical proposition that I do not believe has been adequately tested. "Democracy" is a complex and contested concept, encompassing some mixture of equality, individual freedom, tolerance, rule of law, and communitarian ethics. It is not paradoxical to assume that we could prepare students in partly undemocratic settings to participate later in a robust democracy. In fact, hardly anyone believes that average public schools should operate on a principle of "one person, one vote" (with students and teachers counted equally). Even strong proponents of democratic schooling actually favor a compromise between political equality and adult stewardship. One principal (a participant in Project 540 who had committed to increasing student voice in his own school), put this badly when he said there was a "fine line between letting the monkeys run the zoo and some structure." But even if we drop language about monkeys and zoos, there is a need to balance youth participation and adult responsibility—as the Project 540 experiment showed.[44]

I do not believe that the proper balance can be identified through pure philosophical analysis, because everything depends on the *effects* of empowering students within their own institutions versus providing them with adult guidance. The current empirical literature is not strong enough to settle the issue. However, there is good evidence that students take a greater interest in, and know more about, politics when they have the sense that their own voice counts. That is reason enough to pay attention to students' views and to experiment with mechanisms for substantive input.

7.4 SERVICE-LEARNING

So far, we have considered various forms of discussion. "Service-learning" means an opportunity for students actually to serve in their communities while they study, discuss, or reflect upon their service. It thus implies a deliberate combination of academic study and practical work. Service-learning has a long heritage in the United States and in many other countries and cultures. To consider just one example, as early as the twelfth century in Europe, mendicant friars of the Franciscan and Dominican orders were expected to learn from serving the poor. In the mid-twentieth century there were some excellent programs that we would now call "service learning." For instance, the city planning commission of a small city in the northeast United States asked social studies teachers to recruit high school seniors to design and conduct community surveys, produce maps, and write recommendations.[45] Other settings for service-learning (before the phrase) included settlement houses like Hull-House in Chicago, the Appalachian Folk Schools (of which Highlander in Tennessee was most famous), and the Civilian Conservation Corps, which provided formal civic education programs connected to service work.[46]

The phrase itself seems to have been coined in 1967.[47] Service-learning then developed into a movement, complete with dedicated journals, standards for "best practice," several annual conferences, public and private funding sources, and networks of practitioners and advocates. In 1999, about half of high schools claimed to offer service-learning opportunities.[48]

In practice, both the service and the learning in "service-learning" differ widely. "Service" may mean tutoring, visiting elderly people, raising money for charity, cleaning up public spaces, taking soil or water samples for environmental monitoring, creating Web sites or broadcast segments, or organizing communities for political action. "Learning" may mean discussing a service experience in class, writing journal entries about the underlying issues, or even conducting elaborate research studies.

There is no doubt that the best service-learning works. It not only enhances students' skills and interests, but changes their fundamental identities so that they become—and see themselves as—active citizens.[49] In the context of real public schools, however, service-learning often degenerates into cleaning the school playground and then briefly discussing this experience (or even making photocopies for the principal, and *not* discussing that work with anyone). The best evidence that *average* service-learning has positive effects is Kahne and Sporte's longitudinal study in the Chicago schools, which found a very substantial impact on students' commitment to civic participation.[50] Also Dávila and Mora found that students were more likely to finish high school and graduate from college if they had taken high school courses with mandatory community service—a rough proxy for service-learning.[51]

The federal government funds service-learning through a competitive grants program called Learn & Serve America. A 1999 evaluation found that the program had positive effects on students' civic attitudes, habits of volunteering, and success in school. However, the study was limited to "fully implemented" service-learning projects: ones that involved "substantial hours" of high-quality service, "face-to-face experience with service recipients," and opportunities for reflection. Out of 210 programs funded by Learn & Serve America that the evaluators had randomly selected for their study, only seventeen met the criteria for being "fully implemented," even though the rest would certainly call themselves "service-learning" and had won grants in a competitive process.[52] If all 210 programs had been included, it is not clear that the mean effects of service-learning would have been positive.

That research was conducted more than a decade ago. Practice has probably improved and become more consistent since then. In a smaller study published in 2005, Shelley Billig and colleagues found that average service-learning classes had slightly better civic outcomes than average social studies classes. Students who had been exposed to service-learning gained more knowledge of civics and government and felt more confident about their own civic skills, compared to a matched group of students who had taken conventional social studies classes. However, the apparent effects of service-learning were not positive for students' sense of their own community attachment or their own ability to make a difference. (Possibly, the difficulty of the projects they undertook turned them into pessimists about achieving social change). In any case, these mean results concealed very large differences between the best and worst service-learning. Some classes in Billig's small study that claimed to use service-learning produced notably poor results.[53]

In a public school setting, service-learning may degenerate for two reasons. First, to develop ambitious service projects is difficult and time-consuming; it requires skills, local knowledge, logistical support, patience, and energy. Second, public schools court controversy whenever their students engage in political advocacy and/or "faith-based" community action. Yet forbidding politics and religion drastically narrows the range of discussion and action; as a result, service-learning often becomes trivial.

Many of the best programs are found in Catholic high schools, where service experiences are connected to a challenging normative and spiritual worldview: post–Vatican II Catholic social thought. As Anthony Bryk and colleagues observe, "The formation of each student as a person-in-community is the central educational aim of [American Catholic] schools. From this perspective, schooling involves more than conveying the acquired knowledge of civilization to students and developing in them the intellectual skills they need to create new knowledge. Education also entails forming the basic disposition for citizenship in a democratic and pluralist society."[54] Thus service-learning in Catholic schools is combined with searching moral reflection, exhortation, and examples of commitment. There is no evidence that such programs cause their graduates to agree with the main doctrines of Catholic theology; but students do develop lasting engagement with their community.[55] However, the Catholic model cannot be replicated in public schools, which must be more normatively neutral and respectful of pluralism.

Service-learning is an example of an educational strategy that has strongly positive effects at its best, yet only the Kahne and Sporte study in Chicago has found that *average* practice is truly effective. Most of the best examples occur when teachers (and sometimes also students) are self-selected and highly motivated to try service-learning. There is nothing surprising here; motivated and talented people always provide the best education. They need to be supported and rewarded. However, we should not try to increase rapidly the prevalence of service-learning by *mandating* it or providing very generous funding for it. Rapidly increasing its frequency will simply reduce its quality. Instead, we should try to enhance quality and quantity simultaneously, by linking together motivated volunteers, studying what particular practices work best, recognizing and rewarding the excellent practitioners, and making sure that there are sufficient funds to support the best programs and to launch willing novices.

If a school superintendent asked me what the research shows about service-learning, I would say that it supports creating a small competitive grant program and providing voluntary opportunities for teachers, such as seminars on how to organize a community-service class. The research does not, at this time, support allocating a significant amount of money for service-learning or setting a high target for the rate of student participation. In this respect, service-learning is different from social studies teaching. Standard social studies classes are much more common than service-learning programs and are probably distributed in a normal curve, such that classes of average quality are most common. We can tell from exam results that the average-quality classes have positive effects. Thus I would advise a superintendent or a state official to mandate social studies classes for all students (while also trying to support or weed out the worst teachers and reward the best ones). I would regard service-learning differently: as something to be cherished and admired when it is done well, but not to be mandated.

Although it has not yet been evaluated rigorously, one form of service-learning seems—on the basis of my direct experience with it over several years—especially promising: public-interest research, also called community-based research or youth-led research. (Another closely related activity is youth media production: see 8.2.) Conducting research is consistent with the express purposes of public schools, so it is less controversial than political action. Yet research on public issues can be deeply motivating; it can influence identities and attitudes, not just knowledge. By asking students to study their own communities, we can help them to experience and prize the values of public service, empirical rigor, and critical inquiry. If they give away the fruits of their research, that is a rewarding form of "service."

7.5 EXTRACURRICULAR ACTIVITIES

They also serve who serve at home: for example, within their own school buildings. Almost any school houses a "civil society" composed of organized groups and various informal networks and interest groups. In CIRCLE's 2006 omnibus survey, 62 percent of high school students said that they were "currently participating in any organized groups or clubs in high school such as sports teams, band or chorus, language clubs, or the like." Thirty-one percent said that at least one of the groups to which they belonged was the student government or an "organization concerned with social or political issues." However, all of the most common types of groups (athletics, cheerleading, music, drama, debate, newspaper, yearbook, student government, subject matter clubs, and vocational clubs) drew smaller proportions of the high school population in 1992 than they had twenty years earlier—evidence of a decline in high school civil society during that period.[56]

All students should have opportunities to choose among groups that have serious functions and that are adequately supported with money, equipment, and adults' time. Many longitudinal studies have found lasting relationships between participation in school groups and voluntary membership in adulthood, even when one controls for individuals' characteristics before they entered high school. In some studies, membership in school groups turns out to be a better predictor of adult engagement than is education or income.[57] In turn, adult membership is valuable because voluntary associations do important public work, and their members tend to read the newspaper, vote, and otherwise engage. Thus to recruit students into satisfying extracurricular activities may help make them civic activists, news consumers, and voters, thirty or fifty years later. Presented with this argument at a meeting of the Campaign for the Civic Mission of Schools, Sandra Day O'Connor recalled that she had been a shy high school student until she joined a school group. She was then on a path to become an attorney, an influential state legislator, and the first woman associate justice of the Supreme Court.

There are several plausible reasons for the link between extracurricular participation and lifelong civic engagement. Belonging to school groups may build confidence, or it may be sufficiently satisfying that members develop a taste for participation. People may form networks in school groups that keep them connected to associations as they age. Not least is the educational value of extracurricular activities. In Larson's terminology, students can obtain opportunities for "initiative" by participating in voluntary, purposive, collective activities such as publishing a school newspaper or organizing a dance.[58] Further, as Elinor Ostrom notes, people must learn how to overcome the problems that beset all collective human enterprises: "At any time that individuals may gain from the costly action of others, without themselves contributing time and effort, they face collective action dilemmas for which there are coping methods. When de Tocqueville discussed the 'art and science of association,' he was referring to the crafts learned by those who had solved ways of engaging in collective action to achieve a joint benefit. Some aspects of the science of association are both counterintuitive and counterintentional, and thus must be taught to each generation as part of the culture of a democratic citizenry."[59] Extracurricular participation can teach people, among other things, how to keep records and chair meetings, how to respond when some members shirk their duties, how to handle a budget, how to persuade groups of peers, and how to advertise the benefits of an association to outsiders. Once these skills are learned, they enhance participation in civil society.

We are interested here in whether extracurricular participation helps make students into active and responsible democratic citizens. It is also worth noting that active and responsible civic participation in school helps young people succeed in other aspects of life. That argument may persuade school officials who are not focused on civic education to provide adequate extracurricular opportunities. Dávila and Mora found that "involvement in student government between 1990 and 1992 increased the odds of being a college graduate by 2000 by nearly 18 percentage points."[60] The Eccles and Barber study of "jocks," "brains," and "princesses" (cited in section 4.4, in connection to peer groups) also found strong and lasting correlations between participating in school groups and healthy development: namely, completing high school, succeeding in college, and avoiding drugs and alcohol. Most of the advantages could be explained by determining a student's identity at tenth grade (a factor not measured in the Dávila and Mora study). For example, self-described "jocks" in tenth grade had better chances of attending college but higher rates of alcohol abuse than other students (it did not matter much whether they actually played sports in high school; it was their identity and peer group that counted). However, the advantages of *pro-social* activities—volunteering and church attendance—were evident even after students' identities were controlled.[61]

Several studies have drawn a distinction between "instrumental" groups (those that exist to complete a task, such as publishing a yearbook or a newspaper or organizing student events) and "expressive" groups whose purposes are more intrinsic; the latter category includes athletics, cheerleading, music, and hobby clubs. I am not sure whether this distinction is conceptually clear, but as an empirical matter, membership in groups classified as instrumental predicts political participation, whereas membership in expressive groups does not. One explanation is that students who have to work together to fulfill a function for their community are most likely to develop civic skills.[62]

That finding argues that students should be asked to conduct important school business through voluntary associations such as student government and school media. However, Lopez and Moore, using recent data, found statistically significant, positive relationships between team sports (on the one hand) and volunteering, registering to vote, voting, watching the news, and feeling comfortable making statements at public meetings (on the other). These relationships remained after numerous background conditions were controlled. Apparently, sports are good for civic participation, contrary to some previous scholarship that was critical of athletics (but without using statistical models).[63] Lopez and Moore show that although sports is not "instrumental," not explicitly concerned with political or civic issues, and not particularly discursive or deliberative, it nevertheless seems to boost classic political behavior, such as voting.

We can only speculate about the causal mechanisms. (It could be, for example, that team members occasionally discuss politics before and after games. Or perhaps athletic participation teaches teamwork, which predisposes athletes to join other types of association, some of which are political. Or perhaps athletes gain confidence that encourages them to speak up at community meetings.) In any event, the study reinforces the premise that a wide range of student associations is valuable, and we should not merely support those whose missions are explicitly civic or political. People who participate in extracurricular activities are more likely than others to engage in community service (even once we adjust for background characteristics), which again suggests that being involved is a good thing, almost without regard to the form of involvement.[64]

Nonetheless, special attention should be given to activities that were invented during Dewey's lifetime with the explicit goal of enhancing civic development, especially scholastic journalism and elected student government. Evidence is strong that these activities build civic skills and values for their own members; unfortunately it is less clear that they benefit the whole student population. For example, our probit model based on the Knight Foundation Future of the First Amendment Study finds that students who work for scholastic newspapers hold more positive attitudes toward the press and free speech and consume more news. But whether a school has a student newspaper has no positive effects on average students' attitudes.[65] In the large, comprehensive, public high school where I have worked on after-school projects, members of the newspaper and government are almost completely insulated from the rest of the student body, which pays no attention to them. But obviously the student government and newspaper *could* be important civic resources for all members of a school community, promoting discussion of public issues and supporting other student groups.

In some schools, every student has a roughly equal opportunity to participate; in others, most are left out. In some schools, voluntary groups bridge race, ethnicity, culture, and class; in others, they divide students along those lines. In a given institution, the biggest and most influential groups may emphasize athletic competition, school pride, service, artistic creativity, cultural diversity, or political activism. I am not aware of research that allows us to assess the impact of the overall "ecosystem" of extracurricular groups. However, if we treat a school's collection of clubs as a microcosm of civil society, then some propositions about the adult nonprofit sector ought to apply. For adults, pluralism and choice are valuable; people cannot be "shepherded" into groups that others may consider most valuable.[66] Even more than adults, adolescents must experiment in order to develop their interests and identities; they should be able to try various roles even if we might not fully approve of them.[67] But even if individuals must be allowed to choose their groups, it is better when civil society cultivates what Robert Putnam calls "bridging social capital," not only "bonding social capital." That is, people ought to learn to work together with those different from themselves and develop trust and useful networks that "bridge" differences; they should not merely use associational membership to differentiate in-groups from out-groups.[68] In American schools, voluntary associations tend to be exclusive. Without being excessively manipulative, adults should foster "bridging" activities and groups.

7.6 SIMULATIONS

Service-learning and membership in school groups are ways for students to do actual public work. But there is also a long tradition of asking young people to play *simulated* civic roles. Traditional examples include moot trials, mock elections, model legislatures, and the Model United Nations program. More than half a million students cast ballots every four years in Scholastic's mock presidential election.[69] In one classroom experiment with an imaginary society, students became more tolerant when they observed the unfair effects of simple majority rule.[70]

More recently, computers have been used to help students simulate political situations. In one form of simulation, an individual student plays a leadership role in a historical or hypothetical situation, using software that someone else has written for that purpose. "Oregon Trail" was written in 1971 at Carleton College.[71] It went through various versions and refinements and was later released in popular commercial versions. Players pretended to be pioneers moving west from Independence, Missouri, in 1848. They presumably learned some facts about American history and some civic skills, such as how to negotiate with others (in this case, with computer-generated characters). Another illustrative title is the popular "SimCity" series, in which a player runs an imaginary town by setting the zoning rules and building the public infrastructure. The computer simulates the response of the private sector. To win is to achieve growth and prosperity with low crime.

In another genre of computer-assisted game, many human players interact via networked machines. These games can resemble traditional, face-to-face simulations (such as Model U.N.), but there are important potential differences. Thanks to computers, many more people can play simultaneously, the players can be strangers who are distributed across the globe, participants can face randomly generated events of some complexity, and the visual environment can be rich and complex. In ICONS (International Communication and Negotiation Simulations), students from various countries used such software to simulate diplomatic exchanges. A careful evaluation found that ICONS improved students' sophistication and complexity of thinking.[72]

In recent years, massive multiplayer role-playing games have become popular. Hundreds of thousands of students interact in simulated "worlds." Such simulations can be deliberately designed to teach civic skills. For example, they can have realistic political and economic systems, and winning can require working constructively with others. As an alternative, students could be encouraged to behave in civic ways within standard commercial games as part of class projects. In simulations that are saturated with violence, such as the so-called first-person shooter games, civic behavior would be suicidal. But there are popular environments that are basically nonviolent.

Finally, students could make their own computer-based simulations for civic purposes, thereby learning software skills while also thinking hard about social and political issues in the course of "modeling" an imaginary society. Unless students' products look reasonably professional, they will not be satisfying to play. Thirty years ago, talented students could write games (using the BASIC language) that were as appealing as the most popular ones in circulation. However, the degree to which students can compete with professional designers has changed: games have become more complex, but software languages have become more powerful and in some respects easier to handle. In decades to come, it is not clear whether most young people will feel empowered as game designers. If they are, then game design may be a powerful civic pedagogy.

There is a theoretical argument against using simulations for civic engagement. If young people have actual civic assets, then they should be called upon to play real roles in their communities, thereby learning that they can address serious issues. Asking them to pretend that they are legislators, diplomats, or litigators implies that they are not ready for real citizenship. Besides, those roles are rare enough that most students will not grow up to play them. A simulation might teach them that politics is remote from their real lives and prospects.

Nonetheless, that argument should be weighed against the important advantages of simulations. By creating controlled, imaginary environments, educators (who may include adolescents, as game designers) can ensure that players encounter complex, intellectually challenging problems, tailored to their developmental needs or to educational standards. I often recall sitting on the curb with a group of high school students, waiting in hundred-degree heat for a bus to take us to a service site. We were trying to accomplish real social change, but the failure of the bus ever to appear meant that we mainly experienced frustration. If we had remained inside the high school pretending to be lawyers, members of Congress, or delegates to the United Nations, we might have learned considerably more.

7.7 CONTROVERSIES IN SCHOOL-BASED CIVIC EDUCATION

The previous sections considered forms and venues of civic education in schools. I now turn to philosophical controversies that arise when schools attempt to teach citizenship. These controversies can arise whether the means of civic education is a class, a discussion, a service project, an extracurricular group, or a simulation.

Should Schools be Neutral?

One influential model of the civic educator is a classroom teacher who is careful not to steer her students toward any particular political views, but who tries to enhance their skills of deliberation, critical thinking, and participation. This approach takes open-endedness (see section 1.4) to be a moral obligation. The opposite approach would be to indoctrinate students, who are weaker and more impressionable than their teachers.

Open-endedness is an important aspect of *liberal* education. The root of the word "liberal" is *liberare*, "to make free"; helping young people to develop their own ideals is a good way to give them freedom. An open-ended approach to civic education seems especially consistent with the role of public schools, which often claim political and moral neutrality. They do so in part to defuse tensions in an increasingly pluralistic society, and in part as a response to modern First Amendment jurisprudence. Courts have banned many practices—from organized school prayers to the teaching of Intelligent Design in biology classes—on the ground that schools may not endorse a particular religion without violating the First Amendment's dictum that Congress "shall make no law respecting an establishment of religion." In opposing government salaries for Virginia's Anglican clergy, Thomas Jefferson said that "to compel a man to furnish contributions of money for the propagation of opinions which he disbelieves and abhors, is sinful and tyrannical."[73] Similarly, some believe that for schools to teach any religious doctrine would be tyrannical abuse of taxpayers, who are *required* to fund public education. Court decisions banning the endorsement of religion in schools have caused some Americans to believe that those schools are hostile to faith. Educators often respond that they are not neutral about religion alone, but about all controversial issues. Certainly, it would be a rare teacher or school administrator who would openly teach students to be Democrats or Republicans.

Even so, schools are never neutral about many values relevant to civic engagement. Typically, they teach obedience to authority, order and discipline, some degree of tolerance, and a set of facts and skills that have been selected, in part, because they seem to be preconditions of good citizenship. For example, a high school course in U.S. history is mandatory in thirty-four states and common in the rest.[74] But very few American high school students take a course in Chinese history. Educators and state governments have made judgments about what historical knowledge is most important for American citizenship.

Not only is neutrality impossible, it has a civic cost if it is pushed too far. Students who are taught that there are many opinions about every issue may draw the conclusion that there is never a right answer and that it doesn't matter which side one takes in a political debate. They are then unlikely to take any side with conviction or to act on their own political beliefs (if indeed they form any). Sometimes teachers who are committed to neutrality raise doubts about all available moral theories. But a course "that does no more than critique one theory after another may lead students to believe that all ethical perspectives are seriously flawed and that therefore all ethical questions are matters of personal taste and opinion."[75]

On the other hand, if students are exposed to teachers who believe and act on their own passionately held values, they may realize that impressive adults hold carefully considered political opinions that shape their lives. Students will probably not be brainwashed into agreeing with their teachers, but instead may be inspired to form views of their own. In *On Liberty* (1859), John Stuart Mill famously argued for free speech. His argument did not support neutrality as much as the value of experiencing passionate commitment:

> He who knows only his own side of the case, knows little of that. His reasons may be good, and no one may have been able to refute them. . . . Nor is it enough that he should hear the arguments of adversaries from his own teachers, presented as they state them, and accompanied by what they offer as refutations. That is not the way to do justice to the arguments, or bring them into real contact with his own mind. He must be able to hear them from persons who actually believe them; who defend them in earnest, and do their very utmost for them. He must know them in their most plausible and persuasive form; he must feel the whole force of the difficulty which the true view of the subject has to encounter and dispose of; else he will never really possess himself of the portion of truth which meets and removes that difficulty.[76]

Mill's account is consistent with Youniss and Yates's observations in a Catholic school in Washington, D.C. The teachers and the institution were hardly neutral. One instructor, "Mr. Swirek," demonstrated his liberalism by crossing himself and genuflecting whenever he mentioned the name "Franklin Roosevelt" and by saying that he wanted to "vomit" at the sight of a white woman who argued against a homeless shelter. Mr. Swirek, who was white himself, had been fired from two previous schools but played an important role in this institution, which was devoted to Catholic Social Justice doctrine.[77] It is clearly worth worrying about brainwashing in cases like this. Yet many students expressed disagreement with Mr. Swirek's views. His passion seemed to ignite controversy over such issues as homelessness, rather than automatic assent. Moreover, when alumni of his class were asked their opinions several years later, roughly equal numbers said that they agreed with and disagreed with the views that they had formed while in high school. There was evidence that their ideological views had evolved, but most remained civically engaged.[78]

Public schools face special pressures to be neutral. It is not appropriate for a public school teacher to teach that Jesus is the Lord (or that God is dead), nor should she try to make her students into Republicans or Democrats. But a single-minded dedication to moral and political neutrality is neither necessary nor helpful.

Should Schools Teach Patriotism?

One value that American schools explicitly endorse is patriotism. Reciting the pledge of allegiance is required in forty-three states,[79] and the pledge is hardly the schools' only vehicle for teaching patriotic sentiments. Even so, experts on education are, for the most part, leery of this goal. William Damon writes: "I would guess that patriotism is the most politically-incorrect word in education today. If you think it's hard to talk about morality and values in schools, try talking about patriotism. You really can't get away with it without provoking an argument or, at the least, a curt change of subject. Teachers too often confuse a patriotic love of country with the kind of militaristic chauvinism that 20th Century dictators used to justify warfare and manipulate their own masses. They do not seem to realize that it was the patriotic resistance to these dictatorships, by citizens of democratic republics such as our own, that saved the world from tyranny in the past century and is the best hope of doing so in the future."[80]

Along similar lines, Harry Brighouse quotes a British official, Nick Tate, who complains about his experience on a U.K. curriculum committee: "There was such a widespread association between national identity, patriotism, xenophobia, and racism that it was impossible to talk about the first two without being accused of the rest."[81] I believe Tate exaggerates. Several authors generally associated with the Left endorsed patriotic education—either enthusiastically or with some qualifications—in a special issue of *Phi Delta Kappan* devoted to that topic.[82] However, it is true that discussion of patriotism provokes some discomfort. The *Civic Mission of Schools* report (a consensus statement that I helped to organize) does not use the word at all.

The issue can be divided into two parts: Is patriotism a desirable attitude? Is it an attitude that should be promoted by public schools? I would answer both questions with a qualified yes.

Patriotism is love of country. For most people, it is not a passionate and exclusive and life-altering love. It's more like love for a blood relative, perhaps an aunt. It doesn't involve choice. It doesn't require a tremendously high estimate of the object's intrinsic qualities. (You may admire Mother Teresa more than your Aunt Teresa, but it is the latter you love.) It implies a sense of obligation, including an obligation to understand and be interested in the object. It also implies a sense of entitlement: you can expect your own aunt, or your nation, to help you in ways that others need not. Both the obligation and the entitlement arise because of a sense of identification, a "we-ness," a seeing of yourself in the object and vice versa.

I believe that people should love large human communities in this way. You may put your family first, but to love *only* them is too exclusive. Loving all of humankind is good, but it doesn't mean the same thing as love for a concrete object. For instance, you cannot have an obligation to know many details about humankind.

A nation works as an object of love. One can identify with it and feel consequent obligations and entitlements, including the obligation to know its history, culture, constitution, and geography. Love for a country inspires, enlarges one's sympathies, and gives one a sense of support and solidarity. I would not claim that these moral advantages follow *only* from loving a country. One can also love world Jewry, one's city, or one's fellow Rotarians. But love of country has some particular advantages.

First, patriotism may promote participation in national politics, including such acts as voting, joining national social movements, litigating in federal court, and enlisting in the military or serving in the civil service.[83] In turn, broad participation makes national politics work better and more justly. And national politics is important, because national institutions have supremacy. A system that devolved more power to localities would need less national participation, and hence less patriotism. But it would have its own disadvantages.

Second, patriotism is a flexible concept, subject to fruitful debate. Consider what love of America meant for Woody Guthrie, Francis Bellamy (the Christian socialist author of the Pledge of Allegiance), Frederick Douglass (author of a great 1852 Independence Day speech), Nathan Hale, Presidents Lincoln and Reagan, J. Edgar Hoover, Saul Bellow, or Richard Rorty. All these men believed that they could make effective political arguments by citing—and redefining—patriotic sentiments. One could argue that their rhetoric obfuscated: they should have defended their core values without mixing in patriotic sentiments. Brighouse complains that patriotism can be "used to interrupt the flow of free and rational political debate within a country."[84] But there may not be stand-alone arguments for all moral principles. Rather, reasonable political debate involves allusions and reinterpretions of shared traditions, and patriotism provides a rich and diverse store.

Third, a democratic government can legitimately decide to instill love of country, whereas it cannot legitimately make people love world Jewry or the Rotary Club. Local democratic governments can also promote love of their own local communities (common enough) but such efforts do not negate the right of a national democracy to promote patriotism.

Fourth, patriotism has a role in a theory of human development that Damon has defended.[85] This theory holds that being strongly attached to a community or nation as a child increases the odds that you will care enough about it to scrutinize it critically when you become a young adult. In my own case, as a young boy in the Nixon era, I thought G-men were heroes and wanted to be one. Now I am a strong civil libertarian. I believe my initial attachment to the United States has kept me from simply withdrawing from it. But I am just one person—and a white, male, middle-class person who has been treated justly by the state. Damon's developmental theory may not work as well for children who face evident injustice.

As a moral sentiment, patriotism has benefits. But it can also encourage exclusivity or an illegitimate preference for one's fellow citizens over other human beings. Like all forms of love, it can blind you to faults. These problems are serious, but they can be addressed. After all, some forms of American patriotism identify our particular nation with inclusiveness and the fair treatment of foreign countries.

The teaching of patriotism in public schools raises special problems, several of which Harry Brighouse explores. Here I mention the two most serious concerns. First, legitimate government rests on the sincere or authentic consent of the governed. If the state uses its great power over public school students to promote love of itself, that consent is inauthentic. Brighouse writes: "the education system is an agent of the state; if we allow the state to use that system to produce sentiments in the populace which are designed to win consent for it, it thereby taints whatever consent it subsequently enjoys as being non-legitimizing."[86]

State power is a serious concern, requiring constant vigilance; but I believe it should be put in context. Schools do not have a monopoly on students' attention. They compete against politicians (many of whom love to denounce the national government), religious leaders (who believe that true sovereignty is God's), and big commercial advertisers (who promote consumption instead of political engagement). Within schools there are plenty of teachers and administrators who hold negative views of the national government. I think the dangers of brainwashing are slight, and it remains helpful to present students with an ideal—patriotism in its various forms—that they and their teachers can argue with.

Second, Brighouse fears that a patriotic presentation of history requires whitewashing and distorting the truth about what happened and why. For instance, "an educator who has anywhere in her mind the purposes of instilling love of country will have a hard time teaching about the causal process which led up to the Civil War in the US."[87] That is because pursuit of the truth requires one to consider that the Civil War was perhaps fought for economic reasons—a dispiriting thought for a patriot. Likewise, Brighouse thinks that textbooks depict Rosa Parks as a "tired seamstress" instead of a "political agitator" because the former view (while false) better supports patriotism."[88]

Obviously, Brighouse has a point, but a close look at his cases shows how complicated the issue is. For example, as an American patriot, I find it deeply moving that Rosa Parks was trained at the Highlander Folk School, whose founder, Miles Horton, was inspired by Jane Addams, whose father, John (double-D) Addams was a young colleague and follower of Abe Lincoln in the Illinois State Legislature.[89] That is only one lineage and heritage in the story of Rosa Parks. It is, however, a deeply American and patriotically "Whiggish" one—and it's truer than the cliché of a tired seamstress. It connects Parks to the profound patriotism of Lincoln (who redefined the American past at Gettysburg) and the pacifist patriotism of Jane Addams.

In any case, why study Parks at all unless one has a special attachment to the United States? If the issue is simply nonviolence, then one should study Aung San Suu Kyi, the Burmese human rights advocate, who is still very much alive and in need of support. I believe every young American should know the true story of Rosa Parks, and my reasons are essentially patriotic.

To put the matter more generally: history should be taught truthfully, but it must also be taught selectively. There is no such thing as a neutral or truly random selection of topics. Selecting topics in order to promote patriotism seems fine to me, as long as the love of country that we promote is a realistic one with ethical limitations.

Finally, the causal mechanisms here are unpredictable. Ham-fisted efforts to make children patriotic can backfire. But rigorous investigations of history can make students patriotic. I often think of my own experience helping local students (all children of color) conduct oral-history interviews about segregation in their own school system. They learned that people like them had been deliberately excluded for generations. They took away the lesson that their schools were worth fighting over, that kids could play an active role in history, and that their community was interesting. One girl told a friend from the more affluent neighboring county, "You have the Mall, but we have the history!"

Again, the purpose of our lesson was not simply to teach historical truth and method, but also to increase students' attachment to a community. We were like educators who try to inculcate patriotism, except that we were interested in a county rather than the nation. Our pedagogy involved helping kids to uncover a history of *injustice*. The result was an increase in local attachment. The moral is that truth and patriotism may have a complex and contingent relationship, but they are not enemies.

"Constructivism" in Civic Education

"Constructivism" is one of the most influential words in the whole jargon of education—and a highly divisive one. It is a rallying cry for many progressive educators and reformers, but an irritant to conservatives. Constructivists oppose the kind of scene in which a teacher stands before a disciplined class of children and endlessly tells them what is true. But they oppose that pedagogy for a variety of overlapping reasons, some of which I find more persuasive than others.

Constructivism can be analyzed into the following components:

Creativity: Constructivists often see traditional pedagogy as
   excessively passive, because children are given everything

ready-made in textbooks or by teachers. They want children to be creative, to generate their own works of art, narratives (including factual ones), rules and norms, clubs and other organizations, and social or service projects.

Child-centeredness: Constructivists often want educators to recognize the interests, goals, and "learning styles" of children at particular ages and in particular communities. Teachers are then supposed to tailor classroom experiences in order to capture students' imaginations and interests. Education should "start where the kids are."

Pluralism: Constructivists emphasize that interests, values, and dispositions differ according to the culture, gender, and social class of students. Thus they oppose standardization, as epitomized by textbooks and "standardized" tests.

Experimentalism: Some constructivists want children to discover facts and methods through experimentation, not wait to be given answers. So, for example, it is better for students to rediscover an algorithm for solving a type of mathematical problem than simply to be taught how to solve it. According to constructivists, children will remember and be able to apply the method better if they have "made" it themselves.

Holism: Constructivists oppose the separation of intellectual learning from social and emotional learning and ethical development. They see traditional pedagogy as narrow and dismissive of the "whole child."

Democracy: Many constructivists argue that democracy should not only be an outcome of education, but an integral part of it. Students should share authority and responsibility in schools and classrooms (to various degrees) with adults.

Relativism/Skepticism: It is very common for constructivists to deny explicitly that there is any objective truth. They claim that people or cultures "construct" their own truths. If many truths have been constructed, none is more objective or valid than the others.

These components are not logically identical. For example, one could favor creativity as a core normative value. It is, however, an empirical question whether children use and remember knowledge best if they have rediscovered it for themselves. This may only be true of some knowledge and some children. Likewise, it is an empirical question whether democratically organized classrooms and schools produce the most competent and committed democratic citizens. They may or they may not.

For proponents of civic education, relativism is a problematic part of the constructivist package. Constructivists often deploy a relativist "epistemology" in the belief that it supports their practices. They favor creativity, democracy, experimentalism, holism, pluralism, and child-centeredness. They see positivism as the enemy of all these good things, and relativism as the one alternative to positivism that can support their pedagogy. The classic positivists believed that there were objective, verifiable, empirical (or "positive") facts, in contrast to theories, values, and metaphysical statements, which were merely subjective. In contrast, "constructivists hypothesize that it is the subject who actually invents reality and that knowledge is tied to an internal-subjective perspective where truth is replaced by ways of knowing."[90]

But reality is obdurate. We can invent some things, but other things are real whether we like them or not. Although classical positivism is flawed, there are many ways to defend objectivity without being a positivist. No serious thinker has ever believed that the objective world is obvious, directly apprehended by reason, and uncontroversial. But denying it would be equally foolish. Thus I am very unimpressed by assertions that "subjects invent reality."

Moreover, I think it is ethically bankrupt to pretend that people or groups can and should make up their own worlds. There are many white communities in which everyone would like to believe that chattel slavery was pleasant—or, at the very least, would like to ignore it completely. The vicious wickedness of slavery is not part of their lifeworld. But it should be. If everyone "constructs" reality and individuals may decide what knowledge they want to create, then we have no right to challenge people to face uncomfortable realities.

People who are concerned with civic education, it seems to me, should be constructivists only to the extent that constructivist methods actually enhance civic learning, which is an empirical question. And we should drop epistemological relativism altogether.

7.8 IMPLICATIONS FOR POLICY

In the preceding sections of this chapter, I have argued that it is important to preserve and expand civics courses, service-learning programs, and extracurricular organizations in schools and to give students appropriate "voice" in their own education. Of course, the sheer number of opportunities is not the only important question; quality also matters. We need service-learning programs that truly stretch the minds of students and address authentic issues; extracurricular activities that engage a broad range of students in meaningful activities and connect them to voluntary associations; and teachers who are prepared to explore perennial and emerging issues of politics and justice and to use experiential methods such as projects, debates, and simulations. (It is also important to continue teachers' education about democracy after their careers have begun. Torney-Purta and colleagues find "a statistically significant and relatively substantial effect" on students when educational programs are offered to practicing teachers.)[91]

When Americans discuss what makes a civics class or service program good, they disagree about matters of principle, such as whether teachers should promote patriotism and other values. I have taken a stance on some of these debates, but I think that we should be pluralists and federalists and welcome a fair amount of diversity in civics curricula and teaching across the country. Most important is to invest schools' time and money in courses, service opportunities, and extracurricular activities and to encourage teachers and other educators to think and care about civic themes.

We must worry about *equality* as well as quantity and quality. Civic education is preparation for a democratic system in which all are supposed to be equal. Student government is an example of a civic opportunity that is much more likely to exist in schools in upper-income areas. Some programs mainly serve high-performing schools with college-bound students. They may improve the quantity and average quality of civic education but lower equality.

As we seek to promote schools' civic mission, we must confront the most powerful trend in education: the standards-and-accountability movement. Beginning in the 1980s in some Southern states, this movement called for students to be regularly tested in core academic subjects, especially reading, writing, mathematics, and science. Benefits and penalties were established for students, teachers, schools, and/or states depending on their performance on these pencil-and-paper exams. That movement culminated in the No Child Left Behind (NCLB) Act of 2002. Among other things, NCLB requires all students to be tested annually in reading and mathematics—and regularly in science— between third and eighth grade.

There are arguments in favor and against NCLB as a means of achieving its stated goals of enhancing student outcomes in reading, math, and science. If it were successful, it would benefit democracy, because basic educational success predicts political participation. I am not sure whether it will achieve its explicit goals. For the purposes of *civic* education, however, NCLB raises at least four serious obstacles.

First, teachers and schools spend time on what they must test, especially if the tests have high stakes. NCLB requires testing in three major subject areas but not in civics, history, or government. There is evidence that school districts are cutting those subjects to devote time to the material mandated for regular high-stakes exams. In 2006, the Center for Education Policy found, "To make more time for reading and math in elementary schools, districts cut time for social studies (reduced to a great extent or somewhat by 33% of districts), science (29% of districts), and art and music (22%), among other subjects or activities." One respondent to the CEP survey of administrators said, "[NCLB] has torn apart our social studies curriculum. We are raising tomorrow's leaders and [it's] forcing us to fill their heads with math facts that do not make them better leaders or help students make choices.[92] This trend puts advocates of civic education in a bind. Students are already spending so much time on pencil-and-paper tests—and schools are facing so many unfunded mandates from the federal government—that it seems irresponsible to add a civics test to NCLB. On the other hand, if there is no required civics test, courses will be phased out in many schools.

Second, pencil-and-paper tests measure only skills and knowledge. It is unfortunate if tests drive the curriculum, because we should also seek to impart attitudes, values, habits, and behaviors. It is no solution to add questions about values to our high-stakes written tests. Students can easily provide the desired answers without actually holding the desired values, which makes the tests unreliable. There is also an ethical problem with testing values. I believe, for instance, that we should teach young people to vote, yet we should not penalize those who oppose voting because they hold religious or political objections to the current regime.

Third, the whole framework of NCLB embodies a "deficits" approach. Schools are required to identify students who are failing and intervene to correct their problems. The law does not require anyone to provide positive opportunities, even though the theory of positive youth development suggests that some of the act's explicit goals (such as reducing the high school dropout rate) would be better served by making sure that every student had opportunities to serve, create, collaborate, and lead.

Fourth, NCLB constrains the choices that are available to schools and local communities. It commands a set of essential goals: students must complete high school and pass written tests in a limited set of subjects. But Americans place *other* goals higher on their own agendas for schools.[93] If parents, teachers, other citizens, and students wish to deliberate about what they want their local schools to accomplish, they may find that this discussion is moot; NCLB has already decided. The act's peremptoriness is unfortunate: discussion about goals and priorities would itself be a form of civic education, especially if students were encouraged to participate.

In my view, the basic structure of NCLB is likely to remain in place for at least a decade. It is the outcome of powerful political vectors that originated from both the Democratic and Republican side. Despite disgruntlement in certain quarters, I do not expect it to be repealed. Besides, it is at least plausible that the act, suitably revised and better funded, would increase students' basic academic performance and reduce educational inequality.

Thus I believe we need creative and constructive ways to enhance civic education within the basic framework of NCLB. One idea would be to add a mandatory civics examination *without* increasing the net amount of testing that any student faces during his or her school career. The act could allow states and localities to meet that mandate in several ways, but two approaches are obvious. A civics test could replace one of the subjects that are now mandatory at a particular grade level; or existing tests of reading, writing, and mathematics could be revised to incorporate enough questions about political and historical themes that it would be possible to derive a reliable "civics" score for each student. This reform would motivate schools to enhance students' civic knowledge, but not their civic values, habits, or attitudes. Knowledge is worth enhancing because it is intrinsically valuable as well as an important precondition of effective civic action.

A second idea is to argue that schools should use civic *means* to attain the existing *ends* of NCLB. For example, NCLB requires all American students to pass reading examinations. Those tests already include passages about history and social issues. Some research finds that students need specific experience in interpreting material about politics, history, or social issues before they can handle it on an examination. Partly because of the emphasis on "decoding," and partly because textbook publishers are afraid of controversy, almost all political and social themes have been stripped out of elementary reading texts, which are mostly stories about furry animals or small children in domestic settings. First graders spend less than three minutes per school day reading texts that are rich in information about *any* topic, from dinosaurs to pilgrims.[94] But it is not enough to have read anodyne fictional texts if one is confronted with a passage about Martin Luther King or the Second World War on an exam. Such passages will use specialized vocabulary and allude to background knowledge.

In order to motivate students to read and understand texts (fictional or nonfictional) about social and political themes, it might be wise to make the instruction experiential: to include mock elections, field trips, and service projects. Thus experiential civic education can be used as a way to meet the current NCLB mandates in reading.[95]

NCLB also requires schools to raise high school graduation rates. According to the theory of positive youth development, students are more likely to graduate if they engage in extracurricular activities and service projects and have opportunities to exercise "voice" in their schools. Such directed autonomy would be another example of using civic education as a means to comply with NCLB as currently written.

Given the state of the existing research, the U.S. Department of Education and other authorities cannot yet tell schools to employ civic means to comply with NCLB. Nonetheless, the research is suggestive enough that the federal government at least ought to fund randomized field experiments to test whether civic education would raise reading scores and high school graduation rates.

CHAPTER 8

Civic Learning in Communities

Schools are crucial venues for civic education because they reach almost all children and adolescents and have (in the aggregate) enormous resources that can be used either to promote or to frustrate civic development. Nevertheless, civic education must not occur in schools alone. Community-based organizations have more flexibility to innovate and develop programs, some of which may ultimately migrate to schools. By serving young people who elect to join, they can cement political and civic dispositions and thereby strengthen a cadre of young civic leaders who will, in turn, influence their peers. These organizations can connect young people to institutions, such as churches and municipal agencies, that will remain important in their adult lives.

Community-based organizations are relatively free of political limits that inevitably constrain public schools. For example, Raices is an initiative of the Main Street Project that helps Latino youth in rural Midwestern communities to create digital media. Amalia Anderson, director of the initiative, told me that "our media work is grounded in a right to communicate, to challenge the camera as a tool of colonization, and to use our voices to speak truth to power as well as preserve and protect our culture, languages and identity."[1] That would be a hard set of assumptions to implement in a mainstream public school—as would the premises of a conservative Christian group like Redeem the Vote, whose mission is "to engage America's young people of faith in the political process and educate them on issues pertinent to their lives."[2] Whether you agree with either group's ideology, both exemplify freedom of speech and association and serve young people who hold congruent values.

Furthermore, because they can take on political causes, community-based groups do not artificially separate service from activism. Jane Addams helped provide a rich set of opportunities for learning, service, and politics at Hull-House. She resisted merging that institution with any university, school system, or other large institution, for fear that its independence and democratic character would be lost. As Daynes and Longo write, "Addams' work is a valuable reminder that service-learning may be understood not only as an educational technique, but also as an agile approach to learning whose greatest value is the unpredictable creativity that it brings to public life."[3] This is an argument, they think, for doing at least some service-learning not in schools but in community groups that can decide to move, at times, from service to protest or advocacy.

If many organizations are involved in civic education, there can be greater coordination and less damaging dissonance among aspects of young people's lives. If, for example, students are taught in their social studies classes that they are part of a responsive democracy, yet the municipal government discourages their participation, the net effect may be cynicism. On the other hand, it is valuable when government and community groups *reinforce* the civic lessons that students learn in school. It is not only important to send consistent messages for the sake of credibility; it's also important for students to learn how to "connect" with more than one type of organization and to "navigate" their way through many settings while pursuing a coherent agenda.[4] When schools are the only venues in which they do civic work, they do not gain those skills. As Karen Pittman often says, "Young people do not grow up in programs; they grow up in communities."[5]

Finally, community-based civic education is essential if we view the education of the next generation as a community function—as a matter of deliberating and transmitting values and skills to the next generation—rather than a specialized task reserved for full-time professional schoolteachers. When adults participate in civic education as Big Brothers or Big Sisters, scout leaders, Sunday school volunteers, librarians, coaches, and community activists, they have the experience and stature to participate in local debates about youth and to collaborate with schools. On the other hand, if professional employees of schools are the main educators, then other adults take deferential roles as episodic volunteers, clients, and voters.

I would hypothesize that when many adults—and adolescents—are active as educators, young people gain better civic skills, knowledge, and habits. The relationship between broad participation and student outcomes is an empirical matter for which the evidence is limited but promising (see 2.4). Even so, that causal hypothesis is not the only argument for encouraging citizens to play active roles as educators. People in many walks and stages of life have the *right* to contribute to the common task of reproducing the culture through education. Distributing the locus of education around the community is not merely a way to prepare students for citizenship; it is also a way to make citizenship itself more worthwhile.

The venues for civic education are too numerous to investigate here. A full list would include churches and other religious denominations, labor unions, apprenticeship programs and other jobs, military service, and prisons. The existing research on these institutions varies. For example, much has been written about the effects of religious attendance on civic development, although less on the nuts and bolts of what makes a civic education program effective in a church or other congregation.[6] I am not aware of adequate, relevant research on the military or the penal justice system, even though both institutions are influential and subject to policy change. In this chapter, I focus on organizations that are reasonably well researched *and* amenable to change through public policy: community-based groups that explicitly teach civic engagement using public funds, youth media groups, and municipal agencies.

I intend these three short studies not to be exhaustive, but to represent examples of community-based civic education. In each community, it is important for the various efforts to be made as coherent as possible—while respecting diversity and freedom of association. There have been some promising efforts to bring voluntary coherence at the community level. For example, adolescents in the Saint Paul [Minnesota] West Side Neighborhood Learning Community have identified a multitude of "learning opportunities" in their area. Their research has been the basis of some practical initiatives: an institute for adults who want "to build bridges between formal and informal learning opportunities," "a free bus that provides transportation among learning sites and public places in the neighborhood," and an apprenticeship program that provides youth training in nonprofits and businesses.[7] The Neighborhood Learning Community exemplifies *youth-led research* as well as an effort to coordinate civic education across a community.

8.1 COMMUNITY YOUTH DEVELOPMENT
IN AFTER-SCHOOL SETTINGS

In chapter 6, section 6.2, I summarized positive youth development. This philosophy holds that adolescents are not incomplete adults who are especially prone to various pathologies. Instead, by virtue of their energy, enthusiasm, and fresh outlook, they have special contributions to make: aesthetic, spiritual, athletic, intellectual, and civic. By giving them opportunities to contribute, we actually reduce their odds of getting into trouble more than we would through prevention, surveillance, and discipline.

In principle, there is no reason why this approach should be the province of private associations rather than schools. In fact, if the evidence for positive youth development proves robust, it should become an organizing principle of public schools, thereby reaching millions of young people. However, standard K-12 schools have always been quite hostile to positive youth development and have become more so thanks to recent trends in educational reform. For example, as I noted in section 4.2, schools are more likely to address the serious problem of high school dropouts by testing students in phonics at grade three than by providing adolescents (or young children) with opportunities for creative and constructive participation. In one survey of after-school programs in Chicago, 65 percent of the ones that were based in nonprofit organizations said that young people's civic engagement was a priority, whereas "none of the programs sponsored by the public school or parks district [said] civic engagement [was] a primary outcome."[8]

As the Chicago survey suggests, positive youth development is rare in schools, but it has become a byword in youth-serving voluntary organizations, led by the National 4-H movement, the Boy Scouts, the Girl Scouts, and Big Brothers/Big Sisters of America. When the positive opportunities offered to adolescents include service, community-based research, or political activism, adults often speak of "community youth development." A small subset of those organizations involve youth in political change; they often go under the heading of "youth organizing."[9]

For example, teenagers in Sistas and Brothas United (SBU) have documented the need for better school facilities by showing the New York City Schools chancellor and the local press photographs of "all the things that was messed up—the doors, broken hanging lights, how easily the handrails to the escalators came off, the broken fire alarms, broken steps."[10] Through Community Law in Action (CLIA), Baltimore high school students have collected evidence in support of class-action lawsuits. They were able to force the removal of alcohol and tobacco billboards from their neighborhood and identified violations of the Americans with Disabilities Act in their own schools, among other achievements.[11] The Youth and Farm Market Project operates community gardens in Minneapolis and Saint Paul, sells produce, and works to improve nutrition and provide vegetables and herbs that immigrants need to cook their traditional foods.[12]

These are appealing and highly civic projects chosen, almost at random, from a field that is large and various. In 1998, Judith Erickson identified about five hundred national groups and seventeen thousand state and local ones that provided youth development programs.[13] They were a mixed bag, however, as Roth and Brooks-Gunn's survey of seventy-one such organizations found. Almost all (92 percent) strove to reduce risky behavior such as drug abuse and violence. Two-thirds did so, in part, by offering service opportunities—a sign that they used community youth development. Service was less common than training in "life-skills" and recreational activities, but more common than job placements and remedial education. Most programs also claimed that youth were involved in decision-making. However, on a typical day, in 83 percent of the programs, youth did not participate in a planning meeting, receive training to prepare for a specific experience, or conduct any community service. Only 4 percent of the programs listed as one of their goals helping students to become "advocates."[14]

Most after-school programming exists for reasons other than civic engagement. Perhaps the biggest motive is to change adolescents' use of their discretionary time so that their voluntary activities are less likely to damage their development and more likely to teach them skills and habits useful for college and work. The title of the Carnegie Corporation's major 1992 report reflected this agenda: *A Matter of Time: Risks and Opportunities in the Nonschool Hours.*[15] In 1998, the Clinton administration used the $40 million Community Schools program to "provide expanded learning opportunities for children in a safe, drug-free and supervised environment." Some of those learning opportunities (for example, service projects) were explicitly civic, and others may have had civic benefits because participants became members of small, voluntary groups. In 2002, the Bush administration renamed the program "21st Century Community Learning Centers," expanded the funding to $1 billion, and supported thousands of schools and community-based organizations to provide after-school programs. Now, however, the funds were available only for "academic enrichment" and state agencies were required to assess outcomes.[16] In other words, after-school programming was dramatically expanded but its focus narrowed. Meanwhile, independent organizations like 4-H continued to provide opportunities for service, leadership, and social change without money from the 21st Century Learning Communities program. At this point, it would be valuable to maintain the funding for after-school programs and make civic projects eligible.

8.2 DIGITAL MEDIA CREATION

Some of the after-school programs devoted to positive youth development help teenagers to create "media"—public performances, magazines, broadcasts, artworks, and maps—for the benefit of their communities. This is not a novel concept. Shakespeare's most serious financial competition came from a group of young boys called the "Children of Queen Anne's Revels," who performed plays that had political implications. In fact, the Children were jailed in 1605 for performing a passage in *Eastward Ho* (by Ben Jonson and others) that offended King James I. Much more recently, since the invention of motion pictures, independent nonprofit groups have helped youth to make political documentaries. As I argued in chapter 2, section 2.6, the creation of cultural products is an integral part of civic engagement and a sign of a healthy democracy.

Starting in the late 1980s, digital technology opened new possibilities. Digital still cameras, video cameras, and audio recorders lowered the costs and difficulty of production; the Internet (Web-sites and e-mail) made it much cheaper to distribute products; and search engines enabled people to find materials they wanted instead of the limited supply traditionally available on broadcast channels. The result was a certain euphoria about the demise of mass media and its imminent replacement by an egalitarian, pluralist public sphere. As Justice Stevens observed in *Reno v. American Civil Liberties Union* (1997), "Through the use of chat rooms, any person with a phone line can become a town crier with a voice that resonates farther than it could from any soapbox. Through the use of Web pages, mail exploders, and newsgroups, the same individual can become a pamphleteer. As the District Court found, 'the content on the Internet is as diverse as human thought.'"[17]

Nonprofits began to give young people tools (now relatively inexpensive) and training so that they could make their own movies, audio files, photo galleries, and discussion forums and post them on the Internet for others to find. Often the idea was to enable students to generate speech that was not "free" (in the sense of requiring no money or effort) but that was relatively affordable—yet ambitious. At least some people dreamed that youth might help overthrow the monopoly of commercial mass media and become major producers of culture and free participants in the political dialogue. Yochai Benkler calls this "mid-1990s utopianism."[18]

Projects proliferated in schools, after-school programs that used schools' facilities, and community groups. Funds came from private foundations, local governments, and the federal government through the E-rate program, which subsidized equipment in schools and libraries, and the Technology Opportunities Program, which funded community-based groups. There was always a "digital divide"—a gap in the technological resources and training available to people of different socioeconomic backgrounds—but the divide narrowed after 1995.[19] It seemed possible to give at least the young people who enrolled in community programs all the tools they needed to compete directly with mass media.

It is difficult to conduct a census of such projects or to construct a representative sample in order to make generalizations about them. However, Kathryn Montgomery and her colleagues published a qualitative assessment of scores of sites in 2004,[20] and many of the projects described in their study were *not* among the hundreds that applied for small grants from J-Lab (Center for Interactive Journalism) when I served on the J-Lab selection committee in 2004 and 2005. J-Lab attracted so many applications that it was possible to discern clusters of activity: for example, quite a few community-based groups in various neighborhoods of Chicago applied separately to create Web sites about gentrification in their areas. In the Knight Foundation's Future of the First Amendment survey (2005), 21 percent of randomly selected high schools said that they had a "Student Internet or World-Wide Web publication with a news component that requires students to make judgments about what is newsworthy."[21] Given the goals of the Knight survey, the question was framed so that it missed some other forms of digital media production. Nevertheless, the existence of student-edited Web sites in at least one-fifth of high schools was further evidence that youth media production had become widespread by the early 2000s and had migrated into schools—as the best community-based work should.

However, several developments have dampened many people's optimism. As Benkler notes, "It is common today to think of the 1990s, out of which came the Supreme Court's opinion in *Reno v. ACLU,* as a time of naïve optimism about the Internet, expressing in political optimism the same enthusiasm that drove the stock market bubble, with the same degree of justifiability. An ideal liberal public sphere did not, in fact, burst into being from the Internet, fully grown like Athena from the forehead of Zeus."[22] Benkler explores many reasons for pessimism, ultimately concluding that the Internet, despite its limitations, has helped to create a better public sphere than the mass media system that preceded it. For the purposes of this chapter, I focus on several developments that are especially relevant to youth media projects.

In 1995, with help from a knowledgeable peer or adult, any ordinary group of adolescents could hope to construct a site that looked as good as one owned by a newspaper or a retail chain. Professional graphic designers had not yet made corporate sites look especially appealing, and skilled programmers had not yet made them technically complex. Furthermore, in keeping with the "commons" ethos of the early Internet, one could copy innovative features of other people's Web sites. Anyone could see the underlying "source code" of any site and paste it into her own. However, once major corporations began to construct Web sites in the second half of the 1990s, they made their online products technologically complex and graphically appealing. Companies also protected their innovations with patents and with technology that blocked copying. Microsoft assisted by engineering its software for viewing Web sites and videos in such a way as to reduce transparency.[23] As a result, most youth-generated sites began to look distinctly amateurish compared to corporate sites, and young people gravitated to venues where they could watch professional music videos, purchase clothes, or participate in huge discussion boards.

Sites were now numbered in the billions, but some were far more popular than others. They displayed a "power-law" distribution, in which a tiny proportion had a large fraction of the audience, and most sites received virtually no traffic. The popularity of a site is determined by the number of links that refer to it, because people move along links, and search engines show highly linked sites at the top of their results. Unfortunately, as Benkler notes, "there is a tiny probability that any given Web site will be linked to by a huge number of people, and a very large probability that for a given Web site only one other site, or even no site, will link to it."[24] At the time of writing, the median blog tracked by Truth Laid Bear (a popular ranking service) has two incoming links, whereas the top blog has 4,201. This skewed distribution might be acceptable if the most popular sites were also the best, and if newcomers had a chance to compete. But it is hard to believe, for example, that Instapundit is *thousands* of times better than the average conservative blog with which it competes. It receives more than 100,000 visitors each day, probably because it established early market dominance; now people visit it to see what other people are reading. They also link to it in the hope that Glenn Reynolds, Instapundit's owner, will link back to their commentary. (Reynolds is known as the "BlogFather" for his ability to make other sites temporarily popular by mentioning them.)

The power-law distribution is relevant to youth media production because it means that young people are unlikely to find an audience even if they work hard on a video project, an audio file, or a photo montage and post it on a Web site. There is too much competition, and the field is far from level. Yet young people *want* an audience so that they can get feedback and feel an impact. Global Action Project (GAP) is an independent nonprofit that teaches media production to youth in several countries so that they can "use their media as a catalyst for dialogue and social change."[25] In response to my query, Megan McDermott, the GAP director, asked a group of participants whether and why an audience was important to them. According to her notes, they said that they needed people to watch their videos in order to affect the social issues that concerned them: "Because that's how we're going to make it work to open up the audience's eyes." Students also wanted "honest" feedback from an attentive group, "because it lets you know if your video is hot or not. . . . . They give feedback and point out things you might miss in your own film. They give feedback that might be good and can make your video or film better."[26]

As sites were becoming more numerous and only a few were gaining huge audiences, a third important development occurred. New software was invented to allow people to put material online without much work, and sometimes without any marginal financial cost beyond an Internet connection. For example, early blogs were Web sites that the owners bought, designed, and laboriously updated, which meant that they had to know something about the software language of the World Wide Web. But a service like Blogger provides free blogs that users can automatically design (by choosing customizable templates) and up-date. In the same category belong Flickr and other sites on which one can easily post photographs; "podcasting" sites such as YouTube, through which one can distribute short videos; and social networking services such as MySpace and Friendster. A service like MySpace allows anyone to create a personalized Web site in a few minutes without knowing any-thing about software. Because many millions of other people also have MySpace sites, and they are interlinked, each participant immediately becomes part of a much larger complex. MySpace is the third most popu-lar website in the United States at the time of writing.[27]

These innovations massively increased the number of Web sites, and hence the competition for audiences. But they also reduced the costs of building a Web site; and hence the disappointment when only a few people visited. Most (62 percent) of adolescents who read blogs say that they only read blogs by people they already know.[28] That is no cause for disappointment, because creating a blog need take no more than five minutes. No one expects that it will dethrone major media companies or capture Instapundit's audience; it is simply a way to com-municate with friends.

Luke Walker, education project manager of TakingITGlobal, writes: "The 'old' model of spending hours/days/weeks creating a web site, se-curing server space, and sharing it for all (or no one) to see is both out-dated and largely irrelevant for the average young person, although it's still happening far too often in the school context. As long as that is the production model that teachers are using in their classes, then . . . we are setting children up for failure and disappointment—particularly if we're stopping at the point of posting the content on the web (where many people's knowledge/expertise ends) and not teaching students to employ all the marketing tactics that make commercial/mainstream/high-profile websites successful. More and more, though, young people are moving away from traditional websites to creating a presence in so-cial networking spaces like MySpace."[29]

Given these trends, I think the world of youth media production is about to change dramatically. One option is to abandon elaborate proj-ects and simply help young people to use sites like MySpace and Blog-ger for civic purposes—political organizing and public deliberation. The challenge will be to make such work a form of civic education. It was clear that students who made a video documentary would learn civic skills; the educational advantages of MySpace are more speculative. In particular, I am convinced that young people must learn to use an effective "public voice"—a tone or style that can convince others with whom they are not closely associated to take action on some common or public problem. It is not yet clear to me how students would use social networking sites to develop a public voice.[30]

The second option is to create elaborate media projects and then actively recruit local audiences to see and discuss them, often in face-to-face settings. Steven Goodman, executive director of the Educational Video Center (EVC), described "premiere screenings" at which 50 to 150 people convene face-to-face to watch student videos. He reported, "Our students almost always come away from their screenings feeling a sense of accomplishment, pride, success and recognition they never experience in school or elsewhere in their life. These are times when their parents, friends and teachers see their creative and intellectual potential; the audiences see what they are truly capable of, and the students are just overjoyed."[31]

Goodman and several other interviewees emphasized that it was not the size but the behavior and composition of the audience that matters most to kids. Anderson of the Main Street Project said, for example, that numbers weren't so important as "having the right audience—not just an audience for the sake of people to watch. In my experience youth are most interested in making sure their work (stories) are first screened with family and friends and other people of color. Since their work is often personal, and because they have learned through the workshops the importance of people of color telling our own stories and speaking for ourselves . . . they are far more interested in thinking through where the community screenings will take place, and how sharing their stories can empower others, challenge isolation and lead to organizing campaigns."

Projects like these do not rely on digital technology and networks to disseminate youth media. They actively recruit members of their communities to watch young people's work and respond. Thus digital media production is an element of face-to-face community organizing, not simply an application of new technology.

8.3 YOUTH PARTICIPATION IN LOCAL GOVERNMENT

Participation in local government probably has important educative effects for citizens of all ages.[32] Large-scale politics is rather abstract. We lack direct, personal experience of the locations that we see on national television news. The number of people and amounts of money involved in national politics can be so large as to defy understanding; and our connections to distant human beings can be largely imaginary. We do engage in state, national, and international affairs, but it helps to have experience at a more local level. At the opposite extreme of scale, schools, neighborhoods, and churches and other voluntary associations—while important seedbeds of civic activism—have drawbacks. They tend to be rather homogeneous, so they may not teach skills and ethics of working with people who are different. Also, the issues that arise in such small communities may be different in kind (not just in scale) from the issues that state and national governments address.

A particularly important issue in all modern democracies is the regulation and taxation of private industry. One side recommends deriving the maximum feasible public benefit from industry through taxes and regulations. As Theodore Roosevelt said: "I believe in corporations. They are indispensable instruments of modern civilization; but I believe they should be so supervised and regulated that they shall act for the interest of the community as a whole."[33] Another influential view holds that high taxation and onerous regulation violates private rights and generally harms the community's interests.

This debate does not arise inside schools, churches, and voluntary associations, but it is important at the municipal level, where developers and manufacturers are frequently pitted against public employees, tenant groups, and labor unions. The issues that these groups contest are concrete and understandable, such as whether to offer a tax break to attract or retain a particular business. And these debates involve *diverse* interests, because there are almost always several economic classes within the borders of a city or a county.[34] Only the very poorest cities completely lack a middle class and local businesses. At the opposite extreme, no wealthy suburban county completely lacks poor people. (The county in the United States that has the highest median income is Marin in California, yet almost 7 percent of residents live under the poverty line.)

Because economic issues arise at the local level, city and county governments are important instruments of civic education for Americans of all ages. Thus it is important that cities and counties can make consequential decisions. When they are completely at the mercy of markets or highly constrained by decisions made at higher levels of government, they lose their educative functions. To make municipalities more relevant we should empower them to make economic decisions—conservative, liberal, or libertarian—in response to local opinion. For example, municipalities ought to be permitted to offer services, such as wireless Internet access, that are also provided by companies.[35] I do not assert that this is a wise policy, only that it ought to be allowed so that it can be debated.

Such reforms, however, go beyond the scope of this chapter, which is about interventions to teach young people civic skills and knowledge. For our purposes, the question is whether young people can have direct experiences participating in municipal or county governance. The answer is clearly yes in cities like San Francisco, which has an influential youth commission whose members are between twelve and twenty-three years old. The commission holds hearings, passes resolutions, and considers formal referrals from the board of supervisors. However, the "most ambitious case to date" is Hampton, Virginia, a blue-collar, racially diverse city of 146,000. Hampton not only has a citywide youth commission but also a whole network of youth advisory boards and youth representatives on citizens' boards. Young people have formal roles in each city school, the planning department, the Parks and Recreation Department, and policing. There have also been large-scale youth deliberations in which young people have participated. Training, coaching, and other forms of support are available for participants. In all, Hampton aims to have a "comprehensive system of opportunities for youth to be involved in the life of the community."[36]

We cannot be sure of the impact of such participation on the young people who participate, although Sirianni observed 157 youth discussing the difficult issue of race relations and enjoying themselves. "Despite the seriousness of the comments, there was a spirit of ease, laughter, and spontaneous high-fives among black and white students in the break-out groups and little sign of stereotypical positions based on race."[37] Beane and colleagues studied a case from the 1940s in which youth were employed in city planning. They surveyed the former participants thirty years after the program had occurred. Former participants were still more involved in community affairs than nonparticipants, although they were less optimistic about the likely value of involving youth in planning. This "might be explained by the fact that the recommendations made by students for the city planning project were mostly not implemented."[38] In Hampton, some important recommendations *have* become policy, such as the proposal to build a citywide teen center.

The young people who serve on municipal advisory boards are likely to be a highly motivated and talented. Even when adults work hard to recruit a broad cross section of adolescents, the teenagers who agree to participate in municipal government will always be few and civically inclined. However, that is not a reason to dismiss these programs. We should not merely be interested in interventions that raise the average or total level of civic engagement. It is also important to develop young leaders who can shoulder disproportionate civic responsibility. Besides, there are techniques that can engage larger groups of young people. Hampton sees service-learning projects (which are common in the city) as the base of a pyramid that can lead some participants into advisory roles and even formal leadership positions.[39] Hampton also organizes public meetings and deliberations that engage large numbers of young people.

Third, we should hope that youth input will improve the quality of municipal services for young people. That benefit, in turn, could increase adolescents' sense of attachment to public institutions. According to William Potapchuk and colleagues, youth commissioners in Hampton broke a deadlock over how to design a city park, partly because they had consulted with other young people and could present evidence of public opinion.[40] Police officials in Hampton, who were initially skeptical, now believe that youth advisors enhance public safety—a good thing in itself and possibly a cause of enhanced civic participation.[41]

Finally, placing a few young people in formal advisory roles might have spillover effects on all young citizens. Average youth can observe their peers having an impact and gain confidence and interest in civic affairs, much as students become more interested in politics when some of their peers play significant roles in school governance. One reason that Hampton won the 2005 Innovations in Government award for its youth work was the strikingly high youth turnout rate in the 2004 election, compared to a relatively low statewide rate of 41 percent for ages 18 to 24. Since Hampton is in no way demographically privileged, its high rate of youth voting could reasonably be attributed to a local culture of youth empowerment.[42]

Hampton exemplifies "civic education" that is not simply a function of schools, but a communitywide process, involving broad deliberation, participation, and coordination by citizens, public and private institutions, and students themselves. In the next chapter, I turn our attention to one set of institutions that has special potential for civic education and engagement: colleges and universities.

CHAPTER 9

Developments in Higher Education

In chapter 5, section 5.2, I argued that higher education lost its civic mission over the course of the twentieth century. However, in the last ten to fifteen years, there have been developments in colleges and universities that are relatively small-scale but promising. For the most part, the impact of these experiments on students has not been carefully measured, but they have the potential to develop into more robust and effective programs. These innovative approaches include service-learning at the college level, efforts to capitalize on the increasing diversity of students and faculty, community-based scholarship, and experiments with deliberation.

Although quite varied, most of these practices share two important features: they are experiential (combining practice with reflection or research) and open-ended. Open-endedness does not imply a lack of ideals or commitments. On the contrary, participants are deeply committed to democratic participation, civility, diversity, consensus building, and constructive problem-solving. Those values have deep roots in American political history but were not especially prominent during the campus unrest of the 1960s. They reemerged on college campuses after 1990, and I credit two generations that have interacted constructively since then.

9.1 A GENERATIONAL STORY

First, consider the large cohort of professors who had first encountered the public world—and academia—during the Johnson and Nixon administrations. This was a tumultuous time, marked by war, assassinations, social movements, protests, and a sexual revolution. Campuses were at the center of the tumult. Students provided prominent national leaders for all the major social movements of the day; most male students were confronted with a profound political dilemma in the form of the draft; young people experimented with new lifestyles in revolt against their parents' generation; and urban campuses were sites of struggle as many central cities burned.

Thus a large cohort of professors developed their fundamental attitudes toward the world in general, and academia in particular, at a time of political upheaval in which colleges and members of their own generation, defined as "students," played a leading role—not only in the United States, but also (and with more consequence) in countries like France, South Korea, and Chile. They came of age conscious of a "generation gap" and prone to see colleges as sites of political opposition, critique, and even revolution.[1]

Between the Boomers' formative years on campus and the 1990s, things had calmed down considerably. Some prominent leftist intellectuals had moved to the right. Some had adopted postmodernist theories that, if they were political at all, certainly lacked any political "praxis" (that is, an answer to Lenin's question, "What is to be done?") Some Boomer academics had held onto their radical values but had become disillusioned with colleges' political potential as most of their students had abandoned sixties-style activism. Some, technically part of the baby boom but in graduate school after 1975, faced what David D. Cooper called "the chronically depressed conditions of an insanely competitive job market," making ends meet by teaching adjunct courses at several institutions and never having the time or power to be active politically.[2]

Finally, some had developed a new perspective that, while still reformist and egalitarian, was increasingly pragmatic, open-ended, and solicitous of institutions, of existing communities, of civic culture, and of public deliberation, regardless of its outcome. Cooper wrote that he "was bent on nourishing the fragile bond between the inner life and ethical responsibility to work, institution, and community."[3] He contrasted this civic commitment to the standard approach of his academic discipline, which was "abstract, contentious, and theory-driven." Edward Royce could have been describing Cooper when he wrote about scholars who were not so much interested in "social criticism" as in using "their intellectual capital to inform, empower, and educate ordinary citizens."[4]

In 1990 or 1995, when many professors were Boomers, their students predominantly belonged to Generation X (born between 1966 and 1985). A typical undergraduate of that time had begun to pay attention to the public world during the relatively uneventful administrations of George H. W. Bush and Bill Clinton. Members of "Gen X" formed a relatively small cohort, raised in the shadow of the much more numerous Boomers, and they had the weakest sense of their own distinctness as a generation. However, the Xers at least shared a sense that they had arrived too late for the dramatic events of 1965–1975, yet they lived with the consequences of their parents' choices. Further, they were marked by rising economic anxiety and a belief that their individual performance in school would have profound effects on their economic futures. For "high-performing" students, including those who were female or people of color, some new opportunities seemed to have opened up. But the obverse of opportunity was risk. Students believed that they stood alone in the economy, unable to fall back on unions, neighborhoods, or even intact families. Especially after the recession of the early 1990s, higher education seemed the indispensable key to security. The economic value of college, rather than its potential for social change, was its most salient feature for students and their parents alike.[5]

Leftist students (2.2 percent of freshmen in the 1994 Higher Education Research Institute sample) deserve special consideration, because in my experience they provided a disproportionate percentage of campus activists, leaders of student associations, and partners for the Boomer professors who were working on public projects in the 1990s. These young leftists were different from earlier generations of progressive/activist students, precisely because their formative experiences had occurred during the Clinton administration. Before the 1992 election, most activist students of the Left had favored "community service" if (and only if) it sensitized people to problems like poverty and racism and led to political action. They preferred voting and fundamental change through state action, fearing that service might become an end in itself or a palliative. These were some of the explicit conclusions of a Wingspread summit on service that I attended in 1988 as a student.

Thirteen years later, Campus Compact brought a new group of activist undergraduates (including some conservatives) to Wingspread to discuss civic engagement. These students, summarizing the experience of the 1990s, said:

For the most part, we are frustrated with conventional politics, view-ing it as inaccessible. [However,] while we are disillusioned with con-ventional politics (and therefore most forms of political activity), we are deeply involved in civic issues through non-traditional forms of engagement. We are neither apathetic nor disengaged. In fact, what many perceive as disengagement may actually be a conscious choice; for example, a few of us . . . actively avoided voting, not wanting to participate in what some of us view as a deeply flawed electoral process. . . . While we still hope to be able to participate in our politi-cal system effectively through traditional means, service is a viable and preferable (if not superior) alternative at this time.[6]

I suspect that a major reason for this rejection of formal politics was the failure of the Clinton administration to achieve goals prized by left-ist students, following the built-up hopes of the Reagan and Bush years. The spike in youth voting in 1992 gave way to a substantial turnout decline in 1996 and 2000. Just as turnout fell, however, the rate of stu-dent volunteering increased. As William Galston and I wrote in 1997, "citizens—particularly the youngest—seem to be shifting their pre-ferred civic involvement from official politics to the voluntary sector. If so, the classic Tocquevillian thesis would have to be modified: local civic life, far from acting as a school for wider political involvement, may in-creasingly serve as a refuge from (and alternative to) it. The conse-quences for the future of our democracy could be significant."[7]

In the 1990s, disillusioned leftists could find common ground with some conservative and libertarian youth who were equally skeptical about state action, and equally optimistic about voluntary work in the non-profit sector. Activist students of the Right and Left developed a non–state-centered theory of politics and social change. These young pro-ponents of "service politics"—optimistic about direct work with human beings in need, concerned and self-critical about personal attitudes and behaviors, relatively skilled at interactions with people different from themselves, and disillusioned with formal politics—encountered a group of academics whose own thinking had moved in compatible directions.

9.2 NEW SCHOLARLY ATTENTION TO "THE PUBLIC"

During the 1980s and early 1990s, many scholars had been paying re-newed attention to civil society: voluntary associations and the norms of membership and trust that accompany them. In Marxist thought, "civil

society" is irrelevant to history, a mere symptom of the underlying economic order. But it was civil society that defeated Leninist states in Rus-
sia and Eastern Europe. It was also within civil society that the women's
movement and other revolutionary social forces arose in the West and
achieved major victories. Meanwhile, the quality of civil society in a nation or a neighborhood seemed to explain its economic well-being, political resiliency, and even the outcomes of its schools. A large body of
literature, including influential works by James Coleman in sociology,
Robert Putnam in political science, James C. Scott in anthropology, and
Jean Cohen, Andrew Arato, and Joshua Cohen in political theory, drew
attention to the importance of civil society and the public's role in a democracy. As a result of this literature, older authors such as John Dewey
and Jane Addams enjoyed a renaissance.

A related intellectual development was a renewed concern with *deliberation*. In the 1970s, two of the most influential political philosophers
in the world, the American John Rawls and the German Jürgen Habermas, had argued that justice could not be determined by any abstract
methodology, such as utilitarianism, but had to be discovered by people
reasoning together. For people who use Deweyan vocabulary, the "public" is the population when it deliberates and acts on common concerns. As Maria Farland noted, "despite the enormous diversity of approaches that characterize the new public mindedness among today's
academic professionals, there is ample evidence that 'the public' has
emerged as a common concern in fields as diverse as urban planning
and English literature."[8]

To prize civil society and deliberation is to take a political stance that
is open-ended about outcomes, but strongly committed to values such
as participation, equity in discussion, freedom of speech, civility, and
problem-solving.

9.3 NEW FORMS OF PUBLIC WORK

When Boomer intellectuals, increasingly focused on public deliberation and civil society, encountered young people who were disillusioned
with formal, state-centered politics (but optimistic about the potential
of "service"), the two generations began to experiment with innovative
forms of voluntary public work that exemplified their new theories of
citizen-centered deliberative democracy.

The most prevalent example was service-learning, again defined as
an intentional combination of community service with reflection on the

same issue or topic. In higher education, service-learning grew and was institutionalized rapidly during the 1980s and 1990s, partly thanks to several energetic new advocacy organizations: the Campus Opportunity Outreach League or COOL (founded in 1984), Campus Compact (1985), and Youth Service America (1986). The federal government assisted by creating the Points of Light Foundation, passing the National and Community Service Act of 1990, and launching the Corporation for National Service in 1993.

In colleges and universities, service-learning is now very common and very various. In my view, the best examples are true collaborations among students, professors, and community members; they have a political dimension (that is, they organize people to tackle fundamental problems collectively); they combine deliberation with concrete action; and they are connected to "teaching and learning, research, and the dissemination of knowledge"—the goals that, as Deborah Hirsch argues, "drive the university."[9] In good service-learning, students have the authority to choose their own problems and responses. The professor's stance is open-ended. Much service-learning fails to meet these criteria, but the movement is full of energy and innovation.

One pressing question is how service-learning compares to other experiential approaches that might be more attractive to particular professors, departments, disciplines, and institutions. The Carnegie Foundation for the Advancement of Teaching, though its Political Engagement Project, is evaluating a range of experiential approaches, including service-learning, internships, visiting speakers, simulations, semesters in Washington, dormitories with civic-education programs, and collaborative research projects. "The preliminary findings, based on pre- and post-interviews and surveys, show positive results from the 21 programs studied, with a particularly strong positive influence on students who enter the programs with a low level of political interest.[10]

A second example of the new public work is *concrete experimentation with deliberation*. Examples of organized meetings at which people discuss public issues are National Issues Forums, Study Circles, Deliberative Polls, and Citizens' Juries. Some of these experiments originated in universities. For instance, the Center for Deliberative Polling at the University of Texas both organized and studied deliberative exercises. In other cases, independent groups, such as the National Issues Forum network and the Study Circles Resource Center, have led the experiments, but their reflective practitioners engage in dialogues with academics. And sometimes, higher education is the site or the topic of public deliberation.[11] At Wake Forest, the Democracy Fellows are students who participate in and organize deliberations over their four-year undergraduate careers. A rigorous study with a control group found that the Democracy Fellows gained sophistication about politics, efficacy, and an interest in political participation in contrast to standard volunteering.[12]

A simultaneous and related development was the growth of *practical public scholarship*. It was not a novel idea in the 1990s to conduct research in partnership with laypeople. To name one earlier example, Jane Addams had written her enormously influential works of social analysis by working with her own Chicago neighbors, whom she treated as peers and fellow-investigators. However, as William Sullivan argued, a different conception of scholarship dominated after the Second World War: the idea that experts "'solved problems' by bringing the latest technical knowledge to bear on matters which, it [was] widely presumed, the public as a whole was too limited to understand, much less address."[13] After World War II, academics were impressed (sometimes justifiably) by detached and scientific methods such as large-scale survey research and controlled experiments.

By the 1990s, there were evident countertrends, among them the growth of ethnographic methods. Ethnography had been founded by anthropologists such as Bronislaw Malinowski and Margaret Mead, who lived for substantial periods immersed in distant cultures and used local people as informants. By the 1990s, ethnographic methods were widely employed in America contexts, even to understand the academy itself. A hallmark of "ethnography is its commitment to accurate reflection of the views and perspectives of the participants in the research"; such accuracy requires close and respectful interaction with laypeople.[14] Scott Peters has described the Teen Assessment Project (TAP) in Wisconsin, which "provides a means for communities to collaborate with extension educators and university faculty in conducting their own research on the needs and problems faced by adolescents."[15] This project was one of many such across the country.[16]

A final important development in the 1980s and 1990s was work that capitalized on *diversity as an asset*. In the early to mid-1990s, there were bitter public controversies over diversity, multiculturalism, and "political correctness" versus some notion of a Western educational canon. Carlos E. Cortés observed in 1994 that "multicultural research, teaching, and engagement" had "moved from the margins to center stage" during the previous decade, provoking a powerful reaction.[17] The same year, Eric Liu (then in his early twenties) observed that his own generation had "assiduously read the signals sent out by our public institutions. Be separate. Ask for more. Classify yourselves and stand in line for what is rightly yours. . . . On the other side of the spectrum, young neoconservatives have delighted in exposing the follies of the politically correct."[18]

In 1978, four members of the Supreme Court had ruled that affirmative action was unconstitutional. Four members had supported it as a way to address discrimination and reallocate scarce goods (such as places in college) to disadvantaged groups. The swing vote was Justice Powell's; he argued that affirmative action was permissible only to promote diversity, which in turn could enhance the "robust exchange of ideas," which was a goal "of paramount importance in the fulfillment of [a university's] mission.[19]

Because Powell's opinion was the law of the land after 1978, and because there were substantive reasons for it, many colleges and universities began to see affirmative action (broadly defined as any effort to encourage the participation of women and minorities) as essential to their scholarly and educational missions. Meanwhile, surveys found that young people increasingly saw racial diversity as an asset. As Liu noted, "the twentysomething generation is still key, as confused as we may be now. We are the first American generation to have been born in an integrated society, and we are accustomed to more race-mixing than any generation before us."[20]

Often, multiculturalism has a consumerist feel. One assumes that there is a finite supply of cultural goods, each marked with a gender and ethnic tag; the question is how much of students' finite time should be spent consuming "Western" products, versus works of their own choice, versus assigned works by previously excluded groups. In the 1990s, some scholars and college students struggled for a positive, "win-win" vision in which new generations can not merely consume but also create works that expand the cultural commons, by combining multiple cultural influences.

In 2003, the Supreme Court upheld affirmative action as constitutional if it enhanced the mission of a university (thus converting Powell's lone opinion into a 5–4 majority). The *Michigan* decision was much influenced by supportive testimony from numerous universities and by experiences with creative diversity during the 1980s and 1990s. Independent studies have found positive effects from various programs with "diversity" themes.[21]

I have described recent developments on college campuses as the fruitful result of an encounter between Boomer academics and students born after 1965. Since 1994, however, most Gen X college students have moved on and members of the new Millennial Generation have replaced them.

Some of the undergraduates who were engaged in public scholarship, service learning, or deliberation in 1985–95 went on to obtain doctorates of their own. While that group included people who became civically engaged professors, many responded to the tight job market by becoming knowledge-workers *outside* academia. Their pragmatism, enthusiasm for collaborating with lay publics, and resistance to large organizations—all generational traits—encouraged them to work in nonprofits and communities. In 2000, Maria Farland wrote that these younger Ph.D.s were "going public" by working outside academia; they therefore formed "the vanguard of an exciting professional revolution":

> The scholars of my generation who have chosen to leave academic professionalism as it is narrowly defined within the university's walls . . . address the public, and public problems, in a language and style that differ significantly from the highly specialized language of the academic discipline in which they were trained. Many are rooted in a particular community, especially urban communities. . . . The coming of age of my generation has witnessed the emergence of a population of humanists who see the public conversation as the primary context in which they write, conduct research, and sometimes teach.[22]

As for the new generation that first reached college age in 1993—the Millennials, "Dot-Nets," or "echo-Boomers"—they are another large cohort with a strong sense of a generation gap. Since September 11, 2001, their attention has been directed to news and public events. As noted above, they voted at a relatively high rate in the 2004 and 2006 elections. Although the future is certainly unpredictable, there is a significant chance that the academic innovations of the 1980s and 1990s (especially service-learning, public scholarship, diversity work, and deliberation) will become more *political*—more oriented to fundamental social change—as the Millennials make their mark.

9.4 POLICY IMPLICATIONS

Although civic experimentation is common on college campuses, most students still lack opportunities for service-learning, community-based research, public deliberation, cultural projects that take advantage of diversity, and other forms of civic engagement.[23] As noted in chapter 6, section 6.1, excellent civic education does not enhance institutions' rankings or their ability to attract competitive students and faculty. Partly for that reason, professors are rarely rewarded with tenure or promotion for emphasizing the civic development of their students.

I believe several strategies hold promise for changing these incentives. First, some research exemplifies genuine, mutually respectful collaborations between scholars and laypeople; at the same time, it is methodologically complex and innovative, addressing issues of basic concern to one or more academic disciplines. It is therefore valued highly in the academy. Examples include Elinor Ostrom's discovery of techniques for overcoming the "tragedy of the commons" (discussed in chapter 7) and Jane Mansbridge's analysis of "unitary democracy" in groups that operate by consensus.[24] Both scholars participated closely in communities and social movements and developed their insights only by struggling with lay peers to address practical concerns. Yet both are distinguished members of the political science profession who have presented their findings in highly rigorous, abstract form. Their work avoids the tradeoff between scholarship and service. Promoting such research is a tactic for encouraging civic engagement in departments, disciplines, and institutions that are deeply committed to scholarly excellence.

In programs that are more concerned with professional training, I think the most promising tactic is to persuade professors and administrators that their students need civic skills to succeed. For example, what should an aspiring urban public school teacher know? Before she starts teaching, she should learn the material she is supposed to cover, something about pedagogy and assessment, some instructional techniques—and the ability to address fundamental problems in the system in which she will work. She cannot solve educational problems inside her own classroom, because senior managers and large bureaucratic structures create too many hurdles. She cannot take on managers and bureaucracies alone. Thus she needs to work with other teachers, parents, students, and community members, often quite different from herself, to address common problems together.

Democratic skills (listening, deliberating, organizing, petitioning) are essential for teachers, as they are for many other professionals. For a good teacher, "civic engagement" is not a voluntary after-work activity, but the heart of her professional life. Therefore, it is exciting to watch Minneapolis Community College's Urban Teacher Program embrace "advocacy and activism." Specifically, their associate's degree students lead urban students in Public Achievement projects. In Public Achievement, students choose, define, and address community issues— a genuinely open-ended, nonideological form of politics that will serve teachers well.

Another strategy is to apply outside pressure to colleges and universities. The power of the purse is relevant here. For example, the Federal Work Study (FWS) Program provides work opportunities for college students who qualify for financial aid. Congress currently requires only 7 percent of FWS jobs to involve community service. Most FWS employees do routine work for their institutions, such as sorting departments' mail. If Congress raised the minimum well above 7 percent, colleges and universities would have to provide a great deal more service-learning.

The federal government also funds research, including many projects that have particularly high status within the academy. Some federal grant competitions could be rewritten so that applicants had to show that they would work with communities. Already, proposals to the National Science Foundation generally include a section on "broader impacts," in which applicants must describe their plans for dissemination and the "benefits of the proposed activity to society."[25] It is enough for some projects to disseminate their results and benefit society, but others ought to involve actual partnerships between researchers and laypeople.

Finally, pressure can come from within the university. Peters, Boyte, and others have detected a current of dissatisfaction among professors who entered the academy hoping to have a public role but have found themselves isolated, talking only to fellow specialists.[26] The standard solution to that problem is to try to build a lay audience by writing editorials, appearing on television, or at least lecturing to large undergraduate classes. These solutions involve one-way communication between the professor and a receptive public. One-way communication is not fully satisfying, even for those relatively few academics who can actually find large audiences. It is more fulfilling to work *with* students and communities to define and address tangible problems. That is by no means the only kind of work that should take place in the academy—there is also great value in pure scholarship—but engagement is worthwhile and it can rejuvenate scholars who feel a lack of purpose. As we have seen, there are structural barriers to engaged scholarship (for example, it tends not to count for tenure and promotion). But those barriers could be overcome by senior academics who organized themselves to press for a more civically engaged university.

CHAPTER 10

Institutional Reforms

So far, the programs and reforms discussed in this book have been forms of "civic education," meaning that they are intended to change the knowledge, skills, habits, and values of young people so that youth will become more involved in our existing institutions. However, we may also need to change our institutions so that involvement becomes more rewarding.

The Progressive Era reformers of 1900–1920 sought better education for citizenship *and* better institutions for citizens. We have seen that John Dewey and his contemporaries invented many of the standard forms of civic education, including social studies courses, student governments, service clubs, scholastic newspapers, and 4-H. Dewey rightly argued: "Formal instruction . . . easily becomes remote and dead— abstract and bookish, to use the ordinary words of depreciation." Thus he favored experiential education for democracy and tried to "reorganize" American education "so that learning takes place in connection with the intelligent carrying forward of purposeful activities."[1] A good example would be a school newspaper, which requires sustained, cooperative work, promotes deliberation, and depends upon perennial values such as freedom of the press.

As Diane Ravitch writes in *The Troubled Crusade,* Dewey saw this kind of educational reform as a "vital part" of a broader "social and political reform movement" that aimed at making political participation more meaningful and more equitable. Thus Dewey and his fellow progressives introduced new educational opportunities in schools while also battling corruption, pursuing women's suffrage and civil rights, and launching independent political journals for adults. They saw civic experiences in school as means to help students begin participating in the serious business of democracy, which also needed reform.

Unfortunately, the specific innovations that the progressives introduced into schools often lost their original connection to democracy. When their political purpose was forgotten or ignored, extracurricular activities and social studies classes became means to impart good behavior, academic skills, or "social hygiene"—not ways to begin changing society. Soon, as Ravitch writes, "the progressive education movement became institutionalized and professionalized, and its major themes accordingly changed. Shorn of its roots in politics and society, pedagogical progressivism came to be identified with the child-centered school; with a pretentious scientism; with social efficiency and social utility rather than social reform; and with a vigorous suspicion of 'bookish' learning."[2]

Today, there is a serious risk that we could repeat the same pattern. For example, excellent service-learning programs enhance students' civic capacity: they increase skills and motivations for self-government. The best programs allow students to tackle problems that really matter, sometimes provoking controversy (see section 7.4). But service-learning is being widely advocated as a way to reduce teen pregnancy or drug abuse and as an alternative to "bookish" academic curricula for students who are not succeeding in school. There is merit in both rationales, but there is also the danger that service-learning will be watered down. To use Ravitch's terms, service-learning can be shorn of its connection to politics, made too "child-centered" (instead of academically challenging), and used to enhance "social efficiency" (say, to lower rates of delinquency) as recommended by behavioral scientists.

The alternative is to recall that schools are public spaces in which young people begin the serious business of self-government and have early opportunities to pursue social change. Service-learning, civics courses, and extracurricular activities are useful means for democratic education, but they are not ends in themselves. The point of the whole business is democracy, which begins during the school years and not after graduation.

In the subsequent sections, I will look first at schools and then at political institutions and the news business as institutions that should be reformed while we try to improve civic education.

10.1 COMPREHENSIVE HIGH SCHOOL REFORM

Young people spend a substantial proportion of their time inside schools: more than 18,000 hours if they complete twelfth grade. While in school, almost all participate in some activities that are intended to enhance their civic development, such as social studies classes and various extracurricular projects. But students have other legitimate goals in school, such as mastering academic topics that may be remote from politics and citizenship, making friends, obtaining credentials, exercising, expressing themselves artistically, and simply having fun. In short, schools are not only devices for teaching young people to be citizens. They are also institutions within which groups of human beings—adults and children—spend portions of their lives doing various forms of work.

Some students are "engaged" in these institutions; others are less so. To be fully engaged is to participate in class discussions, to complete academic assignments, to join various extracurricular associations, to have valuable relationships with fellow students and adults, and to care about the whole school community, including those not in one's own peer group. At the opposite extreme, about one-third of American teenagers are so disengaged from school that they simply quit once they reach the legal age. In a 2006 study of recent dropouts, more than half said they had satisfactory grades before they left school ("C" or better), but half said that classes were boring. Further, "only 56 percent said they could go to a staff person for school problems and just two-fifths (41 percent) had someone in school to talk to about personal problems."[3]

Engagement in school enhances students' preparation for college and the workforce. It probably teaches lessons that are useful for civic participation later on, such as how to work together in groups. But it is also intrinsically valuable. Life does not begin at graduation; children and adolescents are already members of communities who can flourish better if they are engaged rather than alienated, and who make institutions better by participating. Thus we should want schools to be engaging communities so that children's lives are better, not only so that they gain civic skills that they can use in adulthood.

High Schools as Communities

I believe we should focus our reform efforts on the high school. High schools are currently organized in ways that are particularly alienating. In addition, the No Child Left Behind Act has made fateful decisions for elementary and middle schools by requiring frequent high-stakes tests. Teachers and administrators can still choose various strategies to increase students' success, but NCLB constrains their priorities. On the other hand, the act has little to say about high schools, yet powerful policymakers and institutions (for example, the National Governors Association, the Business Roundtable, and the Bill & Melinda Gates Foundation) are convinced that high schools must be reformed. Some of the leading reform ideas would make high schools more engaging. Thus there is a chance for positive breakthroughs at the high school level that we do not currently have at earlier grades.

Those who are calling for fundamental high school reform have noticed that many American students attend large, incoherent, "shopping mall" high schools that do not encourage, or even permit, engagement. Thomas Toch, for example, argues that most large high schools fail to "engender a strong sense of community." Instead, they "tend to be intensely impersonal places." The results include "alienation and apathy among students and teachers," a pervasive anonymity that "saps students' motivation to learn and teachers' motivation to teach."[4]

Indeed, the average size of American primary and secondary schools increased fourfold between 1930 and 1970, from 87 students to 440.[5] Toward the end of that period (1959), James Conant identified small high schools as the single biggest problem in American education.[6] He argued that they were economically inefficient, unprofessional, and unable to provide a wide range of equipment and specialized teachers. In addition to these arguments, other factors probably contributed to massive school consolidation in that era, including a tendency to close down historically black schools under court desegregation orders (not to mention the desire to field better football teams). Even so, Conant did not envision or endorse the huge high schools that have become common in recent decades.

In those schools, students are seen as consumers who should be permitted to choose among a wide variety of offerings, both curricular and extracurricular. Students are presumed to have diverse interests and abilities. Thus it is right that some should choose student government and AP courses while others prefer "shop" and basketball. Choice and diversity have been dominant values since the 1960s.

Students who enter such schools on a very good track or who have positive support from peers and family may make wise choices about their courses, friends, cocurricular activities, and next steps after graduation. They can obtain useful civic skills and habits by choosing demanding courses in history and social studies, by joining the student newspaper or serving in the community, and by interacting with administrators. However, relatively few students—usually those on a path to college—can fill these roles in a typical high school. Other students who are steered (or who steer themselves) into undemanding courses and away from student activities will pay a price for the rest of their lives.

The opportunities that a school provides are of no use unless a student has the confidence, motivation, network ties, and knowledge to use them. In a huge high school, there is little chance that any adult will try to steer a student who is on a mediocre track onto a more challenging one. Twenty years later, the student who chose easy courses and avoided clubs may still be paying a price, economically as well as socially and politically.

Typical large high schools also tend to have frequent discipline problems, a general atmosphere of alienation, and internal segregation by race, class, and subculture. Often, they occupy suburban-style campuses, set far apart from the adult community of work, family, religion, and politics. Even worse, some of these huge schools occupy prisonlike urban blocks, secured with gates and bars.

Large high schools sometimes offer venues, such as student governments, school newspapers, video broadcast programs, and arts performances, in which students could discuss issues of schoolwide concern. But most adolescents have no interest in these discussions. Why pay attention to the student government or watch a positive hip-hop video that your peers have produced, if you do not share a community or "public" with them? If a few students produce a school play, only their friends will be motivated to attend. For most other students, the play will be an inferior alternative to slickly produced Hollywood movies. If, however, a high school supports a genuine community in which students deliberate about common concerns, know one another, and feel they can make a difference, then everyone may be quite interested in a school play that is made by their peers and that investigates local concerns. This hypothetical example illustrates a more general theory: strong local communities increase both the supply of, and the demand for, diverse cultural products.

Dewey defined a "community" as any place where "there is conjoint activity whose consequences are appreciated as good by all singular persons who take part in it, and where the realization of the good is such as to effect an energetic desire and effort to sustain it in being just because it is a good shared by all."[7] But the standard American high school is too big and unfocused to support "conjoint activity" or "consciousness of a communal life." It has no common normative framework. As Harry Brighouse describes it: "It is a 2000-plus student institution, in which no individual knows every other individual; in which many children never have any teacher for more than one year of instruction; in which the prevailing values include pep rallies for sports and a slavishly conformist loyalty to school and neighbourhood. These schools maintain a deafening silence about spiritual or anti-materialist values, take sides in the Cola wars, and accept as a given the prevalence of brand names and teen-marketing."[8]

Students who feel that they and their peers have a "voice" in their own schools tend to be confident in their ability to participate in their communities, more interested in public affairs, and more knowledgeable about civics (see section 7.3). However, it is impossible for students— or anyone else—to influence the overall atmosphere and structure of a huge school that offers a wide but incoherent range of choices and that views its student population mainly as consumers.

Young people cannot even observe their *parents* influencing their schools. As noted in previous sections, there have been steep declines in the number of school board seats, the proportion of adults involved in community projects, and membership in the PTA. Given these trends, it is ever less likely that young people will feel that they have roles to play in self-government.

The Small-Schools Movement

At present, three major strategies for making schools more engaging are being attempted fairly widely. The first is to reduce the number of students who learn together. The most dramatic way to do that is to shut down large high schools and replace them with small ones: "New York City is phasing out large high schools and planning for 200 new small schools over the next five years. Chicago is planning 100. Los Angeles is converting 130 middle and high school campuses to smaller units."[9] In some cases, this strategy has had dramatic success. For example, Julia Richman High School in Manhattan was transformed from a chaotic and violent disaster to an effective institution when it was divided into half-a-dozen separate schools.[10]

Notwithstanding such important examples, the evidence is not especially compelling that academic achievement is better in smaller schools once other factors are taken into account. There is stronger evidence that reducing the sheer number of students improves students' attitudes toward their schools and the odds that they will participate in extracurricular activities.[11] These are valuable goals, but reducing the size of school populations has substantial costs. It is expensive and slow to construct new school buildings and disruptive to move students around. Besides, reducing the average number of students per building could become a mindless goal with swiftly diminishing benefits. For the time being, I think we should avoid building new large schools in rapidly growing parts of the country, resist further school consolidation, and continue to experiment on a relatively small scale with small-school models.

Another option is to reorganize large schools so that mixed groups of students are assigned to groups that are variously called "learning communities," "schools within a school" (SWAS), "academies," "clusters," or "houses." These groups may remain together for a student's whole high-school career, so that students take many courses together. Certain teachers, administrators and other adults can be solely assigned to each group. That way, without necessarily reducing the student/teacher ratio, we can reduce the number of students for whom each adult is responsible. These "learning communities" are not the same as academic tracks, which are problematic from a civic point of view because they separate students by performance—hence, by future social class. Each community within the school should contain a cross-section of the whole student body.

A comparison of three types of schools—ordinary large ones that are awaiting reform efforts, large ones that have been divided into "academies," and newly launched small schools—found that the ordinary large schools had much less parental involvement and made less use of the surrounding community in their instruction. Students felt weaker ties to their institutions and less social responsibility. In the small schools and schools with academies, teachers felt more empowered and worked much more closely together as teams. They discussed their students with their colleagues so often—and knew them so well—that some felt overburdened by their intimate knowledge of home lives and problems.[12] These results were adjusted for demographic characteristics and represent promising evidence in favor of smaller learning communities. Even so, this strategy could be watered down if it were widely implemented without the enthusiastic support of teachers and administrators. It is easy to create academies within a large high school that have no sense of community—that are not much more than names.

A second strategy, fully compatible with the first, is to develop strong relationships between each school (or each learning community within a large school) and one or more outside institutions, such as a university or community college, a museum, a hospital, a business, or—more controversially—a religious congregation or military unit. The idea is to break down the barriers between adolescent life and adult life, so that young people can ease into a world of responsibility and "initative." Students should have an easier transition to college and employment if they can gain relevant skills, make connections to helpful adults, and directly experience options for after graduation.[13] For the purposes of this book, the hope is that students will become more integrated into their communities and thus more active citizens if they are less isolated behind school walls. Service-learning can work especially well when schools have partnerships with adult institutions, because students gain opportunities to serve in contexts where real work is being done; and the adult partners can help them to learn relevant academic lessons.

The final strategy for high school reform combines easily with the first two. It is to give each school a strong curricular "theme." Actual examples include the two Cesar Chavez Public Charter Schools for Public Policy in Washington, D.C.; Constitution High School near Independence Hall in Philadelphia; the Academy of American Studies in Queens, New York; the Boston Arts Academy; "New Tech" in Sacramento (which involves teams of students in ambitious technology projects); and Clara Mohammed School in Milwaukee, Wisconsin, which uses an Islamic curriculum in an African American urban cultural setting. Most "themed" schools are small and most have partnerships with one or more adult institutions. They do not focus exclusively on their chosen theme, because they must also meet comprehensive educational standards. But they require courses in the emphasized subject matter and integrate it into their other courses, extracurricular activities, and cultural events. For example, at the Chavez Schools in Washington, most courses (including mathematics and science) involve issues of public policy. Students complete capstone projects and lengthy papers on particular policy issues of their choice and are required to intern in political organizations.[14]

"Themed" schools have several potential advantages. The theme itself ought to provide a common topic of discussion for all students and adults. The concentration on a single topic also allows students to collaborate on lengthy and demanding projects, which are more difficult to sustain in standard schools. In fact, succeeding cohorts of students could sustain a single project, such as a particular advocacy campaign or a series of performances, over many years. Within a "themed" school, regardless of its size, students have less choice about their courses and activities, which means they may segregate less into peer groups that reinforce their members' interests and class backgrounds. We would expect them to collaborate more in groups of mixed ability. Bryk and colleagues note that Catholic schools offer relatively little choice among courses, but they find no negative effects on retention. On the contrary, the stronger sense of community provided by Catholic schools seems to boost academic outcomes.[15]

Clearly, small, "themed" schools pose risks as well as benefits. Students will exercise less individual choice within their school but must make one very consequential choice *among* schools (with varying degrees of input or control from their parents or guardians). That choice could have harmful civic consequences if students placed themselves in different schools based on their class, neighborhood, race, religion, and other background characteristics. It could also have disadvantages if some students chose themes that were far removed from citizenship. I have mentioned schools devoted to public policy and the U.S. Constitution. Such institutions may draw young people who begin with an interest in politics and social issues, segregating them from students who are more interested in the arts or technology. Schools with the latter themes may develop highly apolitical atmospheres in which no one ever mentions social or political topics.

I believe these risks are worth taking. High schools are already strikingly segregated,[16] and it may be better to divide them by theme than by selectivity. Schools devoted to arts, technology, or professions might become apolitical enclaves, but that is by no means inevitable. On the contrary, such schools could provide strong civic educations by encouraging their students to collaborate on creative, technical, or pre-professional projects of their own choice that have social themes.

Providing a panoply of small, "themed" schools or learning communities is a *pluralist* strategy. Pluralism requires us to tolerate values that we do not share, on the ground that human beings who are free and creative will naturally generate diverse communities, and the diversity is a sign of engagement.

In the progressive journal *Rethinking Schools,* Debbie Wei explains how an Asian-American civic group opened a charter school in Philadelphia's Chinatown: "We decided that if we were to build a school, it had to be a school that was consciously a school for democracy, a school for self-governance, a school for creation of community. We needed to build a school that was consciously anti-individualistic, anti-racist, anti-isolationist, and anti-materialist."[17] In the same issue, however, Michelle Fine notes that Philadelphia is also encouraging the creation of small "'faith-based' public schools" that collaborate "with Christian colleges and community organizations." Fine is not pleased. She says, "It breaks my heart to see the small schools movement . . . used to facilitate . . . faith-based education."[18]

A lot of the impetus for the small schools movement has come from progressive people who are antiracist, antimaterialist, and so forth. They want to create alternatives to mainstream schools. However, their strategy is to change policies so that nonprofits may open small schools; inevitably, conservative, religious, and promilitary groups (among others) are getting into the act. Reserving small schools for progressive nonprofits would be both unrealistic and unfair.

My own personal values are aligned with the Philadelphia Chinatown school (to a large degree), not with religious schools. But I see a fundamental parallel; each wants to motivate and inspire children by promoting a rich and compelling philosophical message. That is putting it politely. You could also say that both are sufficiently appalled by the power of mainstream culture that they are willing to *indoctrinate* kids to share their values. I am enough of a classical liberal that I would rather educate students in a more neutral way, to allow them to form their own opinions. For example, I would not want to participate in an "anti-individualistic," "anti-materialistic" school. I would rather teach multiple perspectives on ethics, including religious and libertarian ones.

Nonetheless, there remains a case for diversity of schools (not just within schools). As noted in section 7.7, there is no evidence that students are permanently brainwashed by education that takes a stand. On the contrary, they may be provoked to argue back. In a Catholic school with required religious education and a pervasive ideology of Catholic Social Justice, there is no evidence that the student body (predominantly African American Protestants) converted to Catholicism or adopted ideological positions under their teachers' influence.[19] Certainly, a "themed" school is likely to be more engaging for students, teachers, and parents than a school with no normative core or commitment.

Charter Schools

It is possible to create a small, "themed" school as part of a large educational system. For example, Constitution High School in Philadelphia (which opened in 2006 with a powerful student government and a curricular focus on the Constitution) is a regular high school run by the school district of Philadelphia. However, most small schools—and most large schools that have established truly distinct "academies"—appear to be public charter schools.[20] By the same token, most charter schools are small (they had a median enrollment of just 132 students in 1999) and the larger ones usually have academies.[21] Thus the small school movement and the charter movement overlap considerably.

A charter school is a public institution that operates independently, free from most of the usual bureaucratic tangles. An individual or group develops an idea for a school, organizes a proposal, and petitions the appropriate authorities for authorization to operate. Charter schools are supposed to improve outcomes for the students they enroll by providing alternative approaches precisely tailored to their students. They are also supposed to improve the performance of public education generally, by incubating new models and by increasing parental choice (hence, competition).

Yet charter schools do not seem to work particularly well for these purposes—no better than standard schools.[22] It is too early to say for sure, but charter schools do not look like a magic formula for higher test scores or graduation rates. That finding challenges the thesis that competition will improve education. Chester E. Finn, Jr., Bruno V. Manno, and Gregg Vanourek argue that Federal Express forced the U.S. Postal Service to reinvent itself. Overnight mail "is a welcome product of that reinvention process—and a product of competition." They add: "A similar phenomenon can be observed in public education in some communities, thanks to charter schools (and other forms of school choice). Competition busts monopolies and triggers change."[23]

This theory implies that systems in which there are charter schools should improve overall—a difficult hypothesis to test—and also that charters themselves should perform better than noncharters, at least in the short term (before the noncharters are forced to improve). In a comparison of 2003 data from the National Assessment of Educational

Progress, however, charters performed *worse* than noncharters (although once students' background characteristics were controlled, most of the difference disappeared). Finn, "a supporter of charters" who had called for the comparison and had argued against adjusting the test scores for students' background characteristics,[24] found the charters' scores "low, dismayingly low."[25]

In theory, competition could improve schools in these ways:

1. It could motivate teachers and administrators to work harder. I doubt, though, that a lack of motivation is the major problem in schools. Many educators are already overworked and underpaid. Nor will teachers and administrators be motivated to expand the size of their schools, since they don't profit from expansion, and it may weaken their institutions as communities.

2. It could promote experimentation and the development of better models. But this assumes that there are cost-effective, replicable "solutions" that could be developed in one school and implemented elsewhere. It is not clear that education works like that.

3. It could provide more options to parents or guardians and students. Diversity and choice are good, but they can be provided in many ways—not only through competitive market systems. A typical suburban high school rivals a shopping mall in the number of choices it offers its students. Perhaps well-prepared and motivated children benefit from choice; students who start on the wrong track, however, may simply make bad choices and get into worse trouble.

On the other hand, charter schools do not *reduce* academic performance, at least on average. And they have a huge advantage that is distinct from student educational outcomes. As a society, we need more opportunities to propose solutions to public problems, band together voluntarily, and then work directly to implement our ideas. This is "public work"—one of the most satisfying aspects of citizenship, and a great American tradition. In general, opportunities for public work have shrunk over the last century because of increasing professionalism, standardization and bureaucracy, and a diminished role for the public sector as a whole (see section 6.3). Social work and education used to be excellent fields for public work (especially for women) but they are now exclusively the domains of credentialed specialists who are often unable to innovate because of bureaucratic obstacles.

Here is where charter schools come in. Someone has a new idea, persuades a few friends to join her as teachers, and together they create a new institution. At any rate, that was the story of the charters that I know personally: Cesar Chavez in Washington and the East Bay Conservation Corps in Oakland. Typically, a charter school cannot get off the ground without supportive parents, so the odds are relatively high that parents will play active roles in its governance.[26] Flexibility, creativity, and parental participation do not guarantee better educational results. But they are intrinsically valuable goods—much more important than a few extra points on the SAT.

Some ideas for charter schools are good; others are foolish. And some of the best ideas are not well executed. Although the average test results for charters appear to be about the same as the mean for other public schools, this masks a lot of variation—a wide range from best to worst. That range is a consequence of democracy. The worst charters can be shut down, but the damage they do before they are closed is the price we must pay for creativity in the public sector. Finn and colleagues describe a previous wave of decentralization in New York City in the 1960s, which led to "open schools," "free schools," and other innovations. From their perspective, "Some of this was romantic nonsense, but much of it contained an important truth: schools can afford to be different, need to be responsive, and work best when the people involved with them have a sense of ownership."[27]

Whether charter schools enhance students' *civic* attitudes and skills is an empirical question that has not, to my knowledge, been carefully tested. For the purposes of this chapter, however, they have another rationale. Charters can help to create a society in which citizens have greater scope for creativity and initiative. If citizens take on more important roles, then civic education will be more valued and more rewarding. Charters happen to be educational institutions, but community development corporations, land trusts, and watershed councils are parallel innovations that also allow citizens to do important public work (see section 11.1).

Paying for education with vouchers is an even more radical way of decentralizing educational decisions and allowing many people to innovate at public expense. Even so, I think that civic arguments favor charters over vouchers. With charters, we can balance the influence of local groups that establish schools; chartering authorities, which set rules; and state and national agencies, which regulate and evaluate public education. That means that we can have productive public deliberations at three levels of government. There can be debates not only about what should be taught in the fourth grade at the local charter school, but also about what *everyone* should learn in a city, a state, or nation. Each level can be held accountable to the others. In contrast, vouchers reduce the importance of communitywide discussions, because no one except individual parents has leverage over private schools. To be sure, vouchers could be used only at schools that met a set of rules and standards. But if those rules were detailed, ambitious, and subject to change over time, then a voucher system would begin to look much like a charter system.

10.2 NEW FORMS OF JOURNALISM

The decline in news consumption among young people is deeply troubling. It would be possible to locate the causes of that problem in youth attitudes and daily behaviors. Survey data (summarized in section 3.4) show powerful correlations between following the news and trust in the media. One response, then, is to try to raise young people's confidence in journalists and the news media, in the hope that increased confidence will boost news consumption, which will enhance civic engagement.

That strategy has two drawbacks. First, it appears difficult to increase young Americans' trust in the news media through education. Analyzing a major Knight Foundation–sponsored survey, we found (after controlling for a host of observed factors) rather small effects on students' consumption of newspapers if they took courses that dealt with the First Amendment, journalism, or the role of the press, or if their teachers required them to use the news media. The most positive result was a 5 percent increase in students' trust for journalists if they were required to read the news for courses—a significant impact, but not necessarily a lasting one. The effects of state policies (such as required courses in civics or American government) were mostly negative. Students in states with such requirements were marginally *less* likely to read a newspaper, once other factors were taken into account.[28] Second, it would be inappropriate to try to persuade citizens to trust journalists if the press is not actually trustworthy. If the fault lies with the media, then we should not locate the problem inside citizens' heads, but should rather reform the press to make it more worthy of support.

This book is not an appropriate place to assess the overall merits and demerits of today's journalism, which is a complex and variegated business. It is an empirical fact, however, that the news media have changed in ways relevant to civic development over the last century. The earlier changes offer useful lessons; the most recent developments present opportunities for enhancing civic engagement.

Nineteenth-century newspapers freely combined opinion and news. They printed fiction and poetry along with factual reporting. They often ran whole speeches by favored politicians or clergymen. Standards of evidence were generally low. However, publications were relatively cheap to launch, so they proliferated; 2,226 daily newspapers were in business in 1899.[29] A small voluntary association or independent entrepreneur could break into the news business, hoping to make money or to push a particular ideology, or both.

As noted in chapter 6, section 6.2, the nineteenth century was also an age of partisan citizenship, in which people were expected to show loyalty to a party, a union, a church, a town or state, and sometimes a race or ethnic group. Often such loyalties were ascribed from birth; they were matters of affiliation rather than assent, as Michael Schudson writes.[30] Voting was a public act, an expression of loyalty, not a private choice. Politics involved torchlight parades and popular songs; the essence of civic life was boosterism; and newspapers were written in a similarly rousing, communitarian spirit. Most daily newspapers and magazines reflected the positions of a party, church, or association and aimed to persuade readers or motivate the persuaded. The exceptions, beginning with the New York *Sun* in 1833, were independent businesses that sought mass audiences in big cities.

As Schudson has shown, the new model citizen of the Progressive Era—an independent, well-informed, judicious decision-maker—needed a different kind of newspaper, one that provided reliable information clearly distinguished from opinion, exhortation, and fiction. Leading newspapers were separated from parties and religious denominations and began to claim objectivity and independence. Their intended audience became all good citizens, not just members of particular groups. When they introduced opinion columns and letters pages, they often strove for ideological balance. As Adolph Ochs announced when he bought the *New York Times* in 1896, his intention was to "give the news, all the news, in concise and attractive form, in language that is parliamentary in good society, and give it early, if not earlier, than it can be learned through any other reliable medium; to give the news impartially, without fear or favor, regardless of any party, sect, or interest involved; to make of the columns of *The New York Times* a forum for the consideration of all questions of public importance, and to that end to invite intelligent discussion from all shades of opinion."[31]

The transformation of the American press coincided with the ascendance of logical positivism, which sharply distinguished verifiable facts from subjective opinions.[32] Furthermore, the independent newspaper arose along with the modern research university, whose mission was to create independent, judicious decision-makers instead of loyal members of a community (see 6.3, above). Finally, the new press reflected an ideal of a trained, professional journalist, an ideal that took shape when many other occupations were also striving to professionalize.[33]

At about the time when journalists developed ideals of objectivity, independence, and neutrality, the news business consolidated. For example, the number of daily newspapers in New York City fell from twenty in the late 1800s to eight in 1940. Meanwhile, the first newspaper chains were established.[34] Most people began to obtain news from a daily publication with a mass circulation, and they had relatively little choice. Consolidation of the news business and journalistic professionalism could be justified together with one theory: an excellent newspaper (and later, an excellent evening news show on television) was supposed to provide all the objective facts that a citizen needed in order to make up his or her own mind. The citizen did not need much choice among sources, because any truly professional and independent news organ would provide the same array of facts. Some competition might be valuable to encourage efficiency and rigor, but all credible journals would compete for the same stories. Choice was a private matter to be exercised *after* one had read the newspaper or watched TV. One was to be guided not by an ascribed identity but by making informed selections among policy options.

This new model had idealistic defenders, but it also had several serious drawbacks that became increasingly clear as the century progressed. First, the new journalism was probably not as effective at mobilizing citizens as the old partisan press had been. Although we lack data on individuals' newspaper use and civic engagement from before the 1950s, we know that overall turnout and other measures of participation fell as the press consolidated and aimed at professionalism. It seems likely that the new journalism was less motivating.

Second, it became harder to break into the news business once newspapers needed not only printing presses, ink, and paper, but also credentialed journalists, editors and fact-checkers, and a staff large enough to provide comprehensive coverage ("*all* the news that's fit to print"). Thus the telling of news became the province of a few professionals employed by large businesses, not an activity open to many citizens. That problem worsened once radio and television arrived.

Third, journalistic professionalism often seemed to introduce its own biases. For example, journalists were trained not to editorialize in news stories. That meant that they often simply quoted other people's controversial views, usually aiming for as much balance as possible between voices on either side of a debate. To call the president a liar is to editorialize; to quote someone who holds that view is to report a fact. But one still has to choose whom to quote, and the tendency is to interview famous, powerful, or credentialed sources—often those with talents or budgets for public relations and axes to grind. In 1999, some 78 percent of respondents to a national survey agreed: "powerful people can get stories into the paper—or keep them out."[35] Sometimes the norm of "balance" created a bias in favor of the mainstream left and mainstream right, marginalizing other views. On occasion, it meant that reporters gave excessive space to demonstrably false opinions, because they saw their job as reporting what prominent people said, not what was right.

While professional reporters felt bound not to promote policy positions, they believed that they could write objective stories about campaigns. A poll would tell them who was ahead. Polling data also provided evidence about why each candidate took his or her positions: evidently, to draw particular blocs of voters. Thus newspapers offered readers a relentlessly cynical view of politicians' motives, plus an interminable policy debate among experts who were equally balanced between the Right and the Left, plus polls showing that one side or the other was bound to win. It is no wonder that many lost interest in politics. None of this coverage helped citizens to play a role of their own.

Modern professional journalism placed a tremendous emphasis on politics as a "horse race." Three-quarters of broadcast news stories during the 2000 campaign were devoted to tactics and polls; only one-quarter, to issues.[36] As CNN political director Mark Hannon explained in 1996, his network conducted daily polls because they "happen to be the most authoritative way to answer the most basic question about the election, which is who is going to win."[37] In fact, during a campaign, the most basic question for a citizen is *not* who will win, but which candidate to support. But reporters reflexively see that question as one for the editorial pages, whereas they can cover polls as simple empirical facts. Yet the depiction of politics as a horse race suggests that a campaign is a spectator sport (and not a particularly elegant or entertaining one). Controlled experiments have found that such coverage raises cynicism and lowers engagement.[38]

Finally, the ideal news organ of the Progressive Era demanded a great deal of *trust* from its readers. Perhaps objectivity, independence, and balance are possible in theory; in practice, however, any news source is a fallible human product. Major newspapers, magazines, and broadcast news have powerful effects on politics and public opinion. The newspaper that claims to be objective, independent, and nonpartisan asks us to believe that the consequences of its reporting are involuntary, caused by the facts and not by any political agenda. That defense can be hard to swallow. In 2004, young people were less likely than their elders to see a "great deal" of political bias in the media. Nevertheless, two-thirds of all Americans thought they detected at least a "fair amount" of bias.[39] Almost half of local journalists believe that the owners of their newspapers have a "great deal" or "fair amount" of influence on their coverage.[40]

The most glorious chapter in the history of the modern American press was written between 1965 and 1975, when the *Washington Post* and the *New York Times* published the Pentagon Papers, broke the Watergate scandal, and had their constitutional role as independent watchdogs upheld by the Supreme Court. Their reporting certainly had consequences, helping to end a war and bring down a president. That was all very well if one opposed the Vietnam War and President Nixon. But the same power could also be used against President Clinton or against the welfare state. Anyone whose political goals were frustrated by the press might find it difficult to trust reporters as objective and independent. One's skepticism might be reinforced by the fact that each newspaper has owners, investors, and advertisers with economic interests. Writers and editors, too, form a definable interest group.

The debate about corporate power in the news media is at least a century old and is perennially important. In the 1990s, a new discussion began that concerned reporters' professional norms. Some reporters, editors, and academics argued that the newsroom ideals developed during the Progressive Era no longer served democracy and civic engagement. A newspaper like the *New York Times,* as Ochs had envisioned it, presumed a public that was interested in current events and ready to act on the information it read. But that public was shrinking, and it could be argued that the prevailing style of news reporting was actually making it smaller by increasing cynicism. Adversarial, "watchdog" journalists still played an important role by periodically uncovering scandals, but it was not clear why an individual citizen should spend money and time reading such information every day. When a big scandal broke, the opposition party or law enforcement agencies were supposed to address it. Why should individuals pay for independent oversight as a public good? Only those who were already civically engaged would choose to subscribe to the watchdog press. Their numbers were falling, and they could find ever less information in the newspaper that could inform for their own civic activities.

In the 1990s, under the labels of "public journalism" or "civic journalism," news organs experimented with new forms of reporting that might better serve active citizens and enhance civic engagement. For example, instead of reporting the 1992 North Carolina Senate campaign as a horse race (with frequent polls and numerous articles about the candidates' strategies), the *Charlotte Observer* convened a representative group of citizens to deliberate about issues of their choice and to write questions for the major contenders. The newspaper offered to publish the questions and responses verbatim. Meanwhile, its beat reporters were assigned to provide factual reporting on each of the topics that the citizens chose to explore. When Senator Jesse Helms refused to complete the questionnaire that the citizens had written, the *Observer* published blank spaces under his name.[41]

Careful evaluations have found positive effects from this and other such experiments. But public journalism faltered as a movement by the end of the decade.[42] One of the reasons was the sudden rise of the Internet. The newspaper business, panicked by independent Web sites and bloggers, lost interest in civic experimentation. Meanwhile, many proponents of public journalism began to see the Internet as more promising than reforms within conventional newsrooms.

After all, blogs, podcasts, and other digital media make possible a return to the press that existed before the Progressive Era—for better *and* for worse. The barriers to publication have fallen, not only because Web sites are cheaper than printing presses, but also because a mass audience has moved to products created by individuals and amateurs. Some blogs are specialized sites devoted to careful, factual reporting on particular topics, but most are motivational, ideological, and opinionated, with comparatively low standards of evidence and no trained reporters, fact-checkers, or editors. Nonetheless, there are millions of them and they often check one another's facts. Young people are heavily represented and have better opportunities to enter the fray than at any time since 1900.

Blogs, short videos and audios, and other innovative news media should help many people to mobilize and organize their fellow citizens. Until recently, trust in journalists, consumption of newspapers, and civic engagement were strongly correlated (and declining in tandem), but the links may be weakened if people can gain the information they need to participate from other sources. Those who are not inclined to trust the mainstream press will still be able to participate.

Clearly, there are also dangers. An online audience can screen out uncomfortable ideas, thereby splitting into ideologically homogeneous "echo chambers." There is a relative scarcity of online content devoted to local communities. It can be difficult to distinguish the source and reliability of online information. And the Web provides a sometimes confusing mix of fact, opinion, error, deliberate falsification, and overt fiction.

Each of these dangers can be addressed by citizens working online, and sometimes software can help. For example, Wikipedia provides surprisingly reliable information through a system of peer review involving many thousands of volunteers. Technorati's software increases the chance that bloggers will engage in conversations with their critics, by alerting them whenever their writing has been linked from elsewhere. Social networking software like MySpace (which is currently very popular among the young) can be tweaked so that it helps people identify neighbors with similar political interests.

Because citizens may be able to address the drawbacks of the new online media through voluntary action, we should be cautious about heavy-handed reforms. There are, however, two pressing problems that require attention. First, it is possible to make handsome profits by limiting customers' access to material produced by ordinary citizens and driving them to corporate content. Internet service providers may be tempted to provide quicker access to Web sites that pay them for that advantage; cable companies may charge higher fees for uploading data than for downloading corporate material; and most search engines already sell preferential treatment. Legislation is needed to keep the Internet neutral and open.[43]

Second the "blogosphere" still depends on daily news journalism. Therefore, cuts in newsroom staff and attempts to replace hard news with entertainment are still damaging, even in the Internet era. It's true that people get news, ideas, and values from electronic sources, including the Web portals of Yahoo and other Internet-service providers (which are regular news sources for 15 percent of young people); comedy TV (a regular source for 21 percent of youth); and talk radio (16 percent).[44] However, Yahoo's headlines simply come from wire services—hence, from reporters. Comedy writers get most of their material from print journalism. Lewis Friedland estimates that 90 percent of the news stories on local TV come from a local newspaper.[45] Debates in the blogosphere are very often triggered by reported news. Fictional programs like *Law and Order* are inspired by print journalism. Therefore, influential conversations in the kitchen, the office watercooler, and church often derive ultimately from a newspaper.

Thus we cannot consider citizen media and other new means of communication and discussion in isolation. They are dependent on the state of conventional, professional journalism—which at present isn't good. Newspapers are highly profitable but are cutting their staff and budgets for reporting. Two-thirds of national journalists believe that bottom-line pressure is hurting news coverage—causing the press to avoid complex issues, to be sloppy, and to be timid.[46] Bloggers can complain about newspaper journalists from various angles; they cannot replace them.

10.3 POLITICAL REFORMS

Compared to older people and to youth of past generations, today's young people are relatively uninterested in politics and relatively unlikely to see voting as a duty. Compared to their elders, they are quite uninformed about politics. Those psychological factors may partly explain why they tend to vote at lower rates than older people and youth of the past. Still, there are strong reasons to believe that modern American politics itself discourages or even blocks youth from voting. To the extent this premise is true, we should not try to raise turnout simply by educating young people about politics or exhorting them to participate. The process itself must change.

Imagine two hypothetical political systems. In the first, parties and other large-scale organizations (such as unions and churches) depend on large numbers of citizens: unpaid volunteers and low-paid campaign workers. To keep all those supporters involved and satisfied, these organizations periodically seek their members' advice and offer them opportunities for advancement. Because they need a constant supply of new participants, they are always recruiting. Personal contact is the most effective way to recruit; thus there is much door-to-door canvassing and organizing through local associations, such as congregations and ethnic clubs. Young people represent a large pool of potential recruits with high energy and commitment. If youths can be drawn into one party, they will support it for a long time and *not* join the rival party. (From the 1950s through the 1970s, longitudinal studies found that party identification was "almost perfectly stable" over the course of individuals' lives.)[47] Thus political leaders focus on the next generation, giving them personalized attention and some "voice" through separate youth caucuses.

In the second system, politicians are entrepreneurs, seeking their own election. They employ free-floating professional consultants who advise them on how to raise and spend campaign money. They spend a great deal of time with donors, very few of whom are young. Consultants advise them to maximize the immediate impact of their spending by reaching the most likely voters: people in demographic groups known for participation (such as the elderly and the wealthy) and individuals who have long records of past participation. Candidates spend a high proportion of their budgets on targeted broadcast advertising, and very little on developing future supporters.

The first system is an idealized portrait of American politics circa 1930 or 1960.[48] This portrait overlooks fatal flaws in the old party model, such as racial exclusion, corruption, and male dominance. There were good reasons to weaken the parties by reducing their ability to raise funds and distribute patronage appointments and by creating fair primaries in which insurgent candidates could run.

The second system resembles what prevails in the United States today, except that it, too, is somewhat idealized. In most real U.S. House districts, only the incumbent is able to field a professional campaign with a large budget and the capacity to advertise. In 2002, some $1.6 billion was spent in House and Senate elections, yet the median budget of House challengers was just $50,000, not enough to hire professional advisers, let alone buy any television time.[49] One reason that incumbents have a huge fund-raising advantage is that they are almost guaranteed to win; therefore, groups that seek attention and favorable treatment from Congress give them money. Only four House challengers won in 2002, and only five in 2004.[50] The 2006 election was considered especially competitive, yet only twenty-two incumbent House members and five sitting senators lost in the general election. Almost all electoral districts have been drawn to favor one party or another. A crucial but invisible part of most campaigns is the effort to influence districting through "increasingly sophisticated information technology."[51] If you have the votes to determine the map of legislative districts and a computer that can draw borders to maximize your share of the votes, you are hard to beat.

Regardless of the overall merits of the two systems as they actually work, the system that prevails today is worse for youth development. Entrepreneurial candidates must spend a great deal of time with contributors and must avidly solicit their views. But young people do not make political contributions. In 1998, *none* of the 169 randomly selected young people in the National Election Study sample said that they had given money to a party or candidate (compared to 11 percent of respondents in their forties and fifties).[52] Further, young people are rarely targeted for broadcast ads, because they are known to have a low voter turnout rate. In 1999, Dane Strother, a consultant who worked for Democratic candidates, said, "I help sell politicians and young adults don't participate in the political process. Whenever we buy television and target our advertising spots we just completely discount anyone under thirty."[53] Nor are many young people recruited as volunteers, because unpaid and unskilled workers are not important parts of modern media campaigns. The proportion of young people who said that they had been contacted by a major party fell from 22 percent in the 1960s to 11 percent in the 1990s.[54] (In both periods, I suspect, most of the contacts were perfunctory; but at least they were twice as common forty years ago.) Meanwhile, youth turnout fell by about one-third between 1972 and 2000. Young people were also shrinking as a percentage of the population, owing to relatively low birth rates in the 1960s and 1970s. Because of those two factors, youth (ages 18–24) represented just 6 percent of all voters in the 1994 election, down from 14 percent in 1972.[55]

In short, youth started with the lowest chance of voting, they were a small group, they couldn't increase their power by giving money, their voluntary work was of little perceived value in an age of broadcast advertisements and mass mailings, and entrepreneurial candidates gained little by cultivating them as long-term voters. (It was easier simply to identify those who *did* vote several times and put them on mailing lists). All these factors argued against devoting resources to mobilizing young people. Because they were ever less likely to be contacted, they were ever less likely to vote—a classic vicious cycle.

Parties, especially at the county level, still needed volunteers. Unlike consultants, they were rooted in particular communities, and they would outlast each election cycle. As Cherie Strachan writes, "In modern America, the party organizations, with a vested interest in enhancing strong partisanship in the electorate, are one of the few—if not the only—organizations in society with a self-interested motive" to cultivate new active citizens.[56] Apparently, however, they took their cues from national politics and political consultants and tended to overlook youth. In 2003, Daniel Shea and John Green surveyed more than eight hundred county Democratic and Republican party leaders. As they write:

> We asked an open-ended question: "Are there demographic groups of voters that are currently important to the long-term success of your local party?" We recorded the group listed and then asked for a second and third group. Thus, the local leaders were given three opportunities to mention any group of voters. . . . Overall, just 8.4 percent of the respondents mentioned youth in the first question, another 11.6 percent mentioned it in the second question, and 17.5 percent mentioned it on the third try. Thus, a total of 37.5 percent mentioned young voters—even though the question addressed the "long-term success of the party.[57]

To put it another way, almost two-thirds of local party leaders failed to identify youth as an important demographic group for the future of their party, even given three tries. They were far more likely to name senior citizens.

Several strategies have been proposed to reverse this vicious cycle. All were implemented to some degree before the 2004 election, when youth turnout jumped by eleven percentage points. Thus it is possible that these strategies are beginning to work and should be sustained. Here I will describe them in ascending order of promise.

Celebrity Appeals

First, the entertainment world has embraced youth voting as a cause. If celebrities persuade young Americans that they should vote, and turnout rises, then politicians, parties, and interest groups may invest resources in courting the new generation, reinforcing the rise in turnout. The recording industry founded Rock the Vote in 1990. It enlisted stars such as Madonna (who unfortunately didn't vote herself)[58] to raise youth turnout through nonpartisan videos, endorsements, and public appearances. Rock the Vote was subsequently joined by the World Wrestling Foundation's "Smackdown the Vote" campaign, Christian rockers' "Redeem the Vote" organization, the Hip-Hop Action Summit's Voter Registration Campaign, and Sean Comb's "Vote or Die" project. In all, a remarkable panoply of celebrities from Paris Hilton to Snoop Dogg have made youth voting their main pro bono cause between 1992 and 2004.

Their motives presumably vary. When the recording industry created Rock the Vote, a goal was to mobilize young voters who might be expected to oppose restrictions on "indecent" music.[59] Dr. Randy Brinson of Redeem the Vote and Russell Simmons of Hip-Hop Action Summit have tried to motivate particular segments of the young electorate (respectively, evangelicals and African Americans) in order to promote ideological— although not partisan—goals.[60] Eminem's video *Mosh* (2004), which advocated youth voting as a response to the Iraq war, was sufficiently moving, personal, and idiosyncratic that I thought it was an authentic personal statement. Still, it is likely that some of the entertainment industry's efforts were simply intended to keep young people's attention focused on their brand names without risking controversy. Almost any campaign concerning a public issue would be more controversial than a generic call to vote; that may explain its attraction to the music business.[61]

It is impossible to know whether these celebrity appeals have had any impact. A mass television audience cannot be separated into treatment and control groups to measure the effectiveness of a given broadcast. Youth turnout reached its nadir (22 percent) in 1994, when Rock the Vote was active; but perhaps participation would have been even lower without it. Certainly, companies would spend many millions of dollars to deploy an equal amount of celebrity attention, expecting thereby to affect youth behavior. On the other hand, it is counterintuitive that people would respond to a generic message that they should vote. Normally, we persuade other people to participate by arguing that specific goals will be advanced if someone in particular wins the next election. While celebrity endorsements can make consumer goods more appealing, it seems unlikely that people will undertake the essentially private and ethical act of voting because a star tells them to do so. At best, I think, the Rock the Vote approach drew useful attention to grassroots work that I describe below.

Easing Voting Rules

A second strategy is to remove legal or practical obstacles to voting, especially those that might disproportionately hamper first-time voters. The idea is to make voting easier, thereby raising youth turnout, thereby giving politicians more reason to mobilize young people.

The process of voting has traditionally been complicated in the United States. It requires both the affirmative step of registering and then a visit to a specific polling place during the right hours on Election Day. Many obstacles can arise, either because of a lack of attention on the citizen's part or bureaucratic errors by the government. Recently, however, states have adopted creative reforms. Some have allowed anyone to vote "absentee" without a specific reason, to vote before Election Day in designated locations, to vote early in the morning or after 7 P.M. on Election Day, to register on that day, to register while undertaking other interactions with the government (such as renewing a driver's license), and to register by mail instead of in-person. The last two provisions are universal thanks to the National Voter Registration Act of 1993 (better known as Motor Voter), but were phased in between 1972 and 1995.[62] There are also laws in some states that require public and/or private employers to offer time off for voting; and some states mail information about the next election to all citizens.

The only method that has been used to estimate the impact of these reforms is to compare statewide turnout rates. A reform appears promising if turnout is higher in the states that have it, and if turnout rises after the reform is implemented in a given state. Yet states' turnout rates are also affected by many other factors, such as their historical traditions of participation; the competitiveness of their elections; the average wealth, age, and education of their populations; and the nature of their local media. Often the states with the strongest traditions of turnout are also the ones that first implement reforms to ease the voting process, making it difficult to disentangle the impact of the voting reforms. Although no perfect measures exist for these background factors, we can control for available data. If a reform correlates with higher turnout after observable factors are held constant, it appears to work.

To summarize the existing research, it appears that allowing citizens to register on Election Day has a substantial positive impact on young people's turnout—the estimate is fourteen percentage points—and also makes it much more likely that the parties will contact each young person. That is evidence that Election Day registration can set off a virtuous cycle of higher turnout and more attention. Unfortunately, only seven states had implemented that reform as of 2003.[63]

Sending registrants information about where to vote and/or sample ballots raises turnout, but only for young people who have not attended college. Because their educational background is weaker and because they are out of networks that might inform them about elections, they benefit from the information provided in mailings. Although the overall impact of that reform is not great, it has potential for reducing political inequality.[64] There are also small positive effects from lengthening polling hours and allowing people to vote early or absentee. Providing time off to vote and allowing people to vote or register by mail have no evident benefits for youth turnout.[65]

Other reforms that have been proposed (but cannot yet be assessed because they are not in place) include registering people automatically while they are in high school, allowing online voting, and teaching high school seniors how to use voting machines. The last idea proved extremely successful in a randomized experiment.[66] The most radical reform now in place—Oregon's decision to conduct voting entirely by mail—cannot be accurately assessed because it only exists in one state. But it is interesting that Oregon had one of the biggest gaps in turnout between youth and older people in 2004: twenty-seven percentage points, compared to a national gap of nineteen points. It may be that making it easier to vote increased the number of people who participated, but reduced the proportion of voters who were young.

In conclusion, the most promising evidence favors Election Day registration, and it is possible that more radical reforms would be more effective. But a cautionary story is the Motor Voter Act of 1993, which raised the proportion of people who were registered by easing the registration process, without raising the turnout rate at all. Overall, it has become easier to register and vote in the United States over time, yet turnout has declined.[67] This suggests that ease of voting is not the only factor to worry about.

Mobilizing Young People

A third strategy is to show politicians that they will benefit if they directly mobilize young voters. It may not be in consultants' interests to canvass students and other young adults or to recruit young volunteers who will organize their peers. Consultants typically earn more money by taking a fixed percentage of broadcast advertising contracts. However, if politicians can actually attract more votes by mobilizing youth than by advertising on television programs viewed by senior citizens, then politicians may be persuaded to fire their consultants and find people who can run grassroots, youth-oriented campaigns for them.

Political campaigning is more of an art than a science, and consultants rely heavily on folklore about what works. Starting in the 1990s, however, two Yale political scientists, Donald Green and Alan Gerber, set out to test the effects of canvassing young voters through randomized field experiments. Young registered voters were randomly selected either to be contacted or to be left alone. Actual voting records were used to determine the turnout rate for the treatment and control groups, and the difference was the effect of the contact. When the amount of money spent per contact was recorded, one could also calculate the impact per dollar. Green and Gerber's main motivation was to encourage experimental methods in political science, but The Pew Charitable Trusts, which funded their voting experiments, hoped to generate results that would change political behavior to the advantage of youth.

Green and Gerber's first, small-scale experiments showed that young people could be cheaply mobilized, especially if they were contacted face-to-face. Their students and others have varied those early studies by experimenting in diverse communities—including rural Latino counties, Asian-American enclaves in Los Angeles, and suburban subdivisions— and by using alternative methods of voter mobilization such as direct mailings, phone banks, and prerecorded phone calls. With money from Pew, Carnegie Corporation of New York, the Beldon Fund, the JEHT Foundation, and the Solidago Foundation, CIRCLE funded several additional experiments in 2004 and 2005.

Overall, the results show that young people can be cost-effectively mobilized. The price of each additional vote—beyond what would be cast without the mobilizing effort—is often between $10 and $26, a much better deal than candidates assume they get from broadcast advertising.[68] The results are consistent for various demographic groups, which demonstrates that poor and minority youth can be mobilized at a reasonable cost. When experiments test alternative messages, they usually find no statistically significant differences. As long as an experienced political operative has written the message, one rhetorical approach does not seem to work better than another. For example, appeals to civic duty seem neither better nor worse than partisan arguments. The *quality* of the interaction, however, appears to matter a great deal. Face-to-face contacts by peers are highly effective and work out to be cheapest per vote generated. Volunteer phone banks are somewhat less efficient, but certainly worthwhile. Mass mailings are still less efficient, and "robocalls" (prerecorded telephone messages) generate so few votes that they are a very bad financial deal for the candidate.[69]

The full strategy behind these experiments was not merely to measure the effects of various forms of campaigning, but to influence the behavior of parties, interest groups, and politicians by showing that it is in their interest to recruit young volunteers and to mobilize young voters. Parties and consultants do not like to disclose their strategies or how they allocate their resources. Nonetheless, anecdotal evidence suggests that the major parties *did* change strategies substantially in 2004, putting much more resources into grassroots campaigning (instead of advertising) and specifically targeting the youth vote.[70] Meanwhile, various nonpartisan groups, led by the Pew-funded New Voters Project, spent roughly $40 million on young voter mobilization, using techniques pretested in randomized field experiments.[71] Although I don't believe this thesis can be proved with great rigor, I strongly suspect that the new attention to youth mobilizing caused most of the eleven-point jump in youth turnout in 2004. The hope now is that politicians and parties will sustain their attention to youth even if funding from foundations diminishes. An additional reason for them to do so is the sheer growth of the Millennial generation as a percentage of the population. Young people have numbers and they can be persuaded to vote.

Enhancing Competition

The final strategy for encouraging youth to vote is to make elections more competitive. Youth turnout in the ten most competitive, "battleground" states was seventeen percentage points higher than in the rest of the country in 2004. Growing up in a politically competitive community also turns out to have important educational advantages. Candidates "are compelled to be more specific about their issue positions" when they face competition. More specific campaigning is more educative.[72] James Gimpel and his colleagues find that young people who live in communities with competitive elections are more knowledgeable about politics, more efficacious, more tolerant, and more likely to discuss politics than their peers, holding many other factors constant.

Competition probably enhances civic learning because politicians and parties must reach out to citizens when elections are close. They reach out with messages that make people feel important and that convey interesting information. Also, regardless of how politicians behave, one can learn from growing up among roughly equal groups of Democrats and Republicans. In politically diverse communities, young people are exposed to many political views and understand that disagreement is inevitable. (The same advantage also arises from religious diversity.)

Political competitiveness can compensate for economic disadvantage. In fact, Gimpel and his colleagues studied poor communities with a mix of Democratic and Republican voters in which young people grew up more knowledgeable than their peers who lived in wealthy, single-party suburbs. Political competition boosts the level of discussion "by an amazing 17 percentage points among those with no plans to attend college," because exposure to robust politics compensates for their relatively poor formal educations.[73]

However, most Americans do *not* grow up in competitive districts. As noted above, only a tiny percentage of House incumbents are defeated in most modern elections. The same pattern occurs in many states: for example, in 2004, *none* of California's 153 legislative seats changed parties.[74] The 2006 national election was more competitive than usual, but the change of 31 seats from the Republicans to the Democrats still represented only 7 percent of the House of Representatives.

Three major explanations have been offered for the lack of electoral competition in America. Incumbents have a huge fund-raising advantage, thanks in part to their ability to raise money from groups that have interests before them. Districts have been drawn with increasing sophistication to favor one party over the other. And communities have become politically more homogeneous. No one redraws county lines to benefit politicians, yet the segregation of Democrats and Republicans at the county level increased by 47 percent during the last quarter of the twentieth century.[75] The number of "landslide" counties—where one party or the other wins by at least 60 percent—has increased fourfold since 1994.[76] All this is evidence that people are polarizing: moving to live near people with whom they agree or changing their opinions to conform to their neighbors.

We cannot do much about the last problem; but electoral districts could be drawn to promote rather than reduce competition. Instead of allowing legislatures to establish district boundaries by majority vote, we could give that power to nonpartisan commissions like the one in Iowa. The value of Iowa's reform is demonstrated by the fact that two of the state's five House races were competitive in 2004. In contrast, just one of California's 53 races—for an open seat—was competitive.[77] Nonpartisan commissions could be packed with allies of the incumbent parties. Thus an alternative would be to program a public computer to draw electoral maps. The computer would maximize a set of goals (competitiveness, racial equity, and compactness) and resolve conflicts randomly. Randomness provides procedural fairness, as anyone knows who has flipped a coin to decide who plays first. Federal courts could require such remedies, but they have so far refused to intervene in all but the most extreme cases of partisan gerrymandering. In the absence of court orders, redistricting reform will require a popular movement that can obtain changes through referenda or legislative votes.

The financial advantages of incumbency would be reduced if public funds were available for campaigning. In Maine and Arizona, state candidates receive public subsidies if they agree to limit their private contributions to very low amounts. That reform should help challengers and thereby increase competition. It could be implemented in other states and at the federal level.

An American Political Science Association committee recently recommended changing the way that Electoral College votes are allocated. Today, the winner of a state's popular vote receives all the seats in the Electoral College. That means that if a state leans strongly toward one party or the other, it is not worth campaigning there. The APSA committee recommend that we "give two electoral college votes to the statewide winner and one vote to the winner of each congressional district."[78] Then, for example, Republican presidential candidates would campaign in contested parts of California, and Democrats would campaign in Georgia, even though they have had little chance of winning those states in recent years. The result would be a considerably bigger "battleground."

There are other proposals, including instant runoff voting (in which voters rank candidates in order of preference) and proportional representation (in which seats are awarded in proportion to party support across a whole state.) It is impossible to predict with great certainty the effects of any electoral reform; the Law of Unintended Consequences prevails. Certainly, it is beyond the scope of this book to define the best package of reforms. Yet there is no reason to be satisfied with the status quo. The country at least needs a robust debate about how to enhance political competition.

CHAPTER 11

Youth Civic Engagement within a

Broader Civic Renewal Movement

Our formal political system is coarse, unproductive, uncompetitive, and short-sighted, as young people would be the first to agree. Outside of formal politics, however, there is a robust movement under way for civic renewal in America. In keeping with the ideals described in chapter 1, this movement is dedicated to improving the quality, quantity, and equality of participation in American democracy and civil society. It is concerned with procedures and institutions rather than with specific political objectives (which are left to the participants to choose deliberatively). Just as social-studies teachers in public schools help their students to become skillful and informed deliberators without telling them what to decide, so activists throughout the civic renewal movement empower citizens for self-government in an open-ended way. This broader movement is essential to the future of civic education. Efforts to engage youth in politics and community affairs have no chance unless they are combined with other efforts to strengthen and deepen democracy.

11.1 ELEMENTS OF THE MOVEMENT

At the heart of today's civic renewal movement are concrete, practical experiments, including service-learning, civics courses, community youth development, youth media work, and youth-led research (all described in chapters 7 and 8) plus the following approaches that involve adults as well as young people.

Practical Deliberative Democracy

For some thirty years, nonprofits have been organizing groups of citizens at a human scale (say, five to five hundred people) to discuss public issues, with background materials and some kind of moderation or facilitation. Major organizations in this field include the National Issues Forums (mainly self-selected adults deliberating face-to-face, with published guides), Study Circles (a similar process, but usually more embedded in community organizing), Deliberative Polls (randomly selected citizens who meet for several days), and online forums such as E–The People. Models and practices are proliferating.[1]

Work on deliberation shades into conflict-mediation efforts, intergroup dialogues (which usually involve discussions of identities and relationships rather than issues), and even new mechanisms that governmental bodies are using to "consult" the public.

Community Economic Development

Deliberation also occurs within nonprofit corporations that aim to create jobs and income, and that are formally tied to neighborhoods or to specific rural areas. These corporations include co-ops, land trusts, and community development corporations (CDCs), among others.

One of the biggest weaknesses of democracy today is the mobility of capital. As Gar Alperovitz argues, a corporation can influence political decisions in many ways, including the "implicit or explicit threat of withdrawing its plants, equipment, and jobs from specific locations." Besides, "in the absence of an alternative, the economy as a whole depends on the viability and success of its most important economic factor—a reality that commonly forces citizen and politican alike to respond to corporate demands."[2]

Even people who favor low taxation and light regulation should want democratic communities to make their own choices without undue influence from capital. Unfortunately, if there is no alternative to the standard corporation, then democracies *must* do what firms want. Trying to restrict capital flows simply violates the laws of the market and will impose steep costs. On the other hand, the success of CDCs, land trusts, and similar innovations proves that there is an alternative to the corporation. It is possible to increase the wealth of people in poor communities by creating economically efficient organizations that are tied to places.

Democratic Community-organizing Work

The Industrial Areas Foundation (which has created and worked with many CDCs and other neighborhood corporations) represents a form of community organizing that builds poor people's political capacity as well as their wealth. Instead of defining a community's problems and advocating solutions, IAF organizers encourage relatively open-ended discussions that lead to concrete actions (such as the construction of 2,900 townhouses in Brooklyn, New York), thereby generating civic power. IAF is a major force in this field, but not the only one. A related stream of practice is Asset-Based Community Development, which emphasizes the importance of cataloguing and publicizing the assets of any community as a prelude to development. The goal is to shift from thinking of poor communities as baskets of problems, and instead recognizing their intrinsic capacities. The Pew Partnership for Civic Change is a hub for this kind of work.

Work to Defend and Expand the Commons

The "tragedy of the commons" is the tendency of any resource that is not privately owned to be degraded as people overuse it or fail to invest in it. The "tragedy" is real: consider the collapse of global fish stocks because of overexploitation. However, many unowned resources actually flourish for generations or even centuries. And robust new commons are developing. Land trusts and co-ops are physical examples, but there is also cyberspace, understood as a whole structure, not as a series of privately owned components. Scholars like Elinor Ostrom, working closely with communities, have begun to understand the principles that underlie effective commons—whether they happen to be grasslands, computer networks, or bodies of scientific knowledge.[3]

Practical work to protect and enhance commons is under way within the American Libraries Association, because librarians see themselves as defenders of public artifacts (the books, maps, databases, and Web pages in their collections), public facilities (library buildings, meeting spaces, grounds), and public ideas (including all human knowledge that is not patented or copyrighted, plus copyrighted books that people can borrow and read). Librarians believe that these public goods are threatened in many ways—ranging from patrons' abuse of library books and budget cuts to corporations' efforts to overextend copyright law—and the ALA is fighting back in the courts and legislatures.

Meanwhile, librarians are encouraging constructive public participation in local libraries to enhance the value of these commons. An example is the September Project, an impressive series of discussions, art exhibitions, readings, and performances that now take place in thousands of public libraries every September 11, as a democratic response to the terror attacks.

There is also practical work to defend environmental commons. Collaborative efforts to restore and protect ecosystems are often undertaken under the name of "civic environmentalism." Because the keys to robust, sustainable commons include public deliberation and the wide dispersal of civic skills and attitudes, commons work is closely related to civic renewal.

Work on a New Generation of Public Media

When we hear the phrase "public media," we may think first of publicly subsidized organizations that produce and broadcast shows to mass audiences. Indeed, within the constellation of the Corporation for Public Broadcasting (CPB), NewsHour Productions, and Public Broadcasting Service, there is some interesting work going on that could support civic renewal. "Public media," however, is much broader than CPB; it should include any use of any communications medium to promote the creation and sharing of ideas and cultural products relevant to public issues. So defined, the most compelling public media today originate from thousands of grassroots groups that are creating Web sites, e-mail–based discussions, and audio and video segments.

J-Lab, the Center for Interactive Journalism at the University of Maryland, has made grants to grassroots groups to conduct "micro-news" projects. All across the country, people are producing community blogs (on which citizens can post short news items and comments), elaborate "content management systems" that allow many citizens to contribute news to local Web sites, and "podcasting" projects (short audio clips of news or music that can be downloaded and heard on cell phones and other portable devices). While most of the content created for these media has nothing to do with politics or social issues, nationwide there is a substantial amount of real micro-news.

There is also relevant work inside newspapers. The movement called "civic journalism" or "public journalism" (see 10.2) ran out of steam as a political force, but it left its mark in newsrooms. Furthermore, because of the Internet, newspapers are desperate to become more "interactive." Although interactivity can be a mere gimmick or a way to enhance an individual's experience on a Web site, some journalists are experimenting with interactive features such as blogs for democratic purposes.

Public media work and work to defend the commons come together in the field of positive hip-hop. Youth of all races are now producing music and poetry that confronts serious social problems and that depicts themselves as three-dimensional human beings, not as thugs. Hip-hop culture usually involves borrowing, quoting, and parodying snippets from the mass media. This activity is powerfully democratic. There should be a commons composed of cultural products available for such "fair use." Overrestrictive copyright laws are threatening this commons. Young people in the hip-hop world are increasingly aware that they have a stake in even such dry issues as copyright.

Development of Social Software

I mentioned blogs in the last section. They are one example of a new behavior that is enabled by software. Many developers are working on other software to enhance discussion and collaboration. Examples include "wikis," documents or even whole encyclopedias that can be written and edited by anyone who visits. The Wikipedia is strikingly accurate and well written for an enormous Web site that is edited only by its own readers. It exemplifies a certain kind of deliberation. A good community-oriented example is a whole newspaper, the Bakersfield, California, *Northwest Voice,* that consists entirely of material submitted by citizens. People submit news items that are automatically sorted by location and topic. The result is a Web site that looks exactly like a professional online newspaper, even though it is created by volunteers. Copies are printed with advertising supplements and distributed to every household.

While some of this frenzied innovation is driven by purely technical interests and goals (and by the prospect of making money), there is also a strong subculture of "hackers" who are committed to the commons and to democracy.

The Engaged University

Colleges and universities have great civic potential as producers of knowledge, sites of deliberation, and powerful nonprofit economic institutions, rooted in communities. Since the Second World War, however, they have often overvalued technical knowledge and denigrated public deliberation. They also draw distinctions among research (sophisticated scholarship assessed by academic peers), teaching (the transmission of expert knowledge to students), and service (the application of expertise to community problems). In competitive universities, teaching and service are generally valued less than scholarship, and the three enterprises suffer from being separated.

Today, however, there are evident countertrends, including various impressive scholarly research programs that require close and mutually respectful interactions among scholars, students, and geographical communities, social movements, or professional groups outside the academy. For example, the Jonathan M. Tisch College of Citizenship and Public Service at Tufts University supports service and research in collaboration with local communities. It does not offer its own degrees or certificates but works across the entire campus to strengthen civic engagement. The Center for Community Partnerships at the University of Pennsylvania provides opportunities for distinguished scholars to break new ground in their own disciplines by conducting research that benefits (and takes direction from) residents of West Philadelphia, where the university is situated. Penn has also used its economic leverage in constructive ways, collaborating with community partners.

The Center for Community Partnerships exemplifies several civic trends in higher education: a move from "service" to collaboration; a rediscovery of geographical communities; a reflection on colleges' power as employers, builders, and consumers; and a turn to sophisticated research that requires learning with and from nonacademics.

11.2 THE STRENGTH AND GROWTH OF THE MOVEMENT

I am convinced that the civic renewal movement forms a reasonably tight and robust network. My basis for that claim is the set of social ties that I observe as part of my official work, which involves numerous meetings and conferences in many parts of the United States (probably more than seventy-five per year). I am constantly struck by the appearance of the same people, or of people who know others in the broader network. Of course, this is a mere impression; it could be tested with rigorous network analysis, which I believe would be quite useful. In brief, researchers would begin with several key organizations (such as the ones listed above) and ask decision-makers what other groups they collaborate with. Researchers would then move to those groups and ask, in turn, about their collaborations. Software can automatically generate network maps based on such data. I would hypothesize that a network map of civic renewal would show many links binding the whole field.

Lacking the resources actually to conduct such a study, I have used an imperfect substitute. Instead of asking people to list their partners, I have examined electronic links among organizations' Web sites. A Web link provides imperfect evidence of actual collaboration, but it does show that the person responsible for one site values another. I used software called IssueCrawler to generate figure 9. I began with four nodes that I chose because of my sense that they represent important consolidations of practice since the 1990s: the Civic Practices Network, the Deliberative Democracy Consortium, CIRCLE, and the Pew Partnership for Civic Change. IssueCrawler detected all the sites to which these four linked, and then all the sites linked to these, and so on, until it had built a large database of networked Web sites. It then placed the sites on a two-dimensional plane based on no information about the content of any Web pages, but rather the tendency of sites to link to one another. The resulting map shows that projects of adult public deliberation, civic education, service-learning, higher education reform, and political reform are heavily interlinked. If the map were allowed to display more nodes, it would become too large and complex to present as a single image, but it would reveal that there are also links to the fields of community organizing, urban planning, conflict resolution, and social software.

It is important to note that the civic renewal movement may be robust and coherent, but it is insufficiently diverse. Most of the organizations listed above are predominantly, sometimes exclusively, white. Minorities are best represented in the work that involves community economic development; they are not well represented in civic education or in much of the deliberation field.

My second claim involves growth. I believe that the civic renewal movement is stronger, larger, and more influential than it was ten or twenty years ago. This claim is difficult to substantiate. When we work in social movements, we tend to make two historical assertions without hard evidence. We tend to assert that our problem is getting worse, and that a movement has recently formed to counteract it. Given the "churning" that is endemic to American civil society, it is not obvious that the country's civic condition really has declined or that a civic re-

FIGURE 9 A Map of Civic Renewal

newal movement has recently developed. Maybe every generation could make the same claims.

Nevertheless, some aspects of civic life certainly have declined, and some new strategies and organizations certainly have formed to renew civil society. In September 2006, the National Conference on Citizenship issued an Index of Civic Health (see fig. 10) composed of forty indicators that had been collected regularly since 1975.[4] The forty indicators spanned volunteering, group membership, work on community problems, philanthropy, trust in other people and in government, use of the news media, voting, and expressions of political opinion. The index showed a steep decline from 1975 until the mid-1990s—when talk of civic renewal intensified—followed by some recovery. Most of the indicators that have improved, however, involve political action. The measures of engagement in civil society continue to stagnate or decline.

FIGURE 10 Index of Civic Health

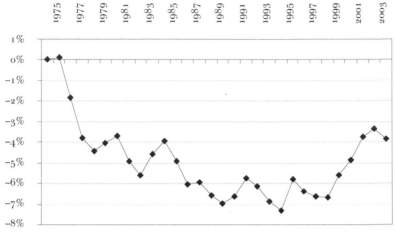

Source: See note 4, page 260.

I believe that several historical factors help to explain the formation of a robust civic renewal movement in America. First of all, this movement (while nonpartisan) has roots in Lyndon Johnson's Great Society. During the War on Poverty, the federal government paid the salaries of thousands of people who worked at the grassroots level, organizing communities and running programs. Granted, the Great Society included elements of bureaucracy and centralization, but it also required the "Maximum Feasible Participation" of citizens. As a result, there was a great deal of civic experimentation. Some people who were heavily involved in those experiments later switched over to electoral politics. Some burned out or lost the opportunity to serve when their budgets were cut. But a considerable number continued to experiment and learn, often moving from federal programs to nonprofits. When they lost their government grants, they developed local financial sources. When they got tired of fighting city hall, they developed collaborative relationships with local governments.[5] Thus there is a generational aspect to the civic renewal movement. The movement partly reflects the maturation of the baby boom and the arrival of younger people whom the Boomers mentored.

Another impetus was the defeat of the Soviet Union at the hands of civil society. Well before 1989, most leftists in the West had become thoroughly disenchanted with the Leninist regimes of the Warsaw Pact.

Nevertheless, the fall of the Soviet Union and the triumph of Havel, Wałesa, Gopnik, Sakharov, and the other dissidents was an important moment for the Western Left. It clearly displayed the moral superiority of civic work over Marxist state-centered politics. And it revealed that civic culture was an important historical force, not merely a phenomenon of the underlying economic system. Because dissidents built healthy civic spaces in Poland, the former Czechoslovakia, and Hungary, those countries could overthrow communism and build democracy. In countries that lacked such a civic culture, the same overthrow led to civil war.

Meanwhile, as authors like James C. Scott and Michael Edwards have argued, economic development is usually disastrous when it relies on social engineering and top-down mandates. Even when governments are reasonably well-meaning, as in Tanzania or India, state efforts to promote growth and equity usually backfire. Again, what seems to matter most are democratic institutions and political culture. As Edwards argues, "It's the polity, stupid."[6] (Edwards had a stint at the World Bank at a time when many of the lending institutions were beginning to recognize the importance of civil society.)

11.3 POLITICAL LEADERSHIP FOR CIVIC RENEWAL

The movement for civic renewal must have an authentic popular base. Such a base cannot be imposed or instigated from above. If politicians try to launch it, not only will they fail to motivate sufficient activity at the grassroots level; they may convey the impression that civic renewal belongs to their party or ideology, thereby alienating citizens on the other side. Because their job is to run the government, they may define civic renewal in state-centered (not citizen-centered) terms. Or else, like Jimmy Carter in 1979, they will call on the public to solve national problems without seeming to take enough responsibility themselves, thereby appearing ineffectual.

President Clinton's 1995 State of the Union address was an inspiring and substantive call to active citizenship. Not only did he identify and thank some specific citizens for addressing serious problems outside of the government; he called for a New Covenant based on "more responsibility for all of our citizens." He said,

> For years, we've mostly treated citizens like they were consumers or spectators, sort of political couch potatoes who were supposed to watch the TV ads—either promise them something for nothing or

play on their fears and frustrations. And more and more of our citizens now get most of their information in very negative and aggressive ways that is hardly conducive to honest and open conversations. But the truth is we have got to stop seeing each other as enemies just because we have different views.

If you go back to the beginning of this country, the great strength of America, as de Tocqueville pointed out when he came here a long time ago, has always been our ability to associate with people who were different from ourselves and to work together to find common ground. And in this day everybody has a responsibility to do more of that. We simply cannot wait for a tornado, a fire or a flood to behave like Americans ought to behave in dealing with one another.

Although this speech was philosophically consistent with the civic renewal movement, nothing concrete came of it. In retrospect, it seems naive to expect a politician's speech, by itself, to spark significant social and cultural change. However, the civic renewal movement has made considerable progress since 1995, working at the grassroots. The most evident need now is at the national level. For example, there are many excellent public deliberations, but none about federal policy. There are fine service-learning programs, but the federal commitment to K–12 service learning has shrunk. Explicit discussion of democratic participation is always marginal in federal campaigns. Meanwhile, the national debate is probably so coarse, superficial, and divisive that its impact on community participation is negative—although that causal claim is difficult to substantiate.

Fortunately, new national political leaders will emerge. Given the strength of the grassroots movement for civic renewal, I believe it would be helpful for at least one of these leaders to make "empowerment" a theme in a national campaign. Alternatively, candidates could speak of "true democracy at home and abroad." Or they could lay claim to an American populist tradition that does not sentimentalize common citizens but calls them to more responsibility.[7] In any case, the message would go something like this:

American citizens have been pushed out of all our major institutions—the government, schools, health care, environmental protection, crime prevention, city planning, and the news media. That is partly because lobbyists and other rich people have bought too much power. Sometimes it's because courts and bureaucracies have made decisions that should be left to communities. Often it's

*because experts claim too much authority. Although we should respect the ex-
pertise of lawyers, economists, regulators, and professional educators, these
people don't know right from wrong better than anyone else. Nor do they
understand everyone's needs and experiences. We must find ways to tap the
energy, creativity, and values of many more Americans if we are going to address our communities' problems.*

To be credible, any such message must be backed up with reasonably specific policy proposals. Appropriate policies might include the
following:

1. *Putting communities back in control of education.* Whole communities
   educate children, not just the professionals who work in K–12
   schools. Although the No Child Left Behind Act has some
   merits, it is making standardized tests all-important, thus
   empowering the testing industry and preventing communities
   from deciding what they value most. Often, people prize moral
   and civic education as well as, or above, reading and math
   scores. The act needs to be revised so that a core of reading,
   math, and language arts remains, yet communities can set
   other priorities and participate in educating their children.

2. *Reforming Congress to check the power of professional lobbyists.*
   Although basic ethics rules are important and must be enforced,
   the fundamental problem is that lawmaking is not transparent.
   Therefore, well-placed insiders can obtain too much power.
   Dramatically simplifying the tax code on a revenue-neutral basis
   would reduce opportunities for special interests to seek special
   breaks. (The current code is about 10,000 pages long and
   generates about 4,000 pages of forms.) Congress should also
   create a bipartisan commission to simplify and regularize the
   Code of Federal Regulations, which is about 150,000 pages long.

3. *A national service agenda.* Instead of cutting or trimming the
   federal voluntary service programs (Americorps, Senior Corps,
   Peace Corps, and others), Congress should expand their
   funding while keeping them competitive and demanding
   evidence of results from grantees. The next president should
   also name a highly respected and famous director for USA
   Freedom Corps who will not only seek adequate funding
   for all the service programs, but also fight to give responsible,
   meaningful roles to volunteers. FEMA, the Defense Department,

and all agencies should use talented and experienced volunteers to their maximum capacities.

4. *Preparing a new generation of active and responsible citizens.* People form attitudes and habits related to civil society when they are young and keep them for the rest of their lives. But civic education has been cut in many school systems, and there are too few opportunities for young people to learn through service and extracurricular activities. Congress should double the small Learn & Serve America program that provides competitive grants for service learning. Congress should also preserve the Education for Democracy Act (slated for elimination in each of President Bush's budgets) and add a new competitive program for school districts that agree to implement districtwide civics programs and collect outcome data. The next president should name an interagency task force on youth civic development that includes the Department of Defense, Homeland Security, and the federal research agencies as well as the departments specifically concerned with education and service.

5. *Rethinking government service.* According to the Partnership for National Service, we would need about 800,000 new federal employees to replace those who are eligible to retire before 2010. Even if we assume that the federal workforce can be cut deeply, we still need about half a million recruits. Many younger people do not view the federal civil service as a desirable lifelong career. To meet the desires of college students as documented in a recent poll,[8] we must create federal jobs that feel less bureaucratic and more interesting. (Raising pay is much less important.) That goal will require a new round of "reinventing government." This time, the goal of reinvention should not be to improve customer service but to find ways to make stints in the civil service feel more creative, collaborative, and rewarding.

6. *Charter schools.* The charter-school movement is not a Trojan horse designed to undermine public education. Charters *are* public schools—funded with tax dollars and authorized by the government. In fact, they stand to rejuvenate public education by giving more people opportunities to serve and innovate in the public sector. If there is any way to create the

equivalent of charters in other areas of federal governance, that would be worth an experiment. An example might be community development corporations (CDCs) that can manage development assistance.

7. *A public voice in policymaking.* Hurricane Katrina showed that the federal government is not ready to convene citizens to deliberate when we face crucial public decisions. Yet we know how to bring diverse citizens together in face-to-face and online settings and harvest their views. The federal government should create an infrastructure that is ready to organize public deliberations when needed. This infrastructure would consist of: standards for fair and open public deliberations, a federal office that could coordinate many simultaneous forums and collect all their findings, and a list of vetted contractors that would be eligible to convene public deliberations with federal grants.

8. *Increase public deliberation through e-rulemaking.* Only paid experts can possibly follow the thousands of new federal regulations that are proposed and enacted each year. That means that special interests that can afford expertise have a huge advantage; indeed, many regulations benefit them alone. Proposed regulations should be issued in a searchable online format with threaded comments, opportunities to vote on the importance of proposals, and opportunities to add links and explanations. Then citizens will sort through this mass of material and add value by collaborating.

9. *New public media.* Without government help, citizens are creating more diverse and interactive forms of media—mostly online— to counteract the consolidation of the commercial news and entertainment businesses. But there remain big holes that require federal attention. First, radio has dramatically consolidated. The Federal Communications Commission must support alternatives, including low-power radio. Second, it is increasingly difficult for people to make fair use of copyrighted media in documentaries, hip-hop, and other cultural forms that rely on borrowing. Congress must protect fair use. Third, most young people are not learning sophisticated media skills. They must have opportunities to work with media in schools. Television is hardest to improve, but the next president should

at least appoint leaders of public broadcasting who are willing to create an entirely new model to replace the current system of using membership drives and corporate advertising to support marginal programs.

10. *Incorporate citizens into civic life.* The many millions of new immigrants need civic skills and opportunities; and the naturalization process should help them to become active and responsible citizens. Until 2006, the Immigration and Naturalization Service (INS) used an exam for citizenship that consisted of pure trivia. The best way to pass it was to memorize the answers, which one could do without learning anything of substance. The proposed revision released late in 2006 was somewhat better, but it still lacked sufficient questions about how American citizens may participate. Along with a better exam, the INS should provide better opportunities to learn the material.

NOTES

INTRODUCTION (pp. xiii–xv)

1. The Hesiod quote is cited widely (e.g., Håkan Holm and Paul Nystedt, "Intra-Generational Trust: A Semi-Experimental Study of Trust among Different Generations," *Journal of Economic Behavior and Organization*, 5., no. 3 (2002): 403), but is not found in the major works securely attributed to Hesiod. William James, "The Moral Equivalent of War" (1906), from www.des.emory.edu/mfp/moral.html.

2. Robert H. Bork, *Slouching Towards Gomorrah* (New York: ReganBooks, 1997), 21 and 1.

3. Cited in Dietlind Stolle and Marc Hooghe, "Emerging Repertoires of Political Action? A Review of the Debate in Participation Trends in Western Societies," paper presented at the European Consortium of Political Research (ECPR) Joint Sessions, April 13–18, 2004.

4. Federal Interagency Forum on Child and Family Statistics, *America's Children: Key National Indicators of Well-Being, 2005* (Washington, D.C., 2006). See also Daniel M. Shea and John C. Green, "The Turned-Off Generation: Fact and Fiction?" in Shea and Green, eds., *Fountain of Youth: Strategies and Tactics for Mobilizing America's Young Voters* (Lanham, Md.: Rowman and Littlefield, 2006), 3–5.

1. WHAT IS CIVIC ENGAGEMENT? (pp. 1–13)

1. Scott Keeter, Cliff Zukin, Molly Andolina, and Krista Jenkins, *The Civic and Political Health of the Nation: A Generational Portrait* (released by CIRCLE, 2002). A more complete analysis is found in Cliff Zukin, Scott Keeter, Molly Andolina, Krista Jenkins, and Michael X. Delli Carpini, *A New Engagement? Political Participation, Civic Life, and the Changing American Citizen* (New York: Oxford University Press, 2006).

2. Mark Hugo Lopez, Peter Levine, et al., "The 2006 Civic and Political Health of the Nation" (CIRCLE, 2006).

3. Likewise, the Pew Charitable Trusts, responsible for considerable funding in the field, defines "civic engagement" as "individual and collective actions designed to identify and address issues of public concern. Civic Engagement can take many forms, from individual volunteerism to organizational involvement to electoral participation. It can include efforts to directly address an issue, work with others in a community to solve a problem or interact with the institutions of representative democracy. Civic Engagement encompasses a range of activities such as working in a soup kitchen, serving on a neighborhood association, writing a letter to an elected official or voting" (quoted by the Pew-funded

Raise Your Voice Campaign, www.actionforchange.org; visited on November 15, 2005).

4. In the focus groups that preceded the survey, the researchers "spent a fair amount of time . . . probing participants about potential subterranean political activity (e.g., boycotts, protests, Internet-organized events) only to come up short. Questions designed to delve into these issues were often greeted with blank stares and moments of silence. Even when prompted with examples, young adults were unlikely to name any sort of activity." Molly M. Andolina, Krista Jenkins, Scott Keeter, and Cliff Zukin, "Searching for the Meaning of Youth Civic Engagement: Notes from the Field," *Applied Developmental Science* 6, no. 4 (2002): 191.

5. Michael X. Delli Carpini and Scott Keeter, *What Americans Know about Politics and Why it Matters* (New Haven: Yale University Press, 1996); Samuel L. Popkin and Michael Dimock, M.A., "Political Knowledge and Citizen Competence," in *Citizen Competence and Democratic Institutions* ed. Stephen L. Elkin and Karol Edward Soltan (Penn State University Press, 1999), 117–46.

6. James C. Scott, *Domination and the Arts of Resistance: Hidden Transcripts* (New Haven: Yale University Press, 1990), 198 and passim.

7. Cf. Stephen Macedo and his eighteen colleagues, *Democracy at Risk: How Political Choices Undermine Citizen Participation, and What We Can Do About It* (Washington, D. C.: Brookings Institution Press, 2005), 16.

8. Cf. Harry C. Boyte and Nancy N. Kari, *Building America: The Democratic Promise of Public Work* (Philadelphia: Temple University Press, 1996), 8.

9. Elinor Ostrom, *Governing the Commons: The Evolution of Institutions for Collective Action* (New York: Cambridge University Press, 1990); Harry C. Boyte, *Everyday Politics: Reconnecting Citizens and Public Life* (Philadelphia: University of Pennsylvania Press, 2004), 162–66.

10. Robert K. Merton, "A Note on Science and Democracy," *Journal of Legal and Political Sociology"* 1 (1942): 115–26.

11. For example, Scott J. Peters, "The Civic Mission Question in Land-Grant Education," *Higher Education Exchange* 6 (2001): 25–37.

12. Boyte, *Everyday Politics,* 138.

13. National Civic Engagement Survey I (2002), CIRCLE via www.civicyouth .org.

14. Harold D. Lasswell, *Politics: Who Gets What, When, How* (New York: McGraw-Hill, 1936; repr. with postcript, New York: Meridian, 1958).

15. David Easton, *The Political System: An Inquiry into the State of Political Science* (New York: Knopf, 1953), 129, 285, and passim.

16. Anthony Downs, *An Economic Theory of Democracy* (New York: Harper and Row, 1957); Peter Levine and Mark Hugo Lopez, "What We Should Know about the Effectiveness of Campaigns but Don't," *Annals of the American Academy of Political and Social Science* 601 (September 2005): 180–91.

17. Jim Yardley, "A Judge Tests China's Courts, Making History," *New York Times,* November 28, 2005, pp. A1, A10.

18. Macedo et al., *Democracy at Risk*, 87.

19. William Talcott, "Modern Universities, Absent Citizenship? Historical Perspectives." CIRCLE Working Paper 39 (2005).

20. Michael Schudson, *The Good Citizen: A History of American Civic Life* (New York: Free Press, 1998), 190; Peter Levine, *The New Progressive Era: Toward a Fair and Deliberative Democracy* (Lanham, Md.; Rowman and Littlefield, 2000), 25–31.

21. Bloggers maintain blogs, which are frequently updated websites with dated entries that often link to other such sites.

22. Quoted in Harold H. Saunders, *Politics Is about Relationship: A Blueprint for the Citizens' Century* (New York: Palgrave Macmillan, 2005), 161.

23. For more than one dozen case studies, see John Gastil and Peter Levine, eds., *The Deliberative Democracy Handbook: Strategies for Effective Civic Engagement in the Twenty-First Century* (San Francisco, Calif.: Jossey-Bass, 2005).

2. WHY DO WE NEED BROAD CIVIC ENGAGEMENT? (pp. 14–45)

1. Confucius, *Analects,* trans. D. C. Lau (London: Penguin, 1979), book 13, nos. 12–13, p. 120 (insertions in brackets based on other translations).

2. Jean-Jacques Rousseau, *The Social Contract,* trans. G. D. H. Cole, in *The Social Contract and Discourses* (London: J. M. Dent, 1993), II:7, II:12 (pp. 214 and 218).

3. James Madison, The Federalist No. 10 (1788), in *The Federalist Papers,* ed. Gary Wills (New York: Bantam, 1982), 44.

4. Madison, The Federalist No. 51, in *The Federalist Papers,* ed. Wills, 262–63.

5. For example, Rousseau, *The Social Contract,* III:3, p. 203: "When intrigues arise, and partial associations are formed at the expense of the great association [i.e., the state], it may then be said that there are no longer as many votes as there are men, but only as many as there are associations."

6. In the 1999–2001 wave of the World Values Survey, the highest rates of belonging to at least one voluntary association were recorded in Sweden (95.6%), Iceland (93.3%) and the Netherlands (92.4%). Compare, for example, France (39.4%) or Italy (42%). The relevant question (A0080) was not reported for the United States (author's tabulations). See also a wealth of international comparative data in Henry Milner, *Civic Literacy: How Informed Citizens Make Democracy Work* (Hanover, NH: University Press of New England, 2002). Cf. Robert D. Putnam, *Bowling Alone: The Collapse and Revival of American Community* (New York: Simon and Shuster, 2000), 281.

7. Based on data in Elinor Ostrom, "A Frequently Overlooked Precondition of Democracy: Citizens Knowledgeable About and Engaged in Collective Action," Workshop in Political Theory and Policy Analysis (2005), 8–9, and population estimates from decennial U.S. Censuses.

8. Joseph P. Marchand, Suzanne Metler, Timothy Smeeding, and Jeff Stonecash, *The Second Maxwell Poll on Civic Engagement and Inequality* (Syracuse, N.Y., 2006), 13 and 15. Cf. American Political Science Association Task Force on Inequality and American Democracy, *American Democracy in an Age of Rising Inequality* (Washington, D.C., 2004).

9. Calculated from U.S. Department of Health and Human Services, *Indicators of Welfare Dependence: Annual Report to Congress* (2005), table TANF 6. Note, however, that the real value of food stamps has grown, even though food stamp recipients report a turnout rate of only 47.2 percent. (Perhaps agricultural lobbying supports the food stamp program.)

10. American Political Science Association Task Force on Inequality and American Democracy, summarizing recent data from numerous sources.

11. The same is true in the Dominican Republic, according to Steven E. Finkel, "Can Democracy be Taught?" *Journal of Democracy* 14, no. 4 (October 2003): 147.

12. Lyn Ragsdale, *Vital Statistics on the Presidency* (Washington, D.C.: Congressional Quarterly Press, 1998), 132–38.

13. Norman H. Nie, Jane Junn, and Kenneth Stehlik-Barry, *Education and Democratic Citizenship in America* (Chicago: University of Chicago Press, 1996), 31.

14. Delli Carpini and Keeter, *What Americans Know about Politics* (see note 5 to chapter 1); James G. Gimpel, J. Celeste Lay, and Jason E. Schuknecht, *Cultivating Democracy: Civic Environments and Political Socialization in America* (Washington, D.C.; Brookings Institution Press, 2003), 197.

15. U.S. Census Bureau, "Voting and Registration in the Election of November 2002," Current Population Report, P20–552, table 12.

16. Nie, Junn, and Stehlik-Barry, *Education and Democratic Citizenship,* chapter 6.

17. Ibid., 162; emphasis mine.

18. CIRCLE omnibus poll, 2006.

19. Nick Bromell, "Freedom Reigns: But it isn't enough," *Boston Review* (March–April 2006), www.bostonreview.net/BR31.2/bromell.html.

20. Alberto Dávila and Marie T. Mora, "Civic Engagement and High School Academic Progress: An Analysis Using NELS Data" and "Do Gender and Ethnicity Affect Civic Engagement and Academic Progress?"; both forthcoming as CIRCLE Working Papers in 2007.

21. Immanuel Kant, *Übergang zur Metaphysik der Sitten* [Groundwork of the metaphysics of morals], (1785–86), Wilhelm Weischedel edition (Frankfurt: Suhrkamp, 1991), 78.

22. Samuel Huntington," The Democratic Distemper," *Public Interest* 41 (1975): 9–38; (emphasis in original).

23. Sources: United Nations Human Development Programme, *Human Development Report 2005,* pp. 221–22; World Values Survey 1999–2004 survey wave (signed a petition, attended a demonstration, boycotted); turnout figures from the International Institute for Democracy and Electoral Assistance.

24. Gregory B. Markus, "Civic Participation in American Cities," draft, February 2002.

25. Robert D. Putnam, "Community-Based Social Capital and Educational Performance," in *Making Good Citizens: Education and Civil Society,* ed. Diane Ravitch and Joseph P. Viteritti (New Haven: Yale University Press, 2001), 69–72.

26. Morton H. Halperin, Joseph T. Siegle, and Michael M. Weinstein, *The Democracy Advantage: How Democracies Promote Prosperity and Peace* (New York: Routledge, 2004).

27. Markus, "Civic Participation," 13.

28. Ibid., 61–62, 48.

29. Ibid., 16–23.

30. Ibid., 48–49.

31. Annette Lareau, *Unequal Childhoods: Class, Race, and Family Life* (Berkeley and Los Angeles: University of California Press, 2003), 210–11.

32. Albert O. Hirschman, *Exit, Voice, and Loyalty: Responses to Decline in Firms, Organizations, and States* (Cambridge, Mass.: Harvard University Press, 1970).

33. Lareau, *Unequal Childhoods*, 99.

34. Ibid., 188.

35. Benkler, *The Wealth of Networks: How Social Production Transforms Markets and Freedom* (New Haven: Yale University Press, 2006), p. 224.

36. Daniel W. Drezner and Henry Farrell, "The Power and Politics of Blogs," APSA conference paper, 2004, at www.danieldrezner.com/research/blogpaper final.pdf.

37. Alexis de Tocqueville, *Democracy in America*, trans. Henry Reeve and Phillips Bradley (New York: Vintage Books, 1954), vol. 2, book 3, chap. 17, p. 239.

38. Hannah Arendt, *The Human Condition* (Chicago: University of Chicago Press, 1958), p. 37.

39. Ibid., 57.

40. Ibid., 179.

41. Ibid., 184 and 193.

42. Ibid., 58, 48, 56.

43. *De la liberté des anciens comparée à celle des modernes* (1819); my translation from the text at www.panarchy.org/constant/liberte.1819.html.

44. Michael Stocker, *Plural and Conflicting Values* (Oxford: Oxford University Press, 1990); Joseph Raz, *The Morality of Freedom* (Oxford: Oxford University Press, 1986); William A. Galston, *Liberal Pluralism: The Implications of Value Pluralism for Political Theory and Practice* (Cambridge: Cambridge University Press, 2002).

45. William Wordsworth, *The Prelude: A Parallel Text* (New York: Penguin, 1995), 438–39 and 442.

46. Yardley and Youniss and Yates quotes are from James Youniss and Miranda Yates, *Community Service and Social Responsibility in Youth* (Chicago: University of Chicago Press, 1997), 39 and 173; emphasis in original.

47. The decline in school board seats is based on data in Ostrom, "Frequently Overlooked Precondition," 8–9; population estimates from decennial U.S. Censuses.

48. John Stuart Mill, *On Liberty*, ed. Currin V. Shields (Indianapolis, Ind.: Bobbs-Merrill, 1956), 133–34.

49. Dewey, *The Public and Its Problems* (New York: Henry Holt, 1927), 74.

50. Ibid., 206.

51. Ibid., 149.

52. Dewey, *Democracy and Education* [1916] (Carbondale: Southern Illinois University Press, 1985), 12 and 93.

53. Ibid., 12.

54. Ibid., 89.

55. Carolyn M. Hendriks, "Consensus Conferences and Planning Cells: Lay Citizen Deliberations," in *The Deliberative Democracy Handbook*, ed. Gastil and Levine, 81 (see note 23 to chapter 1).

56. Dewey, *The Public and its Problems*, 219.

57. Dewey, *Democracy and Education*, 139.

3. MEASURES OF CIVIC ENGAGEMENT (pp. 46–59)

1. CIRCLE omnibus poll, 2006.

2. Putnam, *Bowling Alone*, 18 (see note 6 to chapter 2).

3. Francis Fukuyama, *Trust: The Social Virtues and The Creation of Prosperity* (New York: Free Press, 1996).

4. James S. Coleman, "Social Capital in the Creation of Human Capital," *American Journal of Sociology* 94, supplement (1988): 98 and 113.

5. Walter Lippman, *The Phantom Public* (New York: Harcourt, Brace, 1925), 56.

6. CIRCLE and the Center for Democracy & Citizenship, "Short-Term Impacts, Long-Term Opportunities: The Political and Civic Engagement of Young Adults in America" (results of a survey of 1,500 young Americans conducted in January 2002), pp. 36–40; see Gimpel, Lay, and Schuknecht, *Cultivating Democracy* (17), for a literature review (see note 14 to chapter 2).

7. Focus groups conducted by the author at the University of Maryland, December 2004.

8. Delli Carpini and Keeter, *What Americans Know about Politics* (see note 5 to chapter 1).

9. Ibid., 243 and 253.

10. Popkin and Dimock, "Political Knowledge" (see note 5 to chapter 1).

11. Author's analysis. With 7 degrees of freedom, the chi-squares are: 24.03 for volunteering; 23.07 for working on a community issue; 19.29 for contacting a public official; 28.97 for attending a community meeting; 59.93 for belonging to associations; and 19.93 for belonging to associations that influence the schools.

12. Dhavan V. Shah, Jack M. McLeod, and So-Hyang Yoon, "Communication, Context, and Community: An Exploration of Print, Broadcast, and Internet Influences" *Communication Research* 28, no 4 (August 2001): 485.

13. Tocqueville, *Democracy in America*, vol. 2, book 2, chap. 6, p. 120 ["On the Relation Between Public Associations and Newspapers"] (see note 37 to chapter 2).

14. Madison to William Taylor Barry (August 4, 1822), in *The Writings of James Madison*, Gaillard Hunt, ed. (New York: G.P. Putnam's Sons, 1910), ix: 103.

15. Steven Kull et al., "Americans and Iraq on the Eve of the Presidential Election" (College Park, Md.: Program in International Policy Attitudes, October 38, 2004), report via www.pipd.org.

16. Christopher H. Achen and Larry M. Bartels, "Musical Chairs: Pocketbook Voting and the Limits of Democratic Accountability," working paper, September 2004.

17. David T. Z. Mindich, *Tuned Out: Why Americans Under 40 Don't Follow the News* (New York: Oxford University Press, 2005), 80, 36, 40, 59; Bill Sammon, "Vietnam Fixation Endures," the *Washington Times,* May 11, 2004 via www.washingtontimes.com.

18. Jane Junn, quoted in "CIRCLE Convenes a Meeting on Immigrant Youth Civic Engagement," *Around the CIRCLE: Research and Practice* 3, no. 4 (June 2006): 6.

19. Martin Luther King, Jr., "Our Struggle" (1956), in King, *I Have a Dream: Writings and Speeches that Changed the World,* ed. James M. Washington (Glenview, Ill.: Scott, Foresman, 1992), 3 and 9.

20. Michele Charles, "Giving Back to the Community: African American Inner City Teens and Civic Engagement," CIRCLE Working Paper 38 (August 2005), 15–16.

21. Cf. Scott, *Domination,* 204 (see note 6 to chapter 1).

22. Youniss and Yates, *Community Service,* 32–36, summarizing studies of civil rights activists from the 1960s (see note 46 to chapter 2).

23. According to Michael X. Delli Carpini, Fay Lomax Cook, Lawrence R. Jacobs, "Talking Together: Discursive Capital and Civic Deliberation in America," *Annual Review of Political Science* 7 (May 2004): 315–44, some 25 percent of adults say they have "attended a formal or informal meeting to discuss a public issue in last year."

4. WHY DO WE NEED THE CIVIC ENGAGEMENT OF YOUNG PEOPLE (pp. 60–76)

1. National Exit Poll results, from CIRCLE, "The 2004 Youth Vote" (2005), 5.

2. For a strong generational manifesto with a wealth of stories about struggling young adults, see Tamara Draut, *Strapped: Why America's 20- and 30-Somethings Can't Get Ahead* (New York: Random House, 2005).

3. Office of Management and Budget, *Mid-Session Review, Budget of the United States Government, Fiscal Year 2007,* 8.

4. www.18to35.org/policy/talkingpoints.html.

5. Jagadeesh Gokhale and Kent Smetters, "Fiscal and Generational Imbalances: An Update," National Bureau of Economic Research, August 2005, table II, p. 28.

6. Leonard Green, Joel Myerson, and Pawel Ostaszewski, "Discounting of Delayed Rewards across the Life Span: Age Differences in Individual Discounting Functions," *Behavioural Processes* 46, no. 1 (May 1999): 89–96.

7. Nicholas Zill, Christine Winquist Nord, and Laura Spencer Loomis, "Adolescent Time Use, Risky Behavior and Outcomes: An Analysis of National Data" (Rockville, MD: Westat, Inc., 1995), 52.

8. Monica Kirkpatrick Johnson, Timothy Beebe, Jeylan T. Mortimer, and Mark Snyder, "Volunteerism in Adolescence: A Process Perspective," *Journal of Research in Adolescence* 8, no. 3 (1998): 309–32.

9. Richard M. Lerner, *Liberty: Thriving and Civic Engagement Among America's Youth* (Thousand Oaks, Calif.: Sage, 2004), 85–107 and passim.

10. Dávila and Mora, "Civic Engagement and High School Academic Progress" and "Do Gender and Ethnicity Affect Civic Engagement and Academic Progress?" (see note 20 to chapter 2).

11. Karen J. Pittman, *Promoting Youth Development: Strengthening the Role of Youth Serving and Community Organizations* (Washington, D.C.: Academy for Educational Development, Center for Youth Development and Policy Research, 1991).

12. Jane Addams, *Twenty Years at Hull-House* (1910) (New York: Signet Classic, 1960), p. 94; cf. Lerner, *Liberty*, 138.

13. Erik Erikson, "Eight Ages of Man," *International Journal of Psychiatry* 2 (May 1966): 286; Reed W. Larson, "Toward a Psychology of Positive Youth Development," *American Psychologist* 55, no. 1 (January 2000): 170–83; quotation from p. 177.

14. Robin Abcarian and John Horn, "Underwhelmed by It All: For the 12-To-24 Set, Boredom is a Recreational Hazard," *Los Angeles Times*, August 7, 2006, via www.latimes.com.

15. Larson, "Toward a Psychology"; 176–78, Shirley Brice Heath, "Dimensions of Language Development: Lessons from Older Children," in *Cultural Processes in Child Development: The Minnesota Symposia on Child Psychology*, Ann S. Masten, ed. (Mahway, N.J.: Lawrence Erlbaum, 1999), 29:59–76.

16. Erikson, "Eight Ages of Man," 289–93.

17. NewSchools Venture Fund, quoted from www.newschools.org/portfolio/success.html. The same relationship is cited in a press release by the Business Roundtable, "New Study Uncovers Hidden Dropout Crisis" (Washington, DC: May 14, 2003), www.businessroundtable.org.

18. Summaries of primary literature in Andrew Biemiller, "Oral Comprehension Sets the Ceiling on Reading Comprehension" *American Educator* (Spring 2003), via www.aft.org; and Jeanne S. Chall and Vicki A. Jacobs, "Poor Children's Fourth-Grade Slump," *American Educator* (Spring 2003), via www.aft.org.

19. John M. Bridgeland, John J. DiIulio, Jr., and Karen Burke Morison, "The Silent Epidemic: Perspectives of High School Dropouts," published by Civic Enterprises in association with Peter D. Hart Research Associates for the Bill & Melinda Gates Foundation (Washington, D.C., March 2006).

20. Karen J. Pittman, "Community, Youth, Development: Three Goals in Search of Connection," *New Designs for Youth Development* (Winter 1996), via www.cpn.org.

21. Lerner, *Liberty*, 112.

22. For a list of evaluations, all based on experimental or strong quasi-experimental designs, see Jacquelynne Eccles and Jennifer Appleton Gootman,

eds., *Community Programs to Promote Youth Development*, a report of the National Research Council and Institute of Medicine, Board on Children, Youth, and Families, Committee on Community-Level Programs for Youth (Washington, D.C.: National Academies Press, 2002), 150–65. Some use positive youth development strategies, but many do not.

23. Ibid., 180.

24. Ibid., 36.

25. For a comparison between political organizing and identity development for marginalized youth, see Heather Lewis-Charp, Hanh Cao Yu. Sengsouvahanh Soukamneuth and Joanna Lacoe, *Extending the Reach of Youth Development through Civic Activism: Research Results from the Youth Leadership for Development Initiative* (Takoma, Md.: Innovation Center for Youth and Community, 2003). The sample of programs all appear to reflect left-liberal views (e.g., "marginalized" youth are equivalent to youth of color and sexual minorities and are expected to focus on the causes of their oppression). I have no argument against this frame, but I note that it is not acknowledged or defended in the evaluation. As a matter of definition, "marginalized youth" could include conservatives in predominantly liberal communities.

26. Evaluation by J. P. Allen et al, summarized in Eccles and Gootman, eds., *Community Programs*, 181–84.

27. For a succinct theoretical statement, see Larson, "Toward a Psychology."

28. Marcia W. Baron is typical of modern Kantian moral philosophers in that she emphasizes these two duties rather than the Categorical Imperative as the useful heart of Kant's ethics. See Baron, "Kantian Ethics," in Baron, Philip Pettit, and Michael Slote, *Three Methods of Ethics: A Debate* (Malden, Mass.: Blackwell, 1997), esp. 19 and 35–36.

29. Amartya Sen, *On Ethics and Economics* (Oxford: Basil Blackwell, 1986), 46.

30. Amartya Sen, "Capability and Well-Being," in *The Quality of Life*, ed. Martha Nussbaum and Amartya Sen (Oxford: Clarendon Press, 1993), 40.

31. For a good summary of recent literature, see Constance Flanagan and Lonnie R. Sherrod, "Youth Political Development: An Introduction," *Journal of Social Issues* (54, no. 3 Fall 1998): 447–56. The period between ages 14 and 25 is identified as crucial in R. G. Niemi and M. A. Hepburn, "The Rebirth of Political Socialization," *Perspectives on Political Science* 24 (1995): 7–16.

32. David O. Sears and Sheri Levy, "Childhood and Adult Political Development," in *The Oxford Handbook of Political Psychology*, ed. David O. Sears, Leonie Huddy, and Robert Jervis (Oxford: Oxford University Press, 2003), 82.

33. Steven E. Finkel "Can Democracy be Taught?" (see note 11 to chapter 2). reports positive results from adult civic education programs in Poland, South Africa, and the Dominican Republic, but all three were countries in rapid political transition in which adults might be expected to have fluid attitudes toward politics.

34. Before the 1970s, much of the research focused on early childhood, reflecting a general belief in the importance of early development and a belief

that socioeconomic factors (reproduced in families) were all-important. Empirical evidence since the 1970s, however, underlines the importance of adolescence and young adulthood. See Lonnie R. Sherrod, Constance Flanagan, and, James Youniss, "Dimensions of Citizenship and Opportunities for Youth Development: The *What, Why, When, Where,* and *Who* of Citizenship Development," *Applied Developmental Science* 6, no. 4 (2002): 267.

35. Paul T. Costa Jr. and Robert R. McCrae, "Stability and change in personality from adolescence through adulthood," in *The Developing Structure of Temperament and Personality from Infancy to Adulthood,* ed. C. Halverson, G. Kohnstamm, and R. Martin (Hillsdale, N.J.: Lawrence Erlbaum, 1994), 148.

36. Karl Mannheim, "The Problem of Generations" (1928), in Mannheim, *Essays on the Sociology of Knowledge,* ed. Paul Kecskemeti (London, 1952), 298.

37. Douglas Coupland, *Generation X: Tales for an Accelerated Culture* (New York: St. Martin's, 1991), described in Michael Hoover and Susan Orr, "Youth Political Engagement: Why Rock the Vote Hits the Wrong Note," in Shea and Green, eds., *Fountain of Youth* 160 (see note 4 to the introduction).

38. Keeter, Zukin, Andolina, and Jenkins, "The Civic and Political Health of the Nation" (September 2002), 37.

39. Ibid. The high numbers recorded in 2002 could have been a respose to September 11, 2001. Young people may have felt that growing up in the wake of an unprecedented kind of attack would make them unlike any previous generation; but that feeling may have worn off somewhat when no further attacks occurred. In 2006, according to the CIRCLE omnibus survey, only 59 percent of people between the ages of fifteen and twenty-five said their generation was "unique." This was down 10 percentage points from 2002. Among young people who were between the ages of nineteen to twenty-nine in 2006 (fifteen to twenty-five in 2002), 56 percent said their generation was unique. This was down 13 percentage points from 2002.

40. James Youniss and Daniel Hart, "Motivation, Values, and Civic Participation," paper presented at the Democracy Collaborative–Knight Civic Engagement Project Consultation Meeting, Washington, D.C., October 24, 2002. Portions of this paper appear in James Youniss, Jeffrey A. McLellan, and Miranda Yates, "What We Know About Engendering Civic Identity," *American Behavioral Scientist* 40, no. 5 (March–April 1997): 620–31. See also James Youniss, Jeffrey A. McLellan, Yang Su, and Miranda Yates, "The Role of Community Service in Identity Development: Normative, Unconventional, and Deviant Orientations," *Journal of Adolescent Research* 14, no. 2 (1999): 249–50.

41. M. Kent Jennings and Laura Stocker, "Generations and Civic Engagement: A Longititudinal Multiple-Generation Analysis," paper delivered at the 2001 American Political Science Association Convention, San Francisco, California.

42. Carolyn L. Funk finds that among adults, a commitment to social responsibility predicts community service two years later. But this finding does not show that children and adolescents must change their values before their behaviors will change; the reverse could be true. Funk, "Practicing What We

Preach? The Influence of a Societal Interest Value on Civic Engagement," *Political Psychology* 19, no. 3 (1998): 601–14. See also Edward G. Metz and James Youniss, "Longitudinal Gains in Civic Development through School-Based Required Service," *Political Psychology*, 26, no. 3 (2005).

43. Doug McAdam, *Freedom Summer* (New York: Oxford University Press, 1988).

44. The McAdam study is useful because it compares two groups of students who intended to participate in Freedom Summer: some of whom did and some of whom did not. Their dispositions are presumably similar, but their long-term life courses are fundamentally different, which suggests that Freedom Summer itself had an effect. In a study of alumnae of the University of Michigan conducted in 1992, those who recalled being active in the women's movement and the antiwar movement around 1967 were still much more engaged than those who were not active as college students. Again, it is possible that a disposition or trait was responsible for this pattern of continued involvement. The pattern, however, was the same for participants in both social movements, even though many more women chose to be involved in feminist politics than in antiwar campaigns. It seems most likely that values and dispositions steered some women into one movement rather than the other, but their participation had the same effect regardless. See Abigail J. Stewart, Isis H. Settles, and Nicholas J. G. Winter, "Women and the Social Movements of the 1960s: Activists, Engaged Others, and Non-Participants," *Political Psychology* 19 (1998), 63–94.

45. Youniss, McLellam, Su, and Yates, "Role of Community Service," 250, citing James Coleman and others.

46. Eccles and Gootman, eds., *Community Programs*, 58–60 and 100.

47. Jacquelynne S. Eccles and Bonnie L. Barber, "Student Council, Volunteering, Basketball, or Marching Band: What Kind of Extracurricular Involvement Matters," *Journal of Adolescent Research* 14, no. 1 (January 1999): 31–39.

48. Eccles and Gootman, eds., *Community Programs*, 151 and 187–89.

49. Constance Flanagan and Nakesha Faison, "Youth Civic Development: Implications of Research for Social Policy and Programs," *Social Policy Report* 15, no. 1 (2001): 5–7.

5. HOW ARE YOUTH ENGAGING TODAY? (pp. 77–98)

1. Mark Hugo Lopez and Peter Levine, "Youth Voter Turnout has Declined, by Any Measure," CIRCLE Fact Sheet (June 2002).

2. Mark Hugo Lopez, Emily Kirby, and Jared Sagoff, "The Youth Vote 2004," CIRCLE Fact Sheet (July 2005).

3. Sylvia Hurtado and John H. Pryor, "The American Freshman: National Norms for Fall 2005" (January 26, 2006), via www.gseis.ucla.edu/heri/norms 05.html.

4. Pew Research Center for the People and the Press, "Cable and Internet Loom Large in Fragmented Political News Universe: Perceptions of Partisan Bias Seen as Growing, Especially by Democrats" (Washington, D.C. January 11, 2004), via people-press.org.

5. Times Mirror Center, *The Age of Indifference* (1990), quoted in Mindich, *Tuned Out,* 19 (see note 17 to chapter 3).

6. CIRCLE, "Young People Paying More Attention to News, but Interest and Knowledge Still Lag," press release, January 9, 2002.

7. Summarized in Mindich, *Tuned Out,* 28–29.

8. Cf. Mindich, *Tuned Out:* "we do not know whether dropping out of the once fertile soil social fabric of society pushes us to abandon news or if the reverse is true" (8).

9. In the General Social Survey cumulative datafile for 1972–2004, there is a significant correlation between newspaper readership and trust in the media (chi-squared = 81.85 with 8 degrees of freedom). If we look only at people age thirty or under, or only at data from 2000 and 2004, the relationships remain significant.

10. Author's tabulations.

11. Monitoring the Future data analyzed by Child Trends (www.childtrends databank.org/family/school/32ReligiousServices.htm).

12. Jennings and Stocker, "Generations and Civic Engagement" (see note 41 to chapter 4).

13. Sarah A. Soule and Ann Marie Condo, "Student and Youth Protest in the United States, 1960–1990," presented at the Democracy Collaborative's Spring Research Seminar, University of Maryland, 2005, and cited with permission.

14. Arthur Levine and Jeanette S. Cureton, *When Hope and Fear Collide: A Portrait of Today's College Student* (San Francisco, Calif.: Jossey-Bass, 1998), 68.

15. Levine and Cureton, *When Hope and Fear Collide,* report that "taking issues to court," lobbying, and "going public" have all rapidly increased on college campuses since the 1960s (68).

16. Dean Mohs, "Celebrating and Encouraging Community Involvement of Older Minnesotans: A Snapshot of Current Minnesota Baby Boomers and Older Adults," Minnesota Board of Aging (April 2000), 6, quoted in Harry C. Boyte, "Information Age Populism: Higher Education as a Civic Learning Organization" (Washington, D.C.: Council on Public Policy Education, 2002), May 28, 2002, 7.

17. Lewis A. Friedland and Shauna Morimoto, "CIRCLE Working Paper 40: The Changing Lifeworld of Young People: Risk, Resume-Padding, and Civic Engagement" (September 2005).

18. Michael Olander, Emily Hoban Kirby, and Krista Schmitt, "Attitudes of Young People Toward Diversity," CIRCLE Fact Sheet (February 2005), 5. The source is the General Social Survey. As this is a cross-sectional survey, it assesses different people each year. Still, it is a reasonable assumption that a trend observed in random samples of a population over time would also be observed if a panel of individuals were surveyed repeatedly.

19. General Social Survey, author's tabulations.

20. Olander, Kirby, and Schmitt, "Attitudes of Young People," 5. The percentage of young people who were accepting of homosexuality, however, declined between 2002 and 2006, according to CIRCLE's omnibus survey.

21. On patriotism, see Joseph Kahne and Ellen Middaugh, "Is Patriotism Good for Democracy? A Study of High School Seniors' Patriotic Commitments," *Phi Delta Kappan* 87, no. 8 (April 2006): 600–607.

22. In 1976, some 31.6 percent said that most people could be trusted; the figure was 17.3 percent in 1995: Monitoring the Future data as analyzed in Wendy M. Rahn and John E. Transue, "Social Trust and Value Change: The Decline of Social Capital in American Youth, 1976–1995," *Political Psychology* 19, no. 3 (1998): 548.

23. Ibid., 545–65.

24. Eric M. Uslanser, "Trust as a Moral Value" (forthcoming in Dario Castiglione, ed., *Social Capital*), www.bsos.umd.edu/gvpt/uslaner/uslanerexeter.pdf.

25. Elinor Ostrom, "The Need for Civic Education: A Collective Action Perspective." Workshop in Political Theory and Policy Analysis, Indiana University, Bloomington, Ind., 1998 (Workshop Working Paper W98–26), 1–2.

26. Judith Torney-Purta and Carolyn Barber, "Strengths and Weaknesses in U.S. Students' Knowledge and Skills: Analysis from the IEA Civic Education Study," CIRCLE Fact Sheet (June 2004).

27. Anthony D. Lutkus, Andrew R. Weiss, Jay R. Campbell, John Mazzeo, and Stephen Lazar, *NAEP 1998 Civics Report Card for the Nation* (Washington, D.C.: National Center for Educational Statistics, 1999), 51.

28. Forthcoming research, summarized in Marina Krakovsky, "Teaching Apathy? Researchers Survey High School Student Councils for Clues to why Johnny Won't Vote When He Grows Up," *Stanford Alumni Magazine* (September–October 2004): via www.stanfordalumni.org.

29. Lareau, *Unequal Childhoods,* 130 (see note 31 to chapter 2). All page references in text are to this volume.

30. Ibid., 235. The same finding emerges from focus groups, especially of African American youth. See Sherrod, Flanagan, and Youniss, "Dimensions of Citizenship," 265 (see note 34 to chapter 4).

31. CIRCLE omnibus survey, 2006.

32. Mark Hugo Lopez, "Electoral Engagement Among Latino Youth," CIRCLE Fact Sheet (March 2003).

33. CIRCLE analysis, available on request.

34. CIRCLE omnibus survey, 2006.

35. Mark Hugo Lopez and Emily Hoban Kirby, "Electoral Engagement Among Minority Youth," CIRCLE Fact Sheet (March 2003); the Sentencing Project, "Losing The Vote: The Impact of Felony Disenfranchisement Laws in the United States," via www.hrw.org.

36. CIRCLE omnibus survey, 2006.

37. Richard D. Shingles, "Black Consciousness and Political Participation: The Missing Link," *American Political Science Review* 75, no. 1 (March 1981): 76–91.

38. Gimpel, Lay, and Schucknecht, *Cultivating Democracy,* 68 and 73–74 (see note 14 to chapter 2).

39. Center for American Women and Politics, "Women Officeholders," via www.cawp.rutgers.edu.

40. Sidney Verba, Kay Lehman Schlozman, Henry E. Brady, *Voice and Equality: Civic Voluntarism in American Politics* (Cambridge, Mass.: Harvard University Press, 1995), identify differences in participation among men and women, but consider the gaps "not especially large" (265).

41. Stéphane Baldi, Marianne Perie, Dan Skidmore, Elizabeth Greenberg, Carole Hahn, and Dawn Nelson, *What Democracy Means to Ninth-Graders: U.S. Results from the International IEA Civic Education Study* (U.S. Department of Education, National Center for Education Statistics, NCES 2001–096, pp. 40–41, and 91, At age fourteen, girls are more likely to expect to participate in most ways, save running for office and various forms of antiestablishment protest, such as occupying buildings and painting slogans. See Marc Hooghe and Dietlind Stolle, "Good Girls Go to the Polling Booth, Bad Boys Go Everywhere: Gender Differences in Anticipated Political Participation among American Fourteen-Year-Olds," *Women & Politics*, 26, nos. 3–4 (2004): 10.

42. Krista Jenkins, "Gender and Civic Engagement: Secondary Analysis of Survey Data," Circle Working Paper 41 (June 2005).

43. Putnam, *Bowling Alone*, 438–44 (see note 6 to chapter 2).

44. Amanda Lenhart and Mary Madden, "Teen Content Creators and Consumers," Pew Internet and Public Life Project, November 2, 2005, p. 8.

45. Dietlind Stole in collaboration with Michele Micheletti and Marc Hooghe, "Reconceptualization of Political Participation and Responsibility-Taking," in Peter Levine and James Youniss, "Youth Civic Engagement: An Institutional Turn," CIRCLE Working Paper 45 (2006).

46. Amanda Lenhart, John Horrigan, and Deborah Fallows, "Content Creation Online" Pew Internet and American Life Project, February 29, 2004.

47. Ibid.

48. In *Republic.com* (Princeton, N.J.: Princeton University Press, 2001), Cass R. Sunstein claims that the Internet allows people to choose news and opinion that already interests them, while filtering out any views and facts that they find uncomfortable. As a result, the population splits into small communities of like-minded people who reinforce their shared views. Another predicted result is a widening gap between those who have a great deal of interest in public issues and those who are not interested. Recently, Markus Prior has demonstrated that Internet access correlates with a lower probability of voting among people who start with a low interest in the news. (In other words, these people are more likely to vote if they do *not* have Net access.) The essay is entitled "Liberated Viewers, Polarized Voters: The Implications of Increased Media Choice for Democratic Politics," *Good Society*, 3, (2003): 10–16. The original theoretical account of "cyberbalkanization" is Marshall van Alstyne and Erik Brynjolfsson, "Electronic Communities: Global Village or Cyberbalkans? (1997; see web .mit.edu/marshall/www/papers/CyberBalkans.pdf.).

49. Dean for America, Filing FEC-117872 (April 20, 2004), via the Federal Election Commission.

50. Pew Internet and American Life Project, "Online Communities Survey" (2001), available from www.pewinternet.org.

51. Peter Levine, "The Legitimacy of Labor Unions," *Hofstra Labor and Employment Law Journal* 18, no. 2 (Spring, 2001): 529–73.

6. WHAT ARE THE BARRIERS TO CIVIC EDUCATION? (pp. 99–118)

1. Campaign for the Civic Mission of Schools and Alliance for Representative Democracy, "From Classroom to Citizen: American Attitudes on Civic Education" (December 2004), p. 5 (based on a national sample of 1,219 adult U.S. residents, combining scores of 6 or 7 on a 7-point scale).

2. Focus group conducted for the Campaign for the Civic Mission of Schools in 2004.

3. Campaign for the Civic Mission of Schools and Alliance for Representative Democracy, "From Classroom to Citizen," 5.

4. Friedland and Morimoto, "CIRCLE Working Paper 40" (see note 17 to chapter 5).

5. James Fallows, "The Early-Decision Racket," *Atlantic Monthly* (September 2001), via www.theatlantic.com.

6. Ernest T. Pascarella and Patrick T. Terenzini, How *College Affects Students*, vol. 2, *A Third Decade of Research* (San Francisco, Calif.: Jossey-Bass, 2005), 145–46, 205–6, and 591.

7. Ibid., 286 and 294–95, citing numerous studies.

8. Veblen, *The Higher Learning in America: A Memorandum on the Conduct of Universities by Business Men* (1918), quoted by Andrew Delbanco, "Colleges: An Endangered Species," *New York Review of Books* (March 10, 2005): 20.

9. The Carnegie Foundation for the Advancement of Teaching and CIRCLE, "Higher Education: Civic Mission & Civic Effects" (a consensus statement of twenty-two scholars), (February 2006), 4.

10. Schudson, *Good Citizen,* 6 and passim (see note 20 to chapter 1).

11. CIRCLE, in collaboration with the Center for Democracy and Citizenship and the Partnership for Trust in Government at the Council for Excellence in Government, National Youth Survey, 2002 (released March 4, 2002). Sample: 1,500 Americans between the ages of fifteen and twenty-five.

12. Robert A. Dahl, *Democracy and its Critics* (New Haven: Yale University Press, 1989), 65–79.

13. Of those who felt that politics was understandable, 78 percent voted in the elections between 1948 and 2000. Of those who felt it was too complicated, just 63.6 percent said they voted (National Election Studies, author's tabulations).

14. Rawls, "Reply to Habermas," *Journal of Philosophy* 92, no. 3 (March 1995): 140–41.

15. Boyte, *Everyday Politics,* xi (see note 9 to chapter 1).

16. National Commission on Excellence in Education, *A Nation at Risk: The Imperative for Educational Reform: A Report to the Nation and the Secretary of Education, United States Department of Education* (Washington, D.C.: The Commission [Supt. of Docs., U.S. GPO], 1983).

17. James S. Coleman, Ernest Q. Campbell, Carol F. Hobson, James M. McPartland, Alexander M. Mood, Frederic D. Weinfeld, and Robert L. York, "Equality of Educational Opportunity," Washington, D.C.: National Center for Educational Statistics, 1966.

18. Becker in the Becker-Posner blog, www.becker-posner-blog.com/archives/2006/02/summers_resigna.html.

19. David Mathews, *Reclaiming Public Education by Reclaiming our Democracy* (Dayton, Ohio: Kettering Foundation Press, 2006), 16–17.

20. David Mathews, "Public-Government/Public-Schools," *National Civic Review* 85, no. 3 (Fall 1996): 15.

21. Putnam, *Bowling Alone,* 442 (see note 6 to chapter 2).

22. Lareau, *Unequal Childhoods,* 112 (see note 31 to chapter 2).

23. Ibid., 66.

24. Nina Eliasoph, "What if Good Citizens' Etiquette Requires Silencing Political Conversation in Everyday Life? Notes from the Field," paper presented at conference on the Transformation of Civic Life, Middle Tennessee State University, Murfreesboro, Tennessee, November 12–13, 1999.

25. Diane Ravitch, "A Brief History of Social Studies," in *Where Did Social Studies Go Wrong?* ed. James Leming, Lucien Ellington, Kathleen Porter-Magee (Washington, D.C.: Thomas B. Fordham Institute, 2003), 1.

26. Arold W. Brown, The *Improvement of Civics Instruction in Junior and Senior High Schools* (Ypsilanti, Mich.: Standard Printing, 1929), 28.

27. Richard G. Niemi and Julia Smith, "Enrollments in High School Government Classes: Are We Short-Changing Both Citizenship and Political Science Training?" *PS: Political Science and Politics* 34, no. 2 (June 2001): 282.

28. Nathaniel Schwartz, "How Civic Education Changed (1960 to the present)," master's paper, quoted with the permission of the author. On the other hand, observers have long complained that schools devote "the time almost entirely to a detailed study of the structure of government, with extremely little attention to the problem of behavior as a citizen." This latter quotation is from Charles Clinton Peters, *Objectives and Procedures in Civic Education: An Intensive Study in Curriculum Construction* (New York: Longmans, Green, 1930), but cf. Arnold R. Meier et al., *A Curriculum for Citizenship: A Total Approach to Citizen Education* (New York: Greenwood, 1969), pp. 134–41.

29. Quoted in R. Claire Snyder, "Should Political Science Have a Civic Mission? An Overview of the Historical Evidence," *PSOnline* (June 2001).

30. Arthur Twining Hadley, "Political Education," in *The Education of the American Citizen* (New York: Scribner's, 1901), 135.

31. Harold D. Lasswell and Abraham Kaplan, *Power and Society: A Framework for Political Inquiry* (New Haven: Yale University Press, 1950), xiv; Lasswell, *Politics: Who Gets What, When, and How* (New York: Meridian Books, 1958), 13. Citations from Saunders, *Politics Is about Relationships*, 16 (see note 22 to chapter 1).

32. Quoted in Talcott, "Modern Universities," 2 (see note 19 to chapter 1), 2.

33. Quoted in Schwartz, "How Civic Education Changed," 10.

34. APSA Committee of Seven (1914, p. 263; quoted in Stephen T. Leonard, "'Pure Futility and Waste': Academic Political Science and Civic Education," *PSOnline* (December 1999).

35. Quoted in Snyder, "Should Political Science Have a Civic Mission?"

36. Plato, *Protagoras* 325e–326a (author's translation).

37. Francis Bacon, *The Advancement of Learning*, ed. William Aldis Wright (Oxford: Oxford University Press, 1880), II.xviii.i.

38. R. S. Crane, *The Idea of the Humanities and Other Essays Critical and Historical*, (Chicago: University of Chicago Press, 1967), 2:12.

39. Leibniz, *Theodicy*, II:148.

40. Carl Becker, "Everyman His Own Historian," annual address of the president of the American Historical Association, delivered at Minneapolis, Minnesota, December 29, 1931, from the *American Historical Review* 37, no. 2 (1932): 221–36. (www.historians.org/info/AHA_History/clbecker.htm).

7. CIVIC LEARNING IN SCHOOL (pp. 119–155)

1. Joseph Kahne and Susan Sporte, "Developing Citizens: A Longitudinal Study of the Impact of Classroom Practices, Extra-Curricular Activities, Parent Discussions, and Neighborhood Contexts on Students' Commitments to Civic Participation" (unpublished paper, October 2006).

2. Gregory A. Strizek, Jayme L. Pittsonberger, et al., "Characteristics of Schools, Districts, Teachers, Principals, and School Libraries in the United States, 2003–04," National Center for Education Statistics, April 2006, table 1, p. 13.

3. Carnegie Corporation of New York and CIRCLE, *The Civic Mission of Schools* (Washington, D.C., 2003), 23. The report reflected consensus among sixty participants who deliberated during the fall of 2002. Those experts represented diverse ideologies, professions, and disciplines (including political science, psychology, education, law, and philosophy). The report remains a useful template for discussing civic education within k–12 schools; here I will summarize, expand, and update its findings.

4. Richard G. Niemi and Jane Junn, *Civic Education: What Makes Students Learn* (New Haven: Yale University Press, 1998), 16.

5. Melissa K. Comber, "Civic Curriculum and Civic Skills: Recent Evidence," CIRCLE Fact Sheet (November 2003), uses the IEA data to compare civic skills (mostly as self-reported by the students) and the subjects that they report having studied. Many of the relationships are positive and statistically significant even after all other factors observed in the study are controlled. Because the

civic skills are self-reported, I see them as evidence of confidence more of than actual ability. But confidence is important for participation.

6. Niemi and Junn, *Civic Education.* Jay Greene's reanalysis found a smaller effect that only lasted while students were enrolled in a course: "Review of *Civic Education: What Makes Students Learn,*" *Social Science Quarterly* 81 (2000): 696–97.

7. Gimpel, Lay, Schuknecht, *Cultivating Democracy,* 149 (see note 14 to chapter 2).

8. Karl Kurtz, Alan Rosenthal, and Cliff Zukin, "Citizenship: A Challenge for all Generations" (Denver, Colo.: National Conference of State Legislatures, 2003), 6.

9. Comber, "Civics Curriculum and Civic Skills", p. 5.

10. Melissa K. Comber, "The Effects of Civic Education on Civic Skills," CIRCLE Fact Sheet (October 2005).

11. California Campaign for the Civic Mission of Schools, "The California Survey of Civic Education" (Los Angeles, 2005), p. 9 (based on a regression model with controls for demographics): available via www.cms-ca.org.

12. Michael McDevitt and Spiro Kiousis, "Experiments in Political Socialization: Kids Voting USA as a Model for Civic Education Reform," CIRCLE Working Paper 49 (August 2006).

13. To put the matter more formally, whether one voted last time is a positive correlate of voting this year, even after other variables are controlled. See Eric Plutzer, "Becoming a Habitual Voter: Inertia, Resources, and Growth," *American Political Science Review* 96, no. 1 (March 2002): 41–56.

14. Benjamin Highton and Raymond E. Wolfinger, "The First Seven Years of the Political Life Cycle," *American Journal of Political Science* 45 (2001): 202–9.

15. David E. Campbell, "Voice in the Classroom: How an Open Classroom Environment Facilitates Adolescents' Civic Development," CIRCLE Working Paper 28 (February 2005), 8.

16. Bruce Frazee and Samuel Ayers, "Garbage In, Garbage Out: Expanding Environments, Constructivism, and Content Knowledge in Social Studies," in Leming, Ellington, and Porter-Magee, eds., *Where Did Social Studies Go Wrong?* 111–23 (see note 25 to chapter 6).

17. Chester E. Finn, Jr., foreword to Leming, Ellington, and Porter-Magee eds., *Where Did Social Studies Go Wrong?*

18. James B. Murphy, "Tug of War: The Left, the Right, and the Struggle over Civic Education," *Education Next* 3, no. 4 (2003): 70–76. Peter Levine, "Civic Education" (letter), *Education Next* 4, no. 2 (2004): 5, disputes some of Murphy's premises.

19. Peter Levine and Mark Hugo Lopez, "Themes Emphasized in Social Studies and Civics Classes: New Evidence," CIRCLE Fact Sheet (February 2004), based on a survey of one thousand Americans between the ages of fifteen and twenty-five, sponsored by the Center for Excellence in Government and CIRCLE (November 17–24, 2003).

20. I have not found long-term research on the effects of teachers' ideologies. However, community service increases "unconventional" political activity, such as boycotting and protesting. This finding implies that "service does not merely stand for naïve compliance with adult norms. . . . [It] does not necessarily lead to acceptance of adult norms but affords exposure to reality that might, in turn, challenge extant norms while fostering exploration of possible ideals." See Youniss, McLellan, Su, and Yates, "Role of Community Service," 259 (see note 40 to chapter 4).

21. Carnegie Corporation of New York and CIRCLE, *Civic Mission of Schools*, xx.

22. Gimpel, Lay, and Schucknecht, *Cultivating Democracy*, 150–52 (see note 14 to chapter 2).

23. Ibid., 153–54, 212.

24. John R. Hibbing and Elizabeth Theiss-Morse, *Stealth Democracy: Americans' Beliefs about How Government Should Work* (New York: Cambridge University Press, 2002).

25. Sharareh Frouzesh Bennett, "An Analysis of the Depiction of Democratic Participation in American Civics Textbooks," conference paper, 2005, available from the Center for Civic Education via www.civiced.org, 16, 15.

26. For example, Jürgen Habermas, *The Structural Transformation of the Public Sphere: An Inquiry into a Category of Bourgeois Society* (1962), trans. Thomas Burger, with the assistance of Frederick Lawrence (Cambridge, Mass.: MIT Press, 1989, 54; Joshua Cohen, "Deliberation and Democratic Legitimacy," in *The Good Polity: Normative Analysis of the State*, ed. Alan Hamlin and Phillip Pettit (Oxford: Blackwell, 1989), or Bernard Manin, "On Legitimacy and Political Deliberation," *Political Theory* 15 (1987): 338–68.

27. Cf. focus-group results reported in Carole L. Hahn, "Challenges to Civic Education in the United States," in *Civic Education Across Countries: Twenty-Four National Case Studies From the IEA Civic Education Project*, ed. Judith Torney-Purta, John Schwille, and Jo-Ann Amadeo (Amsterdam: International Association for the Evaluation of Educational Achievement, 1999), 601–2.

28. Campbell, "Voice in the Classroom."

29. Carole L. Hahn, *Becoming Political: Comparative Perspectives on Citizenship Education* (Albany: State University of New York Press, 1998), Diana Hess, "Discussing Controversial Public Issues in Secondary Social Studies Classrooms: Learning from Skilled Teachers" (Ph.D. diss., University of Washington, 1998); Judith Torney-Purta, "The School's Role in Developing Civic Engagement: A Study of Adolescents in Twenty-Eight Countries," *Applied Developmental Science* 6, no. 4 (2002): 209; Judith Torney-Purta, Carole L. Hahn, and Jo-Ann M. Amadeo, "Principles of Subject-Specific Instruction in Education for Citizenship," in *Subject-Specific Instructional Methods and Activities*, ed. Jere Brophy (Amsterdam and New York: JAI, 2001), 388–89.

30. Michael McDevitt, Spiro Kiousis, Xu Wu, Mary Losch, and Travis Ripley, "The Civic Bonding of School and Family: How Kids Voting Students Enliven the Domestic Sphere," CIRCLE Working Paper 7 (July 2003).

31. Ibid., 32.

32. Campbell, "Voice in the Classroom," 19.

33. I owe this idea to Diana Hess (personal communication).

34. Project 540, "Students Turning into Citizens: Lessons Learned from Project 540" (Providence, R.I.: Providence College, 2004), 11, 16–17; Richard Battistoni, "Democracy's Practice Grounds: The Role of School Governance in Citizenship Education," forthcoming in a volume edited by Judith Pace and Janet Bixby.

35. Eugene Borgida and James Farr, "Final Report to The Pew Charitable Trusts" (unpublished), 3–4.

36. Project 540, "Students Turning into Citizens," 29–30.

37. Carnegie and CIRCLE, *Civic Mission of Schools,* 27.

38. In "The California Survey of Civic Engagement," the only approach to civic education that enhanced students' trust in others and confidence in institutions was giving them voice in their own schools (California Campaign for the Civic Mission of Schools, 9).

39. Flanagan and Faison, "Youth Civic Development," 4 and 7 (see note 49 to chapter 4).

40. Gary Homana, Carolyn Henry Barber, and Judith Torney-Purta, "School Citizenship Education Climate Assessment" (Denver: Education Commission of the States, 2006), via. www.ecs.org.

41. Flanagan and Faison, "Youth Civic Development," 5–7.

42. Gimpel, Lay and Schuknecht, *Cultivating Democracy,* 38 and 147.

43. Carl D. Glickman, *Holding Sacred Ground: Essays on Leadership, Courage, and Endurance in Our Schools* (San Francisco, Calif.: Jossey-Bass, 2003), 267.

44. Project 540, "Students Turning into Citizens," 23.

45. James Beane, Joan Turner, David Jones, and Richard Lipka, "Long-Term Effects of Community Service Programs," *Curriculum Inquiry* 11, no. 2 (Summer 1981): 145–46.

46. Gary Daynes and Nicholas V. Longo, "Jane Addams and the Origins of Service-Learning Practice in the United States," *Michigan Journal of Community Service Learning* 11, no. 1 (Fall 2004): 5–13; Melissa Bass, "National Service in America: Policy (Dis)Connections Over Time" (CIRCLE Working Paper 11, 2004) and "Civic Education through National Service" (CIRCLE Working Paper 12, 2004).

47. Peter Titlebaum, Gabrielle Williamson, Corinne Daprano, Janine Baer, and Jayne Brahler, "The Annotated History of Service-Learning: 1862–2002" at www.servicelearning.org/welcome_to_service-learning/history/index.php.

48. Almost half of U.S. high schools offer service-learning programs. See U.S. Department of Education, National Center for Education Statistics, "Service Learning and Community Service in K–12 Public Schools" (September 1999), table 1.

49. Youniss and Yates, *Community Service,* 115–34 (see note 46 to chapter 2).

50. Kahne and Sporte, "Developing Citizens."

51. Dávila and Mora, "Civic Engagement" (see note 20 to chapter 2).

52. The Center for Human Resources, Brandeis University, *Summary Report, National Evaluation of Learn and Serve America School and Community-Based Programs* (Washington, D.C.: The Corporation for National Service, July 1999), 1–3.

53. Shelley Billig, Sue Root, and Dan Jesse, "The Impact of Participation in Service-Learning on High School Students' Civic Engagement," CIRCLE Working Paper 33 (2005), 26–27. In the California Survey of Civic Education, service learning was found to increase students' civic skills (as did several other pedagogies), but service learning did not enhance interest in politics, political knowledge, or intentions to vote.

54. Anthony S. Bryk, Valerie E. Lee, and Peter B. Holland, *Catholic Schools and the Common Good* (Cambridge, Mass: Harvard University Press, 1993), 289.

55. Youniss and Yates, *Community Service*, 141 and passim; David E. Campbell. "Making Democratic Education Work," in *Charters, Vouchers, and Public Education,* ed. Paul E. Peterson and David E. Campbell (Washington, D.C.: Brookings Institution Press, 2001), 241–67.

56. Patricia Green, Bernard L. Dugoni, and Steven J. Ingels, "Trends Among High School Seniors," Statistical Analysis Report (Washington, D.C.: National Center For Education Statistics, 1995).

57. Mary Kirlin, "The Role of Adolescent Extracurricular Activities in Adult Political Participation," CIRCLE Working Paper 2 (March 2003) has a summary, including eight studies that find positive correlations between extracurricular activities and adult civic participation, controlling for various other measured variables. See Michael Hanks, "Youth, Voluntary Associations, and Political Socialization," *Social Forces,* 69, no. 1 (1981): 211–23; Paul Beck and M. Kent Jennings, "Pathways to Participation," *American Political Science Review* 76, no. 1 (1982): 94–108; Verba et al., *Voice and Equality* (see note 40 to chapter 5); Elizabeth S. Smith, "The Effects of Investments in the Social Capital of Youth on Political and Civic Behavior in Young Adulthood: A Longitudinal Analysis," *Political Psychology* 20, no. 3 (1999): 553–80; Jennifer L. Glanville, "Political Socialization or Selection? Adolescent Extracurricular Participation and Political Activity in Early Adulthood," *Social Science Quarterly* 80, no. 2 (1999): 279–90; and Margaret M. Conway and Alfonso J. Damico, "Building Blocks: The Relationship Between High School and Adult Associational Life" (unpublished, 2001). A later study with similar results is M. Kent Jennings and Laura Stocker, "Social Trust and Civic Engagement across Time and Generations," *Acta Politica* 39 (2004): 342–79 (see 361–63).

58. Larson, "Toward a Psychology of Positive Youth Development" (see note 13 to chapter 4); Eccles and Barber, "Student Council, Volunteering, or Marching Band" (see note 47 to chapter 4).

59. Ostrom, "The Need for Civic Education: A Collective Action Perspective" (see note 25 to chapter 5).

60. Dávila and Mora, "Civic Engagement," (forthcoming).

61. Eccles and Barber, "Student Council, Volunteering, or Marching Band," 38; Bonnie L. Barber, Jacquellyne S. Eccles, and Margaret R. Stone, "Whatever happened to the Jock, the Brain, and the Princess? Young Adult Pathways Linked to Adolescent Activity Involvement and Social Identity," *Journal of Adolescent Research* 16 (2001): 429.

62. Kirlin, "Role of Adolescent Extracurricular Activities," 15.

63. Mark Hugo Lopez and Kimberlee Moore, "Participation in Sports and Civic Engagement," CIRCLE Fact Sheet (February 2006); Robert K. Fullinwider, "Sports, Youth and Character: A Critical Survey," CIRCLE Working Paper 44 (February 2006).

64. Youniss, McLellan, Su, and Yates, "Role of Community Service," 258.

65. Mark Hugo Lopez, Peter Levine, Kenneth Dautrich, and David Yalof, "Schools, Education Policy, and the Future of the First Amendment" (in progress).

66. Nancy Rosenblum, "The Moral Uses of Pluralism," in *Civil Society, Democracy, and Civic Renewal*, ed. Robert K. Fullinwider (Lanham, Md.: Rowman and Littlefield, 1999), 261.

67. Erikson, "Eight Ages of Man," 290 (see note 13 to chapter 4).

68. Putnam, *Bowling Alone*, 22–24 (see note 6 to chapter 2).

69. Via teacher.scholastic.com/scholasticnews/.

70. Patricia G. Avery, "Teaching Tolerance: What Research Tells Us," *Social Education*, 66, no. 5 (2002): 273.

71. "The Oregon Trail (computer game)" entry in Wikipedia, via http://en.wikipedia.org.

72. Judith Torney-Purta, "Cognitive Representations of the International Political and Economic Systems in Adolescents," in *The Development of Political Understanding*, ed. H. Haste and J. Torney-Purta (San Francisco, Calif.: Jossey-Bass, 1992), 11–25; Torney-Purta, "Conceptual Changes in Adolescents Using Computer Networks in Group-Mediated International Role Playing," in *International Perspectives on the Design of Technology-Supported Learning Environments*, ed. Stella Vosniadou et al. (Hillsdale, N.J.: Erlbaum, 1996), 203–22.

73. Jefferson, preamble to a Bill for Establishing Religious Freedom, reproduced in *The Papers Of Thomas Jefferson*, ed. Julian P. Boyd (Princeton: Princeton University Press, 1950), 2:304ff.

74. Source: Education Commission of the States (www.ecs.org/html/Issue Section.asp?issueid=108&subissueid=145&ssID=0&s=Quick+Facts).

75. Anne Colby, Thomas Ehrlich, Elizabeth Beaumont, and Jason Stephens, *Educating Citizens: Preparing America's Undergraduates for Lives of Moral and Civic Responsibility* (San Francisco, Calif.: Carnegie Foundation for the Advancement of Teaching and Jossey-Bass, 2003), 109.

76. Mill, *On Liberty*, 45 (see note 48 to chapter 2).

77. Youniss and Yates, *Community Service*, 41, 103, and 42.

78. Ibid., 80 and 122.

79. Peyton Cooke, "Pledge of Allegiance Statutes, State by State" (June 19, 2006), via the First Amendment Center at www.firstamendmentcenter.org/.

80. William Damon, "What Schools Can Do to Prepare Students for Democracy," in ed. Levine and Youniss, 8 (see note 45 to chapter 5).

81. Harry Brighouse, *On Education* (New York: Routledge, 2006), 99.

82. See, especially, Gloria Landson-Billings, "Once Upon a Time When Patriotism Was What You Did," *Phi Delta Kappan*, 87, no. 8 (April 2006): 585–88 and Joel Westheimer, "Politics and Patriotism in Education," *Phi Delta Kappan*, 87, no. 8 (April 2006) 608–20.

83. However, Gimpel, Lay, and Shucknecht found "contrary to [their expectations]," that patriotic or nationalistic sentiments did *not* predict intentions to vote among high school students (*Cultivating Democracy*, 119–200).

84. Brighouse, *On Education*, 105.

85. William Damon, "Restoring Civil Identity Among the Young," in *Making Good Citizens: Education and Civil Society*, ed. Diane Ravitch and Joseph Viteritti (New Haven, Conn.: Yale University Press, 2001).

86. Brighouse, On Education, 109.

87. Ibid., 112.

88. Ibid., 113.

89. Nicholas V. Longo, "Recognizing the Role of Community in Civic Education: Lessons from Hull House, Highlander Folk School, and the Neighborhood Learning Community," CIRCLE Working Paper 30 (April 2005).

90. Mark Viner, "Constructivism and Educational Implications for Teaching and Learning," *Journal of Educational Computing, Design & Online Learning* 3, no. 1 (Fall 2002): online at coe.ksu.edu/jecdol/Vol_3/.

91. Judith Torney-Purta, Carolyn Henry Barber, and Wendy Klandl Richardson, "How Teachers' Preparation Relates to Students' Civic Knowledge and Engagement in the United States: Analysis from the IEA Civic Education Study," CIRCLE Fact Sheet (April 2005): "Students who had teachers with in-service professional development but no degree had civic knowledge scores (117.33) that were a half of a standard deviation above those of students who had teachers with neither degree nor in-service (106.31)" (p. 6).

92. Center for Education Policy, *From the Capital to the Classroom: Year 4 of the No Child Left Behind Act* (Washington, D.C., March 2006), xi and 20.

93. Mathews, *Reclaiming Public Education by Reclaiming our Democracy*, 16–17 (see note 19 to chapter 6).

94. Nell K. Duke, "3–6 Minutes per Day: The Scarcity of Informational Texts in First Grade," *Reading Research Quarterly* 35, no. 2 (2000): 202–24.

95. Nell K. Duke, S. Bennett-Armistead, and E. M. Roberts, "Filling The Great Void: Why We Should Bring Nonfiction into the Early-Grade Classroom," *American Educator* 27, no. 1 (2000): 1–8; Mariam J. Dreher, "Motivating Struggling Readers By Tapping The Potential Of Informational Books," *Reading and Writing Quarterly* 19, no. 1 (2003): 25–38; J. Flood and D. Lapp, "Types Of Text:

The Match Between What Students Read in Basals and What They Encounter In Tests," *Reading Research Quarterly*, 21, no. 3 (1986): 284–97.

8. CIVIC LEARNING IN COMMUNITIES (pp. 156–169)

1. Anderson, e-mail, July 17, 2006 (quoted by permission).

2. Quoted from www.redeemthevote.com.

3. Daynes and Longo, "Jane Addams," 6 (see note 46 to chapter 7).

4. Nan Skelton, Nan Kari, Kari Denissen, David Scheie, and Harry Boyte, "A Community Alive with Learning: The Story of the West Side Learning Community, 2001–2005," (St. Paul, MN, 2005); 8 via www.publicwork.org.

5. See, for example, Thaddeus Ferber and Karen Pittman, "Framing the Challenge," in Benjamin Butler and Donna Wharton-Fields, "Finding Common Agendas: How Young People Are Being Engaged in Community Change Efforts: Report on a National Survey of Community Development Organizations" (Washington, D.C.: Forum for Youth Investment, 1999), 4.

6. For example, Verba, Schlozman, and Brady, *Voice and Equality*, 282–83 (see note 40 to chapter 5).

7. Skelton, Kari, et al., "A Community Alive with Learning," 2.

8. Joel Tolman, Karen Pittman, Nicole Yohalem, Jean Thomases, and Ming Trammel, "Moving an Out-of-School Agenda, Task Brief #7" (Washington, D.C.: Forum for Youth Engagement, 2002), 1–2.

9. Michell Alberti Gambone, Hanh Cao Yu, Heather Lewis-Charp, Cynthia L. Sipe, and Johanna Lacoe, "A Comparative Analysis of CommunityYouth Development Strategies," CIRCLE Working Paper 23 (October 2004).

10. "'We could start a school!' How one Bronx youth group is taking on the future," What Kids Can Do, via www.whatkidscando.org.

11. CLIA website, via www.law.umaryland.edu/specialty/clia.

12. www.youthfarm.net.

13. Judith B. Erickson, *Directory of American Youth Organizations* (Minneapolis, Minn.: Free Spirit Publishing, 1998), also discussed in Jodie L. Roth and Jeanne Brooks-Gunn, "What Exactly is a Youth Development Program? Answers from Research and Practice," *Applied Developmental Science* 7, no. 2 (2003): 95.

14. Roth and Brooks-Gunn, "What Exactly is a Youth Development Program?" 100, 103.

15. Carnegie Corporation of New York, *A Matter of Time: Risks and Opportunities in the Nonschool Hours* (New York: Task Force on Youth Development and Community Programs, 1992).

16. The Forum for Youth Investment, "Reflections on System Building: Lessons from the After-School Movement," Out of School-Time Policy Commentary 3 (May 2003), 2.

17. *Reno v. American Civil Liberties Union*, Supreme Court of the United States, no. 96–511.

18. Benkler, *Wealth of Networks,* 260 (see note 35 to chapter 2).

19. "Between December 1998 and September 2001, Internet use by individuals in the lowest-income households (those earning less than $15,000 a year) increased at a 25 percent annual growth rate." U.S. Department of Commerce, National Telecommunications & Information Administration (NTIA), *Falling Through the Net: Defining the Digital Divide: A Report on the Telecommunications and Information Technology Gap in America* (Washington, D.C.: U.S. Department of Commerce, National Telecommunications and Information Administration, 1999), 1. This increase meant that poor people were adopting the Internet at an accelerating pace, and faster than upper-income people (most of whom were already online). The gender gap had completely disappeared. Whereas the U.S. Commerce Department's 1999 report on Internet use was called "Falling Through the Net," the 2002 report was entitled "A Nation Online."

20. Kathryn Montgomery, Barbara Gottlieb-Robles, and Gary O. Larson, "Youth as E-Citizens: Engaging the Digital Generation," report, Center for Social Media, School of Communication, American University, Washington, D.C., March 2004.

21. Future of the First Amendment, High School Profile component (544 schools), via http://firstamendment.jideas.org

22. Benkler, *Wealth of Networks,* 233.

23. David Bollier, *Public Assets, Private Profits: Reclaiming the American Commons in an Age of Market Enclosure* (Washington, D.C.: New America Foundation, 2001), 52.

24. Benkler, *Wealth of Networks,* 241.

25. Global Action Project "Mission & History," via http://www.global-action .org/main.html.

26. McDermott, e-mail, July 27, 2006 (quoted by permission).

27. This according to Alexa, Inc. at www.alexa.com, accessed on August 17, 2006.

28. Lenhart and Madden, "Teen Content Creators," 8 (see note 44 to chapter 5).

29. Walker, e-mail, July 12, 2006.

30. See Peter Levine, "A Public Voice for Youth: Digital Media and Civic Education," forthcoming in *Digital Media and Youth Civic Engagement,* ed. W. Lance Bennett.

31. Goodman, personal communication, July 11, 2006.

32. Macedo et al., *Democracy at Risk,* 68–72 (see note 7 to chapter 1).

33. Roosevelt (from a 1905 speech), in John Milton Cooper, Jr., The *Warrior and the Priest: Woodrow Wilson and Theodore Roosevelt* (Cambridge, Mass: Harvard University Press, 1983), 83.

34. Stephen L. Elkin, *Reconstructing the Commercial Republic: Constitutional Design after Madison* (Chicago: University of Chicago Press, 2006), 194–206.

35. Ibid., 280.

36. Carmen Sirianni, "Youth Civic Engagement: Systems and Culture Change in Hampton, Virginia," CIRCLE Working Paper 31 (April 2005), 2 and 6 (quoting Hampton Coalition for Youth).

37. Ibid., 9.

38. Beane et al., "Long-Term Effects of Community Service Programs," 151 (see note 45 to chapter 7).

39. Coalition for Youth, "Pathways to Civic Engagement for Youth," www .hampton.gov/foryouth/youth_pathways.html.

40. William R. Potapchuk, Cindy Carlson, and Joan Kennedy, "Growing Governance Deliberatively: Lessons and Inspiration from Hampton, Virginia," in *The Deliberative Democracy Handbook: Strategies for Effective Civic Engagement in the 21st Century,* ed. John Gastil and Peter Levine (San Francisco, Calif.: Jossey-Bass, 2005), 262.

41. Sirianni, "Youth Civic Engagement," 14 (and personal communication).

42. Sirianni, personal communication.

9. DEVELOPMENTS IN HIGHER EDUCATION (pp. 170–181)

1. As noted above, even in 2002, half of the "Boomer" generation agreed that "my age group is unique," compared to just 42 percent of the Generation-Xers who followed them. Keeter, Zukin, Andolina, and Jenkins, *Civic and Political Health,* 37 (see note 1 to chapter 1).

2. David D. Cooper, "Bus Roads and Forks in the Road: The Making of a Public Scholar," *Higher Education Exchange* (*HEX*) (2002), 29.

3. Ibid., 32.

4. Edward Royce, "The Practice of the Public Intellectual," *HEX* (1998): 26.

5. Friedland and Morimoto, "CIRCLE Working Paper 40" (see note 17 to chapter 5).

6. *The New Student Politics: The Wingspread Statement on Student Civic Engagement* (2002), available at www.actionforchange.org/getinformed/nsp-download .html. Discussed at length in David D. Cooper, "Education for Democracy: A Conversation in Two Keys," *HEX* (2004): 30–43.

7. William A. Galston and Peter Levine, "America's Civic Condition: A Glance at the Evidence," *Brookings Review* 15, no. 4 (Fall 1997): 26. This article is reprinted in *Community Works: The Revival of Civil Society in America,* ed. E. J. Dionne, Jr. (Washington, D.C.: Brookings Institution Press, 1998), 30–36.

8. Maria Farland, "Academic Professionalism and the New Public Mindedness," *HEX* (1996): 54.

9. Deborah Hirsch, "An Agenda for Involving Faculty in Service," *HEX* (1997): 35.

10. The Carnegie Foundation for the Advancement of Teaching and CIRCLE, "Higher Education," 3 (see note 9 to chapter 6).

11. D. Connor Seyle, "NIF at A&M," *HEX* (2002): 52–58; Douglas Challenger, "The College as Citizen: One College Evolves through the Work of Public Deliberation," *HEX* (2002): 68–81; Anne Wolford, Larkin Dudley, and

Diane Zahm, "Supporting the Mission of a Land Grant University and Cooperate Extension," *HEX* (2002): 72–80.

12. Katy J. Harriger and Jill J. McMillan, *Speaking of Politics: Preparing College Students for Democratic Dialogue,* forthcoming from Kettering Foundation Press.

13. William M. Sullivan, "The Public Intellectual as Transgressor," *HEX* (1996): 20.

14. Margaret D. LeCompte and Jean J. Schensul, *Ethnographer's Toolkit,* vol. 1, *Designing & Conducting Ethnographic Research* (Walnut Creek, Calif.: Altamira/Sage Publications, 1999), 12.

15. Scott J. Peters, "Public Scholarship and the Land-Grant Idea," *HEX* (1997): 55–56.

16. Cf. the University of Kentucky's partnership with the Public Life Foundation Organization, described by Douglas Scutchfield, Carol Ireson, and Laura Hall in "Bringing Democracy to Health Care: A University-Community Partnership," *HEX* (2004): 55–63.

17. Carlos E. Cortés, "Backing into the Future: Columbus, Cleopatra, Custer & the Diversity Revolution," *HEX* (1994): 6–8.

18. Eric Liu, "Shredding the Race Card," *HEX* (1994): 21.

19. *University of California Regents v. Bakke,* 438 U.S. 265 (1978).

20. Liu, "Shredding the Race Card," 22.

21. Pascarella and Terenzini, *How College Affects Students,* 306 (see note 6 to chapter 6).

22. Maria Farland, "Talking About My Generation: The Public Work of Today's Young Scholars," *HEX* (2000): 59 and 64–65.

23. The Carnegie Foundation for the Advancement of Teaching and CIRCLE, "Higher Education."

24. Elinor Ostrom, *Governing the Commons* (see note 9 to chapter 1); Jane J. Mansbridge, *Beyond Adversary Democracy* (Chicago: University of Chicago Press, 1983).

25. National Science Foundation, Grant Proposal Guide, NSF 04–23, September 2004.

26. Peters, "Public Scholarship"; Boyte, *Everyday Politics* (see note 12 to chapter 1).

10. INSTITUTIONAL REFORMS (pp. 182–213)

1. Dewey, *Democracy and Education,* 11 and 144 (see note 52 to chapter 2).

2. Diane Ravitch, *The Troubled Crusade: American Education, 1945–1980* (New York: Basic Books, 1983), 46.

3. John M. Bridgeland, John J. DiIulio, Jr., and Karen Burke Morrison, "The Silent Epidemic: Perspectives of High School Dropouts" (Washington, D.C.: Civic Enterprises and Peter D. Hart and Associates for the Bill and Melinda T. Gates Foundation, March 2006), v.

4. Thomas Toch, *High Schools on a Human Scale: How Small Schools can Transform American Education* (Boston: Beacon Press, 2003), 7.

5. Christopher Berry, "School Size and Returns to Education: Evidence from the Consolidation Movement, 1930–1970," p. 5: www.educationnext.org/unabridged/20044/56.pdf.

6. James Conant, *The American High School Today* (New York: McGraw-Hill, 1959).

7. Dewey, *The Public and Its Problems*, 149 (see note 49 to chapter 2).

8. Brighouse, *On Education*, 87–88 (see note 81 to chapter 7).

9. "The Small Schools Express," *Rethinking Schools* 19, no. 4 (summer 2005): 4.

10. Toch, *High Schools*, 18–40.

11. Kathleen Cotton, "School Size, School Climate, and Student Performance," Northwest Regional Education Laboratory, School Improvement Research Series, May 1996, via www.nwrel.org.

12. American Institutes for Research and SRI International, *High Time for High School Reform: Early Findings from the Evaluation of the National School District and Network Grants Program* (Bill & Melinda Gates Foundation, 2003), v-15, v-17, 93, and III-8.

13. Barbara Ferman, "Leveraging Social Capital: The University as Educator and Broker," in *Social Capital in the City: Community and Civic Life in Philadelphia,* ed. Richardson Dilworth (Philadelphia: Temple University Press, 2006), 81–100.

14. See www.cesarchavezhs.org/homeoffice/history/. I have visited the school on several occasions.

15. Bryk et al., *Catholic Schools*, 272 (see note 54 to chapter 7).

16. The clearest data are available for racial segregation, but schools are also segregated by family income and students' performance. On race, see Gary Orfield and Chungmei Lee, "Racial Transformation and the Changing Nature of Segregation," report, The Civil Rights Project (Cambridge: Harvard University, 2006), 9, available via www.civilrightsproject.harvard.edu.

17. Debbie Wei, "A Little School in a Little Chinatown," *Rethinking Schools* 19, no. 4 (Summer 2005): 30–31.

18. Michelle Fine, "Not in Our Name," *Rethinking Schools* 19, no. 4 (Summer 2005): 11–14.

19. Youniss and Yates, *Community Service*, 38–39 (see note 46 to chapter 2).

20. American Institutes for Research and SRI Internationa, v-2.

21. Chester E. Finn Jr., Bruno V. Manno, and Gregg Vanourek, *Charter Schools in Action: Renewing Public Education* (Princeton: Princeton University Press, 2000), 229–30.

22. Richard Buddin and Ron Zimmer, "Academic Outcomes," in Zimmer, Buddin, et al., *Charter School Operations and Performance: Evidence from California* (Santa Monica, Calif.: RAND Education, 2003), 37–62; F. Howard Nelson, Bella Rosenberg, and Nancy Van Meter, "Charter School Achievement on the 2003 National Assessment of Educational Progress" (Washington, D.C.: American Federation of Teachers, 2004); U.S. Department of Education, Institute of Education Sciences, *America's Charter Schools: Results From the NAEP 2003 Pilot Study* (Washington, D.C.: The Institute, 2005).

23. Finn, Manno, and Vanourek, *Charter Schools,* 204.

24. Quoted in Nelson, Rosenberg, and Van Meter, "Charter School Achievement," i.

25. Diana Jean Schemo, "Charter Schools Trail in Results, U.S. Data Finds," *New York Times,* August 17, 2004, p. A1.

26. Finn, Manno, and Vanourek, *Charter Schools,* 228–36.

27. Ibid., 226.

28. Lopez, Levine, Dautrich, and Yalof, "Schools, Education Policy" (see note 65 to chapter 7).

29. Bruce M. Owen, *Economics and Freedom of Expression: Media Structure and the First Amendment* (Cambridge, Mass.: Ballinger, 1975), table 2A-1.

30. Schudson, *Good Citizen,* 6 (see note 20 to chapter 1).

31. Quoted by Schudson, *Good Citizen,* 178, who notes that Ochs also pledged to promote "right-doing" and to maintain a commitment to political principles, such as "sound money and tariff reform." But it was the section I quote that was most influential.

32. An influential defense in English was Alfred J. Ayer's *Language, Truth, and Logic* (London: V. Gollancz, 1936). The prestige of logical positivism, however, owed more to the apparently unambiguous progress of science before World War II than to any theoretical defense.

33. Burton J. Bledstein, *The Culture of Professionalism: The Middle Class and the Development of Higher Education in America* (New York: Norton, 1976); Schudson, *Good Citizen,* 179–82.

34. Mitchell Stephens, "Newspaper," *Collier's Encyclopedia* (1994), available via www.nyu.edu/classes/stephens.

35. American Association of Newspaper Editors, "Examining Our Credibility," August 4, 1999, available via www.asne.org/kiosk/reports/99reports.

36. Annenberg Public Policy Center, "Networks Only Aired About One Minute of Candidate-Centered Discourse a Night in the Days Leading to the Election: More Stories Focused on Horse-Race & Strategy than Issues & Substance," press release, December 20, 2000.

37. James Bennet, "Polling Provoking Debate in News Media on its Use," *New York Times,* October 4, 1996, p. A24.

38. Joseph N. Cappella and Kathleen Hall Jamieson. *Spiral of Cynicism: The Press and the Public Good* (New York: Oxford University Press, 1997).

39. Pew Research Center for the People and the Press, "Cable and Internet Loom Large in Fragmented Political News Universe: Perceptions of Partisan Bias Seen as Growing, Especially by Democrats," January 11, 2004.

40. Pew Research Center for the People and the Press, "Striking the Balance, Audience Interests, Business Pressures and Journalists' Value," March 30, 1999.

41. Peter Levine, *The New Progressive Era: Toward a Fair and Deliberative Democracy* Lanham, MD.: Rowman and Littlefield, 2000), 156–57.

42. Lewis A. Friedland, *Public Journalism: Past and Future* (Dayton, Ohio: Kettering Foundation Press, 2003).

43. Jeffrey Chester, "The Death Of The Internet : How Industry Intends To Kill The 'Net As We Know It," TomPaine.com, October 24, 2002.

44. Pew Research Center for the People and the Press, "Cable and Internet Loom Large in Fragmented Political News Universe: Perceptions of Partisan Bias Seen as Growing, Especially by Democrats," January 11, 2004.

45. Friedland, personal communication, January 20, 2006.

46. Pew Research Center for the People and the Press, "Bottom-Line Pressures Now Hurting Coverage, Say Journalists: Press Going Too Easy on Bush," May 23, 2004.

47. Sears and Levy, "Childhood and Adult Political Development," 79–80 (see note 32 to chapter 4).

48. E. E. Schattschneider, who was famous for his analysis of the unequal distribution of power in a political system dominated by organized interests and parties, nevertheless noted that parties were instruments for increasing participation. See Schattschneider, *Party Government* (New York: Farrar and Rinehart, 1942), 47.

49. Alan Abramowitz, "The 2004 Congressional Elections," American Political Science Association website, www.apsanet.org/content_5179.cfm.

50. Fair Vote, Voting and Democracy Research Center, "2004 Facts in Focus: The Least Competitive U.S. House Elections in American History" via www.fair vote.org.

51. Macedo et al., *Democracy at Risk,* 45 (see note 7 to chapter 1).

52. Author's tabulation from NES. Over the whole period from 1948 to 2000, just 4.9 percent of 17–26-year-olds said that they had given money to a party or candidate—compared to 12 percent of people in middle age—but the youth rate declined over the decades.

53. Interview on National Public Radio's *All Things Considered,* quoted in Hoover and Orr, "Youth Political Engagement," 145 (see note 37 to chapter 4).

54. Author's tabulations from NES. I have collapsed the years into ten-year categories to increase the youth sample size.

55. Peter Levine and Mark Hugo Lopez, "Youth Voter Turnout has Declined, by Any Measure," CIRCLE Fact Sheet (September 2002), 9.

56. J. Cherie Strachan, "Building Party Identification in the Young and Revitalizing Democracy," in *Fountain of Youth,* ed. Shea and Green, 83 (see note 4 to introduction).

57. John C. Green and Daniel M. Shea, "Throwing a Better Party: Local Political Parties and the Youth Vote," in *Fountain of Youth,* Shea and Green, 34.

58. Hoover and Orr, "Youth Political Engagement," 149.

59. Ibid., 155.

60. I have had lengthy conversations with Brinson and believe that he is a genuinely nonpartisan conservative who wants to cooperate with Democrats and liberals whenever his principles allow.

61. Hoover and Orr, "Youth Political Engagement," 155.

62. Mary Fitzgerald, "Easier Voting Methods Boost Youth Turnout," CIRCLE Working Paper 1 (February 2003), 4. North Dakota does not have voter registration at all.

63. Ibid., 4, 8, and 12.

64. Raymond E. Wolfinger, Benjamin Highton, and Megan Mullin, "How Postregistration Laws Affect the Turnout of Registrants," CIRCLE Working Paper 15 (June 2004).

65. Fitzgerald, "Easier Voting Methods," 8; Wolfinger et al., "How Postregistration Laws Affect the Turnout," 6.

66. Elizabeth Addonizio research in progress, available from CIRCLE.

67. Macedo et al., *Democracy at Risk,* 48.

68. Most results prior to 2004 are collected in Donald P. Green and Alan S. Gerber, *Get Out the Vote: How to Increase Voter Turnout* (Washington, D.C.: Brookings Institution Press, 2004). For more recent efficiency estimates, see, for example, Ricardo Ramirez, "Giving Voice to Latino Voters: A Field Experiment on the Effectiveness of a National Nonpartisan Mobilization Effort," in *The Science of Voter Mobilization,* special editors Donald P. Green and Alan S. Gerber, *Annals of the American Academy of Political and Social Science,* 601 (September 2005): 66–84; David W. Nickerson, "Partisan Mobilization Using Volunteer Phone Banks and Door Hangers," in *The Science of Voter Mobilization,* special editors Donald P. Green and Alan S. Gerber, *Annals of the American Academy of Political and Social Science* 601 (September 2005): 10–27; and David W. Nickerson, "Volunteer Phone Calls Can Increase Turnout: Evidence from Eight Field Experiments," *American Politics Research* 34 (2006):271–92. Those studies produce estimates in the range of $22–$26 per vote. Experiments assessed by Kevin Arceneaux (in progress) have been more efficient.

69. Ramirez, "Giving Voice to Latino Voters"; Alan S. Gerber and Donald P. Green, "Comparing Experimental and Matching Methods using a Large-Scale Field Experiment on Voter Mobilization," *Political Analysis* 14 (2006):37–62.

70. Evidence includes a confidential e-mail from one of the parties' senior organizers.

71. Heather Smith and Ivan Frishberg, "Mobilizing the Youth Vote in 2004 and Beyond," in *Fountain of Youth,* ed. Shea and Green, 163–80.

72. Macedo et al., *Democracy at Risk,* 45.

73. Gimpel, Lay, and Schucknecht, *Cultivating Democracy,* 32, 163, 50–51, 54, 140, and 159 (see note 14 to chapter 2).

74. Alan I. Abramowitz, "Don't Blame Redistricting for Uncompetitive Elections" (May 26, 2005) via www.centerforpolitics.org/crystalball/.

75. Bill Bishop, "The Cost of Political Uniformity: People are Becoming More Extreme Versions of What they Were Before," *Austin American-Statesman,* April 8, 2004, via www.statesman.com.

76. Philip A. Klinkner and Ann Hapanowicz, "Red and Blue Déjà Vu: Measuring Political Polarization in the 2004 Election," *The Forum* 3, no. 2 (2005): 4. The proportion of landslide counties, however, was higher in many years be-

tween 1920 and 1968, probably because there were so few Republicans in the "Solid South."

77. Cook Political Report, "2004 Competitive House Race Chart," October 29, 2004.

78. Macedo et al., *Democracy at Risk*, 60.

11. YOUTH CIVIC ENGAGEMENT WITHIN A BROADER CIVIC RENEWAL MOVEMENT (pp. 214–228)

1. Gastil and Levine, *Deliberative Democracy Handbook* (See note 26 to chapter 1).

2. Gar Alperovitz, "America Beyond Capitalism: Reclaiming Our Wealth, Our Liberty, and Our Democracy," *Philosophy & Public Policy Quarterly* 25, nos. 1–2 (Winter–Spring 2005): 29.

3. Ostrom, *Governing the Commons* (see note 9 to chapter 1).

4. National Conference on Citizenship, "Broken Engagement; America's Civic Health Index," report (Washington, DC: National Conference on Citizenship, 2006).

5. This human trajectory is a major theme in Carmen Sirianni and Lewis Friedland's *Civic Innovation in America: Community Empowerment, Public Policy, and the Movement for Civic Renewal* (Berkeley and Los Angeles: University of California Press, 2001).

6. Michael Edwards, *Future Positive: International Co-operation in the 21st Century* (London: Earthscan Publications, 1999), 46 (borrowing the phrase from *The Economist*).

7. Boyte, *Everyday Politics*, 17–35 (see note 9 to chapter 1).

8. Partnership for Public Service, "Back to School: Rethinking Federal Recruiting on College Campuses," (Washington, D.C.: Partnership for Public Service, 2006).

SELECTED BIBLIOGRAPHY

Note: All items published or written by CIRCLE (the Center for
Information & Research on Civic Learning & Engagement) are
available from www.civicyouth.org

Addams, Jane. *Twenty Years at Hull-House.* 1910 (New York: Signet Classic, 1960).
American Political Science Association Task Force on Inequality and
    American Democracy. *American Democracy in an Age of Rising Inequality*
    (Washington, DC: American Political Science Association, 2004).
Andolina, Molly M., Krista Jenkins, Scott Keeter, and Cliff Zukin. "Searching
    for the Meaning of Youth Civic Engagement: Notes from the Field." *Applied
    Developmental Science* 6, no. 4 (2002), 189–95.
Arendt, Hannah. *The Human Condition* (Chicago: University of Chicago Press,
    1958).
Avery, Patricia G. "Teaching Tolerance: What Research Tells Us." *Social
    Education* 66, no. 5 (2002), 270–275.
Baldi, Stéphane, Marianne Perie, Dan Skidmore, Elizabeth Greenberg, Carole
    Hahn, and Dawn Nelson. *What Democracy Means to Ninth-Graders: U.S.
    Results from the International IEA Civic Education Study.* U.S. Department of
    Education, National Center for Education Statistics, NCES 2001–96.
Barber, Bonnie L., Jacquellyne S, Eccles, and Margaret R. Stone. "Whatever
    happened to the Jock, the Brain, and the Princess? Young Adult Pathways
    Linked to Adolescent Activity Involvement and Social Identity." *Journal of
    Adolescent Research* 16 (2001), 429–55.
Baron, Marcia, Philip Pettit, and Michael Slote. *Three Methods of Ethics*
    (Oxford: Blackwell, 1997).
Bass, Melissa. "National Service in America: Policy (Dis)Connections Over
    Time." CIRCLE Working Paper 11 (2004).
———. "Civic Education through National Service." CIRCLE Working Paper
    12 (2004).
Beck, Paul and M. Kent Jennings. "Pathways to Participation." *American
    Political Science Review* 76, no. 1 (1982), 94–108.
Beane, James, Joan Turner, David Jones, and Richard Lipka. "Long-Term
    Effects of Community Service Programs." *Curriculum Inquiry* 11, no. 2
    (Summer 1981), 143–155.
Benkler, Yochai. *The Wealth of Networks: How Social Production Transforms
    Markets and Freedom* (New Haven, Yale University Press, 2006).
Billig, Shelley, Sue Root, and Dan Jesse. "The Impact of Participation in
    Service-Learning on High School Students' Civic Engagement." CIRCLE
    Working Paper 33 (2005).

Boyte, Harry C. *Everyday Politics: Reconnecting Citizens and Public Life* (Philadelphia: University of Pennsylvania Press, 2004).

———. "Information Age Populism: Higher Education as a Civic Learning Organization" (Washington: Council on Public Policy Education, 2002).

———, and Nancy N. Kari. *Building America: The Democratic Promise of Public Work* (Philadelphia: Temple University Press, 1996).

Brown, Arnold. *The Improvement of Civics Instruction in Junior and Senior High Schools* (Ypsilanti, MI: Standard Printing Co., 1929).

Bryk, Anthony S., Valerie E. Lee, and Peter B. Holland. *Catholic Schools and the Common Good* (Cambridge, Mass: Harvard University Press, 1993).

Bridgeland, John M., John J. DiIulio, Jr., and Karen Burke Morison. "The Silent Epidemic: Perspectives of High School Dropouts." published by Civic Enterprises in association with Peter D. Hart Research Associates for the Bill & Melinda Gates Foundation (Washington, DC, March 2006).

Brighouse, Harry. *On Education* (Abingdon and New York: Routledge, 2006).

Campbell, David E. "Voice in the Classroom: How an Open Classroom Environment Facilitates Adolescents' Civic Development," CIRCLE Working Paper 28 (February 2005).

———."Making Democratic Education Work." In *Charters, Vouchers, and Public Education,* Paul E. Peterson and David E. Campbell, eds. (Washington, DC: Brookings Institution Press, 2001), 241–67.

California Campaign for the Civic Mission of Schools. "The California Survey of Civic Education" (2005), available from www.cms-ca.org.

Carnegie Corporation of New York. *A Matter of Time: Risks and Opportunities in the Nonschool Hours* (New York: Task Force on Youth Development and Community Programs, 1992).

———, and CIRCLE. *The Civic Mission of Schools* (Washington: DC, 2003).

Carnegie Foundation for the Advancement of Teaching, and CIRCLE. "Higher Education: Civic Mission & Civic Effects" (2006), via www.civic youth.org.

Charles, Michele. "Giving Back to the Community: African American Inner City Teens and Civic Engagement." CIRCLE Working Paper 38 (2005).

Colby, Anne, Thomas Ehrlich, Elizabeth Beaumont, and Jason Stephens. *Educating Citizens: Preparing America's Undergraduates for Lives of Moral and Civic Responsibility* (San Fransciso: Carnegie Foundation for the Advancement of Teaching and Jossey-Bass, 2003).

Coleman, James S. "Social Capital in the Creation of Human Capital," *American Journal of Sociology,* 94 (1988), supplement 95–120.

———, Ernest Q. Campbell, Carol F. Hobson, James M. McPartland, Alexander M. Mood, Frederic D. Weinfeld, and Robert L. York. "Equality of Educational Opportunity." ("The Coleman Report") Washington, DC: National Center for Educational Statistics, 1966.

Comber, Melissa K. "Civic Curriculum and Civic Skills: Recent Evidence." CIRCLE fact sheet, November 2003.

———. "The Effects of Civic Education on Civic Skills." CIRCLE Fact Sheet, October 2005.

Dahl, Robert A., *Democracy and its Critics* (New Haven: Yale University Press, 1989).

Damon, William. "Restoring Civil Identity Among the Young." In *Making Good Citizens,* Diane Ravitch and Joseph Viteritti, eds. (New Haven, Conn.: Yale University Press, 2001), 122–41.

———, Jenni Menon, and Kendall Cotton Blank. "The Development of Purpose During Adolescence." *Applied Developmental Science,* 7 no. 3 (2003), 119–28.

Dávila, Alberto, and Marie T. Mora. "Civic Engagement and High School Academic Progress: An Analysis Using NELS Data." CIRCLE working paper (forthcoming in 2007).

Dávila, Alberto, and Marie T. Mora, "Do Gender and Ethnicity Affect Civic Engagement and Academic Progress?" CIRCLE working paper (forthcoming in 2007).

Daynes, Gary, and Nicholas V. Longo. "Jane Addams and the Origins of Service-Learning Practice in the United States." *Michigan Journal of Community Service Learning,* 11, no. 1 (Fall 2004), pp. 5–13.

Delli Carpini, Michael X., and Scott Keeter, *What Americans Know about Politics and Why it Matters* (New Haven: Yale University Press, 1996).

Delli Carpini, Michael, Fay Lomax Cook, and Lawrence R. Jacobs. "Talking Together: Discursive Capital and Civic Deliberation in America." *Annual Review of Political Science,* 7 (May 2004), 315–44.

Dewey, John, *Democracy and Education,* 1916 (Carbondale and Evansville: Southern Illinois University Press, 1985).

———. *The Public and Its Problems* (New York: Henry Holt, 1927).

Downs, Anthony. *An Economic Theory of Democracy* (New York: Harper & Row, 1957).

Draut, Tamara. *Strapped: Why America's 20- and 30-Somethings Can't Get Ahead* (New York: Random House, 2005).

Duke, Nell K. "3–6 Minutes per Day: The Scarcity of Informational Texts in First Grade." *Reading Research Quarterly,* 35, no. 2 (2000), p. 202–24.

Easton, David, *The Political System: An Inquiry into the State of Political Science* (New York: Knopf, 1953).

Eccles, Jacquelynne, and Jennifer Appleton Gootman, eds. *Community Programs to Promote Youth Development,* a report of the National Research Council and Institute of Medicine, Board on Children, Youth, and Families, Committee on Community-Level Programs for Youth (Washington, DC: National Academies Press, 2002).

Eccles, Jacquelynne S., and Bonnie L. Barber. "Student Council, Volunteering, Basketball, or Marching Band: What Kind of Extracurricular Involvement Matters." *Journal of Adolescent Research,* vol. 14, no. 1 (January 1999), pp. 31–39.

Elkin, Stephen L. *Reconstructing the Commercial Republic: Constitutional Design after Madison* (Chicago: University of Chicago Press, 2006).

Erikson, Erik. "Eight Ages of Man," *International Journal of Psychiatry,* 2 (May 1966), 281–300.

Federal Interagency Forum on Child and Family Statistics. *America's Children: Key National Indicators of Well-Being 2005* (Washington, DC, 2006).

Ferman, Barbara. "Leveraging Social Capital: The University as Educator and Broker," ed. Richardson Dilworth, in *Social Capital in the City: Community and Civic Life in Philadelphia* (Philadelphia: Temple University Press, 2006), 81–100.

Finkel, Steven E. "Can Democracy Be Taught?" *Journal of Democracy,* 14, no. 4, (October 2003), 137–51.

Finn, Chester E. Jr., Bruno V. Manno, and Gregg Vanourek. *Charter Schools in Action: Renewing Public Education* (Princeton: Princeton University Press, 2000).

Flanagan, Constance, and Nakesha Faison. "Youth Civic Development: Implications of Research for Social Policy and Programs," *Social Policy Report,* 15, no. 1 (2001), 3–15.

Flanagan, Constance, and Lonnie R. Sherrod. "Youth Political Development: An Introduction." *Journal of Social Issues* (Fall, 1998).

Friedland, Lewis A. and Shauna Morimoto. "The Changing Lifeworld of Young People: Risk, Resume-Padding, and Civic Engagement," CIRCLE Working Paper 40 (2005).

Fukuyama, Francis. *Trust: The Social Virtues and The Creation of Prosperity* (New York: The Free Press, 1996).

Fitzgerald, Mary. "Easier Voting Methods Boost Youth Turnout." CIRCLE Working Paper 1 (2003).

Fullinwider, Robert K. "Sports, Youth and Character: A Critical Survey." CIRCLE Working Paper 44 (February 2006).

———. *Civil Society, Democracy, and Civic Renewal* (Lanham, Md.: Rowman & Littlefield, 1999).

Funk, Carolyn L. "Practicing What We Preach? The Influence of a Societal Interest Value on Civic Engagement." *Political Psychology,* 19, no. 3 (1998), 601–14.

Galston, William A. "Political Knowledge, Political Engagement, and Civic Education." *Annual Review of Political Science,* 4 (2001), 217–34.

———. "Civic Knowledge, Civic Education, and Civic Engagement: A Summary of Recent Research." In *Constructing Civic Virtue: A Symposium on the State of American Citizenship.* (Syracuse: Campbell Public Affairs Institute, 2003), 33–58.

———, and Peter Levine. "America's Civic Condition: A Glance at the Evidence." *The Brookings Review,* 15, no. 4 (Fall 1997), 23–26.

Gambone, Michell Alberti, Hanh Cao Yu, Heather Lewis-Charp, Cynthia L. Sipe, and Johanna Lacoe. "A Comparative Analysis of Community Youth Development Strategies." CIRCLE Working Paper 23 (October 2004).

Gastil, John, and Peter Levine, eds. *The Deliberative Democracy Handbook: Strategies for Effective Civic Engagement in the Twenty-First Century* (San Francisco: Jossey-Bass, 2005).

Gerber, Alan S., and Donald P. Green. "Comparing Experimental and Matching Methods using a Large-Scale Field Experiment on Voter Mobilization." *Political Analysis* 14, (2006) 37–62.

Gimpel, James G., J. Celeste Lay, and Jason E. Schuknecht. *Cultivating Democracy: Civic Environments and Political Socialization in America* (Washington, D.C.: Brookings Institution Press, 2003).

Green, Donald P., and Alan S. Gerber. *Get Out the Vote: How to Increase Voter Turnout* (Washington, Brookings Institution Press, 2004).

Green, Leonard, Joel Myerson, and Pawel Ostaszewski. "Discounting of Delayed Rewards across the Life Span: Age Differences in Individual Discounting Functions." *Behavioural Processes,* 46, no. 1 (May 1999), 89–96.

Glanville, Jennifer L. "Political Socialization or Selection? Adolescent Extracurricular Participation and Political Activity in Early Adulthood." *Social Science Quarterly,* 80, no. 2 (1999), 279–90.

Glickman, Carl D. *Holding Sacred Ground: Essays on Leadership, Courage, and Endurance in Our Schools* (San Francisco: Jossey-Bass, 2003).

Hadley, Arthur Twining. "Political Education," in *The Education of the American Citizen* (New Haven, Conn.: Yale University Press, 1901).

Hahn, Carole L. "Challenges to Civic Education in the United States." In *Civic Education Across Countries: Twenty-Four National Case Studies From the IEA Civic Education Project,* ed. Judith Torney-Purta, John Schwille, and Jo-Ann Amadeo (Amsterdam: International Association for the Evaluation of Educational Achievement, 1999), 583–607.

———. *Becoming Political* (New York: SUNY Press, 1998).

Halperin, Morton H., Joseph T. Siegle, and Michael M. Weinstein. *The Democracy Advantage: How Democracies Promote Prosperity and Peace* (Routledge, 2004).

Hanks, Michael. "Youth, Voluntary Associations, and Political Socialization." *Social Forces,* 69, no. 1 (1981), 211–23.

Heath, Shirley Brice. "Dimensions of Language Development: Lessons from Older Children." In *Cultural Processes in Child Development: The Minnesota Symposia on Child Psychology,* ed. Ann S. Masten. (Mahway, N.J.: Lawrence Erlbaum, 1999), 29: 59–76.

Hibbing, John R., and Elizabeth Theiss-Morse. *Stealth Democracy: Americans' Beliefs about How Government Should Work* (Cambridge University Press, 2002).

Highton, Benjamin and Raymond E. Wolfinger. "The First Seven Years of the Political Life Cycle," *American Journal of Political Science,* 45 (2001), 202–9.

Hirschman, Albert O. *Exit, Voice, and Loyalty: Responses to Decline in Firms, Organizations, and States* (Cambridge: Harvard University Press, 1970).

Hooghe, Marc and Dietlind Stolle. "Good Girls Go to the Polling Booth, Bad Boys Go Everywhere: Gender Differences in Anticipated Political Participation among American Fourteen-Year-Olds." *Women & Politics,* 26, no 3/4 (2004), 1–23.

Janoski, Thomas, March Musick, and John Wilson. "Being Volunteered? The Impact of Social Participation and Pro-Social Attitudes on Volunteering." *Sociological Forum* 13, no. 3 (1998), 495–519.

Jenkins, Krista. "Gender and Civic Engagement: Secondary Analysis of Survey Data." Circle Working Paper 41 (June 2005).

Jennings, M. Kent, and Laura Stocker. "Social Trust and Civic Engagement across Time and Generations." *Acta Politica* 39 (2004), 342–79.

Johnson, Monica Kirkpatrick, Timothy Beebe, Jeylan T. Mortimer, and Mark Snyder. "Volunteerism in Adolescence: A Process Perspective." *Journal of Research in Adolescence* 8, no. 3 (1998), 309–32.

Kahne, Joseph, and Ellen Middaugh. "Is Patriotism Good for Democracy? A Study of High School Seniors' Patriotic Commitments." *Phi Delta Kappan* 87, no. 8 (April 2006), 600–607.

Kant, Immanuel. *Übergang zur Metaphysik der Sitten (Groundwork of the Metaphysics of Morals),* 1785, Wilhelm Weischedel ed. (Frankfurt: Surkamp, 1991).

Keeter, Scott, Cliff Zukin, Molly Andolina, and Krista Jenkins. *The Civic and Political Health of the Nation: A Generational Portrait* (released by CIRCLE, 2002).

King, Martin Luther Jr. *I Have a Dream: Writings and Speeches that Changed the World,* ed. James M. Washington (Glenview, Ill.: ScottForesman, 1992).

Kirlin, Mary. "The Role of Adolescent Extracurricular Activities in Adult Political Participation." CIRCLE Working Paper 2 (March 2003).

Ladson-Billings, Gloria. "Once Upon a Time When Patriotism Was What You Did." *Phi Delta Kappan* 87, no. 8 (April 2006), 585–88.

Lareau, Annette. *Unequal Childhoods: Class, Race, and Family Life* (Berkeley and Los Angeles: University of California Press, 2003).

Larson, Reed W. "Toward a Psychology of Positive Youth Development," *American Pyschologist,* 55, no. 1 (January 2000), 170–83.

Lasswell, Harold D. *Politics: Who Gets What, When, and How* (New York: Meridian Books, 1958).

———. *Power and Society* (New Haven, CT: Yale University Press, 1950).

Leming, James, Lucien Ellington, Kathleen Porter-Magee, eds. *Where Did Social Studies Go Wrong?* (Washington, D.C.: Thomas B. Fordham Institute, 2003).

Leonard, Stephen T. "'Pure Futility and Waste': Academic Political Science and Civic Education," *PSOnline* (December 1999).

Lerner, Richard M. *Liberty: Thriving and Civic Engagement Among America's Youth* (Thousand Oaks, Calif.: Sage, 2004).

Levine, Peter. *The New Progressive Era: Toward a Fair and Deliberative Democracy* (Lanham, Md.: Rowman & Littlefield, 2000).

———, and James Youniss, "Youth Civic Engagement: An Institutional Turn." CIRCLE Working Paper 45 (2006).

————, and Mark Hugo Lopez. "What We Should Know about the Effectiveness of Campaigns but Don't." *Annals of the American Academy of Political and Social Science,* 601 (Sept. 2005), 180–91.

————, and Mark Hugo Lopez. "Themes Emphasized in Social Studies and Civics Classes: New Evidence." CIRCLE Fact Sheet (February 2004).

Levine, Arthur, and Jeanette S. Cureton. *When Hope and Fear Collide* (San Francisco: Jossey-Bass, 1998).

Lewis-Charp, Heather, Hanh Cao Yu, Sengsouvahanh Soukamneuth, and Joanna Lacoe. *Extending the Reach of Youth Development through Civic Activism: Research Results from the Youth Leadership for Development Initiative* (Takoma Park, Md.: Innovation Center for Youth and Community, 2003).

Lippman, Walter. *The Phantom Public* (New York, 1925).

Longo, Nicholas V. "Recognizing the Role of Community in Civic Education: Lessons from Hull House, Highlander Folk School, and the Neighborhood Learning Community." CIRCLE Working Paper 30 (2005).

Lutkus, Anthony D., Andrew R. Weiss, Jay R. Campbell, John Mazzeo, and Stephen Lazar. *NAEP 1998 Civics Report Card for the* Nation (Washington, DC: National Center for Educational Statistics, 1999).

Lopez, Mark Hugo. "Electoral Engagement Among Latino Youth." CIRCLE fact sheet, March 2003.

————, and Emily Hoban Kirby, "Electoral Engagement Among Minority Youth." CIRCLE Fact Sheet, March 2003.

————, Emily Kirby, and Jared Sagoff. "The Youth Vote 2004." CIRCLE Fact Sheet, July 2005.

————, and Peter Levine. "Youth Voter Turnout has Declined, by Any Measure." CIRCLE Fact Sheet, June 2002.

————, Peter Levine, and others. "The 2006 Civic and Political Health of the Nation" (CIRCLE, 2006), via www.civicyouth.org.

————, and Kimberlee Moore. "Participation in Sports and Civic Engagement." CIRCLE Fact Sheet, February 2006.

Macedo, Stephen, and 18 colleagues. *Democracy at Risk: How Political Choices Undermine Citizen Participation, and What We Can Do About It* (Washington: Brookings Institution Press, 2005).

Madison, James, Alexander Hamilton, and John Jay. *The Federalist Papers,* 1788. Gary Wills, ed., (New York: Bantam, 1982).

————, letter to William Taylor Barry (August 4, 1822), in *The Writings of James Madison,* Gaillard Hunt, ed (New York: G.P. Putnam's Sons, 1910), ix: 103.

Mannheim, Karl. "The Problem of Generations," 1928. In *Essays on the Sociology of Knowledge,* ed. Paul Kecskemeti (London, 1952), 276–322.

Mansbridge, Jane J. *Beyond Adversary Democracy* (Chicago: University of Chicago Press, 1983).

Marchand, Joseph P., Suzanne Metler, Timothy Smeeding, and Jeff Stonecash. *The Second Maxwell Poll on Civic Engagement and Inequality* (Syracuse, N.Y., 2006).

Mathews, David. *Reclaiming Public Education by Reclaiming our Democracy* (Dayton, Ohio: Kettering Foundation Press, 2006).

———, "Public-Government/Public-Schools." *National Civic Review* 85, no. 3 (Fall 1996), 14–22.

McAdam, Doug. *Freedom Summer* (Oxford University Press, 1990).

McDevitt, Michael, and Spiro Kiousis. "Experiments in Political Socialization: Kids Voting USA as a Model for Civic Education Reform." CIRCLE Working Paper 49 (2006).

McDevitt, Michael, Spiro Kiousis, Xu Wu, Mary Losch, and Travis Ripley. "The Civic Bonding of School and Family: How Kids Voting Students Enliven the Domestic Sphere." CIRCLE Working Paper 7.

Metz, Edward G., and James Youniss. "Longitudinal Gains in Civic Development through School-Based Required Service." *Political Psychology,* 26, 3 (2005), 413–37.

Mill, John Stuart. *On Liberty,* 1859. Currin V. Shields, ed. (Indianapolis: Bobb-Merrill, 1956).

Milner, Henry. *Civic Literacy: How Informed Citizens Make Democracy Work* (Hanover, N.H.: University Press of New England, 2002).

Mindich, David T. Z. *Tuned Out: Why Americans Under 40 Don't Follow the News* (New York: Oxford University Press, 2005).

Murphy, James B. "Tug of War: The Left, the Right, and the Struggle over Civic Education." *Education Next,* 3, no. 4 (2003), 70–76.

Nickerson, David W. "Volunteer Phone Calls Can Increase Turnout: Evidence from Eight Field Experiments." *American Politics Research,* 34 (2006), 271–92.

———. "Partisan Mobilization Using Volunteer Phone Banks and Door Hangers." *The Annals of the American Academy of Political and Social Science* 601 (September 2005), 10–27.

Nie, Norman H., Jane Junn, and Kenneth Stehlik-Barry. *Education and Democratic Citizenship in America* (Chicago: University of Chicago Press, 1996).

Niemi, Richard G., and Jane Junn. *Civic Education: What Makes Students Learn* (New Haven: Yale University Press, 1998).

Niemi, Richard G., and Julia Smith. "Enrollments in High School Government Classes: Are We Short-Changing Both Citizenship and Political Science Training?" *PS: Political Science and Politics* 34, no. 2 (June 2001), 281–87.

Niemi, Richard G., and Mary A. Hepburn. "The Rebirth of Political Socialization." *Perspectives on Political Science* 24 (1995), 7–16.

Olander, Michael, Emily Hoban Kirby, and Krista Schmitt. "Attitudes of Young People Toward Diversity." CIRCLE Fact Sheet, February 2005.

Ostrom, Elinor. "The Need for Civic Education: A Collective Action Perspective." Workshop in Political Theory and Policy Analysis, Indiana University, Bloomington, Ind. 1998 (Workshop Working Paper W98–26).

———. *Governing the Commons: The Evolution of Institutions for Collective Action* (New York: Cambridge University Press, 1990).

Pascarella, Ernest T., and Patrick T. Terenzini. How *College Affects Students: Vol. 2, A Third Decade of Research* (San Francisco: Jossey-Bass, 2005)

Peters, Scott J. "The Civic Mission Question in Land-Grant Education." *Higher Education Exchange* 6 (2001), 25–37.

Peters, Charles Clinton. *Objectives and Procedures in Civic Education* (New York: Longman, Green and Co., 1930).

Pittman, Karen J. *Promoting Youth Development: Strengthening the Role of Youth Serving and Community Organizations* (Washington, D.C.: Academy for Educational Development, Center for Youth Development and Policy Research, 1991).

———. "Community, Youth, Development: Three Goals in Search of Connection." *New Designs for Youth Development* (Winter 1996), via www.cpn.org.

Plutzer, Eric. "Becoming a Habitual Voter: Inertia, Resources, and Growth." *The American Political Science Review* 96 no. 1 (March 2002), 41–56.

Popkin, Samuel L., and Michael Dimock. "Political Knowledge and Citizen Competence." In *Citizen Competence and Democratic Institutions*, ed. Stephen L. Elkin and Karol Edward Soltan (Penn State University Press, 1999), 117–46.

Putnam, Robert D. "Community-Based Social Capital and Educational Performance." In *Making Good Citizens: Education and Civil Society*, ed. Diane Ravitch and Joseph P. Vitcritti (New Haven: Yale University Press, 2001), 58–95.

———. *Bowling Alone: The Collapse and Revival of American Community* (New York: Simon & Shuster, 2000).

Rahn, Wendy M., and John E. Transue. "Social Trust and Value Change: The Decline of Social Capital in American Youth, 1976–1995." *Political Psychology* 19, no. 3 (1998) 545–65.

Ramirez, Ricardo. "Giving Voice to Latino Voters: A Field Experiment on the Effectiveness of a National Nonpartisan Mobilization Effort." *The Annals of the American Academy of Political and Social Science* 601 (September 2005), 66–84.

Ravitch, Diane, *The Troubled Crusade* (New York: Basic Books, 1983).

Roth, Jodie L., and Jeanne Brooks-Gunn. "What Exactly is a Youth Development Program? Answers from Research and Practice." *Applied Developmental Science* 7, no. 2 (2003), 94–111.

Rousseau, Jean-Jacques. *The Social Contract*, 1762. G. D. H. Cole, trans. in *The Social Contract and Discourses* (London: J.M. Dent, 1993).

Saunders, Harold H. *Politics is about Relationship* (New York: Palgrave Macmillan, 2005).

Sears, David O., and Sheri Levy. "Childhood and Adult Political Development." In *Oxford Handbook of Political Psychology*, ed. Leonie Huddy Sears and Robert Jervis (Oxford: Oxford University Press, 2003), 60–108.

Scott, James C. *Domination and the Arts of Resistance: Hidden Transcripts* (New Haven: Yale University Press, 1990).

Sen, Amartya. *On Ethics and Economics* (Oxford: Basil Blackwell, 1986).

———. "Capability and Well-Being." In *The Quality of Life*, ed. Martha Nussbaum and Amartya Sen (Oxford: Clarendon Press, 1993), 30–53.

Shah, Dhavan V., Jack M. McLeod, and So-Hyang Yoon. "Communication, Context, and Community: An Exploration of Print, Broadcast, and Internet Influences." *Communication Research* 28, no. 4 (August 2001), 464–506.

Shea, Daniel M., and John C. Green. *Fountain of Youth: Strategies and Tactics for Mobilizing America's Young Voters* (Lanham, Md.: Rowman & Littlefield, 2006).

Sirianni, Carmen. "Youth Civic Engagement: Systems and Culture Change in Hampton, Virginia," CIRCLE Working Paper 31 (2005).

———, and Lewis A. Friedland. *Civic Innovation in America: Community Empowerment, Public Policy, and the Movement for Civic Renewal* (Los Angeles: University of California Press, 2001).

Stewart, Abigail J., Isis H. Settles, and Nicholas J. G. Winter. "Women and the Social Movements of the 1960s: Activists, Engaged Others, and Non-Participants." *Political Psychology* 19 (1998), 63–94.

Michael Schudson. *The Good Citizen: A History of American Civic Life* (New York: The Free Press, 1998).

Sherrod, Lonnie R., Constance Flanagan, and James Youniss. "Dimensions of Citizenship and Opportunities for Youth Development: The *What, Why, When, Where,* and *Who* of Citizenship Development." *Applied Developmental Science*, 6, no. 4 (2002), 264–72.

Shingles, Richard D. "Black Consciousness and Political Participation: The Missing Link." *The American Political Science Review* 75, no. 1 (March 1981), 76–91.

Smith, Elizabeth S. "The Effects of Investments in the Social Capital of Youth on Political and Civic Behavior in Young Adulthood: A Longitudinal Analysis." *Political Psychology* 20, no. 3 (1999), 553–80.

Snyder, R. Claire. "Should Political Science Have a Civic Mission? An Overview of the Historical Evidence," *PSOnline,* June 2001.

Sunstein, Cass. *Republic.com* (Princeton University Press, 2001).

Talcott, William. "Modern Universities, Absent Citizenship? Historical Perspectives." CIRCLE Working Paper 39 (2005).

Toch, Thomas. *High Schools on a Human Scale: How Small Schools can Transform American Education* (Boston: Beacon Press, 2003).

Tocqueville, Alexis de. *Democracy in America,* 1835, 1840. Henry Reeve and Phillips Bradley, trans. (New York: Vintage Books, 1954).

Torney-Purta, Judith. "The School's Role in Developing Civic Engagement: A Study of Adolescents in Twenty-Eight Countries." *Applied Developmental Science* 6, no. 4 (2002), 203–12.

———. "Conceptual Changes in Adolescents Using Computer Networks in Group-Mediated International Role Playing." In *International Perspectives on the Design of Technology Supported Learning Environments,* ed. Stella Vosniadou et al. (Hillsdale, N.J.: Earlbaum, 1996), 203–22.

———. "Cognitive Representations of the International Political and Economic Systems in Adolescents." In *The Development of Political Understanding,* ed. Helen Haste and Judith Torney-Purta (San Francisco: Jossey-Bass, 1992), 11–25.

———, and Carolyn Barber. "Strengths and Weaknesses in U.S. Students' Knowledge and Skills: Analysis from the IEA Civic Education Study." CIRCLE Fact Sheet, June 2004.

———, Carolyn Henry Barber, and Wendy Klandl Richardson. "How Teachers' Preparation Relates to Students' Civic Knowledge and Engagement in the United States: Analysis from the IEA Civic Education Study." CIRCLE Fact Sheet, April 2005.

———, Carole L. Hahn, and Jo-Ann M. Amadeo. "Principles of Subject-Specific Instruction in Education for Citizenship." In *Subject-Specific Instructional Methods and Activities,* Jere Brophy, ed. (New York: Elsevier Science, 2001), 347–72.

Verba, Sidney, Kay Lehman Schlozman, and Henry E. Brady. *Voice and Equality: Civic Voluntarism in American Politics* (Cambridge: Harvard University Press, 1995).

Westheimer, Joel. "Politics and Patriotism in Education," in *Phi Delta Kappan* 87, no. 8 (April 2006), 608–20.

Wolfinger, Raymond E., Benjamin Highton, and Megan Mullin. "How Postregistration Laws Affect the Turnout of Registrants." CIRCLE Working Paper 15 (2004).

Youniss, James, Jeffrey A. McLellan, and Miranda Yates. "What We Know About Engendering Civic Identity." *American Behavioral Scientist* 40, no. 5 (March/April 1997), 620–31.

———, Jeffrey A. McLellan, Yang Su, and Miranda Yates. "The Role of Community Service in Identity Development: Normative, Unconventional, and Deviant Orientations." *Journal of Adolescent Research* 14, no. 2 (1999), 248–61.

———, and Miranda Yates. *Community Service and Social Responsibility in Youth* (Chicago: University of Chicago Press, 1997).

Zill, Nicholas, Christine Winquist Nord, and Laura Spencer Loomis. *Adolescent Time Use, Risky Behavior and Outcomes: An Analysis of National Data* (Rockville, Md.: Westat, Inc, 1995).

Zukin, Cliff, Scott Keeter, Molly Andolina, Krista Jenkins, and Michael X. Delli Carpini. *A New Engagement? Political Participation, Civic Life, and the Changing American Citizen* (New York: Oxford University Press, 2006).

INDEX